Pepe Nummi

HANDBOOK OF PROFESSIONAL FACILITATION

Theory, Tools, and Design

ISBN 978-952-69073-5-2 (nid.)
ISBN 978-952-69073-6-9 (PDF)
ISBN 978-952-69073-7-6 (EPUB)

Drawings: Encore Digital Marketing OY
Layout: Taru Tarvainen
Cover design: Nik Nummi
Printed by Kindle Direct Publishing

This book has been financially supported by The Association
of Finnish Non-fiction Writers.

Table of Contents

VOLUME 1

VOLUME 2

*In the course of writing this book, not a single precious idea
was distorted through the practice of grouping.
Each idea was considered important and sovereign
so that its true meaning would not be obscured.*

About the Author

Pepe Nummi began his leadership career
in 1990 and worked as a facilitator since
1998. He has served as the inaugural chairman of the Finnish Association of Facilitators. Pepe is a facilitation trailblazer and is
a co-founder of Grape People, a facilitation
training company. On top of all this, Pepe
is the developer of the Idealogue Method,
and is the author of *The Handbook of Facilitation* (2007), *The Handbook
of Virtual Facilitation* (2012), *Beyond Brainstorming – Idealogue* (2016),
and *Handbook of Facilitative Leadership* (2018). Over the course of his
long career, Pepe has provided facilitation services in over 20 countries
and has trained over 15,000 facilitators.

Acknowledgements

I could not have completed this project alone, and thankfully I did not
have to try. The content was developed over years of collaboration and
experience with my colleagues at Grape People. I want to single out
Miikka Penttinen for always having the time to share his thinking
with me and help me organise my cluttered thoughts. I also want
to express my deep gratitude to Andrew Ullom for his professional
support throughout the writing and editing process. Finally, thanks
to the thousands of people who participated in one of my workshops
where I tested and refined the ideas I share here; I could not have done
it without you!

Handbook of
Professional Facilitation
Theory, Tools, and Design

VOLUME 1

INTRODUCTION:

Dinner in Shanghai

I was overwhelmed as I stood in the centre of Shanghai's Fangbang Lu Market; I smelled smoky grease as noodles were fried, saw fresh lobster and fish being tossed into huge pots of boiling water, and heard the cries of vendors hawking endless varieties of dumplings. My wife Lena was with me, and we were both hungry. In that moment, my objective was crystal clear: I was going to find and eat the largest hot pot I could find.

Lena had not been to Shanghai before, so I wanted to show her the delicious stew of noodles, seafood, tofu, and vegetables known as hot pot. "You will absolutely love it," I said, as I led her by the hand towards a restaurant stall advertising the best hot pot dinner in the city. Lena, however, had a drastically different idea.

"I saw a pizza place over by our hotel. Let's go there," she said.

I smiled and laughed a bit, but once I realised that she was serious, I could not believe it. "Lena, you didn't come all the way to Shanghai for the pizza, did you? We are literally standing in a place that probably has some of the best hot pot in the world!"

Unconvinced, Lena countered by asking why I always got to choose the place to eat, and off we went in a predictable tug-of-war; bickering and talking over each other without listening to a word of what the other person was saying.

Lena accidentally improved the situation with an insult; "You know, you are a pretty bad listener for someone who talks with people for a living."

Her comment stopped me in my tracks. I decided to try to see things from her point of view and said, "Enough arguing. Let's try to understand each other. Why do you want pizza instead of hot pot?"

She remarked, "I'm starving, and I want to have cheese because I know it will energise me for the rest of tonight. How about you? Is hot pot something special to you?"

I replied, "The whole flight over I imagined sitting down with you and sharing a special meal and a good bottle of wine. I just wanted a nice moment together. I am open to other options, but I know that the pizza in this city is notoriously bad. I guess that's why I reacted so negatively to your suggestion."

Once we began to understand each other, the argument faded away. I pointed across the street to a restaurant called Hello Switzerland, full of happy couples sharing cheesy fondue dishes.

"Does that look good to you?" I asked.

She smiled and began walking into the restaurant. "Perfect, let's eat."

From a fight to fondue

Lena and I managed to pivot away from a potentially nasty fight to a tasty dinner. But how? Let's start at the top. We both were in a new place with empty stomachs, circumstances which can make even the most patient person snappy and irritable. We wanted to enjoy some tasty food together instead of remaining hungry, so we needed to find a solution. Our argument began over what our best option was. Fighting over solutions (or options, or choices, or decisions, or plans of action, etc.) is quite common. If you do not understand the reasons behind someone else's solution, it will not seem like a good option. At face value, it may feel illogical or cold, making it difficult to see the positive parts of it, let alone agree to it. In fact, understanding the available options and the logic behind them is a non-negotiable requirement for effective decision making.

Lena and I managed to understand each other's logic. I learned that Lena wanted energising comfort food and she understood that I was imagining sharing a special meal together. It was a positive step for us to understand what the other person wanted, but we did not stop there; we came up with a solution that met both of our needs and made us both happy—this is breakthrough decision making.

The six pitfalls

I love my job. I have been fortunate enough to spend my career traveling the world teaching the tools, techniques, and leadership style needed to help groups make better decisions. It is a worthy objective that is becoming more popular each year. Now, there are all sorts of professionals dedicated to helping groups make better decisions—coaches, mentors, facilitators, strategists, and mediators are all teaching people how they can work more effectively together. This is a great goal, so I should be thrilled about this, right? Well, not quite.

It fills my heart with joy to see people spend time and energy trying to help groups effectively together, but at the same time I notice the same mistakes happening again and again that make group decision making more difficult than it should be. Some people don't design workshops correctly, which causes a lack of alignment and understanding among the workshop participants. Some group leaders love the sound of their own voice and just talk and talk without saying much at all. They may know the names of the tools and have an array of buzzwords, but they can't tell you the methodology and theory behind the methods that explain why they work.

In *Handbook of Professional Facilitation: Theory, Tools, and Design*, I help to eliminate these errors by sharing my knowledge and experience that I have acquired over the past 25 years. Among the pile of mistakes that I see again and again, six reoccurring themes emerge.

The six common pitfalls in group decision making

1. **Individual decision-making processes instead of group processes:** Sometimes people rush decision making by using tools that focus on the individual instead of the group.

2. **Complicated decision-making processes:** It can be easy to try to include too many stages in a workshop or tool in order to make everything clear and perfect, but this actually causes people to get confused and lose focus.

3. **Grouping:** Combining similar ideas actually changes their meaning and loses nuance and small details.

4. **Choosing ideas without understanding them:** People may want to commit an idea with only a surface-level understanding. It is important to understand the logic behind an idea before making a decision.

5. **Hasty decisions:** Usually too much focus is spent on creating ideas (divergence) instead of dedicating time on selecting the best ideas (convergence). This leads to a lack of agreement within the group.

6. **Being the centre of attention:** A key part of leading groups to make decisions is to step back and let the participants do it. Yet, many people feel that they need to lead the process by being in the middle of every discussion and interaction.

Individual processes instead of group processes

Years ago, I attended an innovation workshop where a well-known guru was demonstrating his methods. This man was at the head of his field and had achieved the type of success which found him head-lining an international conference with expensive tickets. The guru led us through a 7-part innovation process: explore, define, ideate, prototype, test, refine and implement. This framework was detailed and structured in such a way to allow for all ideas to be fully explored. By the end of the workshop, people were happy because they had all produced new and exciting ideas.

I was happy, too, but despite the careful design of the guru's workshop, there was a key problem. We were 16 individuals that were happy with our own ideas, but we did not have any understanding about where they fit in relation to what other people produced. What were the best ideas? How could they be prioritised as a group? Without a common agreement concerning solutions and action points, what was the point of the workshop? The guru spent too much time helping us develop our own thoughts, but then neglected to explore them as a group. The workshop results were incomplete, and our work remained unfinished.

Group leaders often take a short cut and help people create individual decisions instead of helping the entire group decide together. Sometimes they do not even understand the difference, and think individual processes are simply faster and easier. For effective group decision making, the leader should make sure all ideas are understood and agreed upon during each stage of a meeting or workshop.

Complicated decision-making processes

The guru led a well-planned workshop that yielded some great individual results, but it was still too complicated. Groups should not be required to follow a complicated decision-making process. People often lose focus transitioning between stages, so it is best to keep things as simple as possible. I use a 3-stage framework called CSA for my workshops. CSA is an abbreviation for clarifying, solutions, and action. The clarifying stage is where content is reviewed so that it is mutually understood by the group. In the solutions stage, people create proposals and then choose the best ones together as a group. In the action stage, the group creates actions on how to proceed and prioritises them together. CSA is simple enough for the group to understand the workshop structure, and there is still enough time for the leader to help the group reach a consensus.

Think back to Lena and I searching for dinner—we managed to understand each other and quickly come to an agreement. Now imagine if we had followed a complex 10-stage process to resolve our difference and come to agreement? It could have taken us until breakfast time to come to an agreement. Simplicity is both beautiful and practical. Communicating in a clear way and using logical tools and a clear workshop structure is an important part of how I lead groups.

Grouping

Being an old man means that I have my fair share of age-related problems. My knees hurt, I wake up with a headache most mornings, and my elbow makes a clicking noise when I bend it. When I think about these ailments, I group them all together and call them health problems. What happens when I do this? These individual problems that have separate causes and solutions are lumped together. This oversimplifies things. To find the right solutions, it makes more sense to study each problem individually. Perhaps I need to stop running each morning and my knees will feel better, and maybe some more sleep will cure my headaches, but if I group these problems together and try to solve all of them at once, I might try a broad solution that does little to fix the actual issues. Grouping similar things together is a natural process as our minds try to make sense of the constant inflow of information, but we sometimes need to fight this tendency. Grouping obscures the root cause of a problem and oversimplifies things.

If grouping is counterproductive, then why do people do it? First, because they are taught to. There are many popular group methods where a part of the process dictates that you cluster the ideas, although many of these techniques were created over 50 years ago and are outdated. They should be replaced by more effective techniques.

Second, clustering is an easy way to avoid true—and sometimes painful—decision making. When you bunch ideas together there is something for everyone, and it's easy for people to agree with one another on the whole package. It is efficient and tidy, but you did not decide anything concrete. You only made nice clusters and perhaps even gave them neat names that will be forgotten very soon. Think back to Lena and me in Shanghai, and our disagreement about eating pizza or hot pot. Imagine if we thought to ourselves, "Pizza is a food, so is hotpot...our problem is food!" This would not help us decide at all, and Lena's reasons for wanting pizza and my motivation for eating hot pot would be lost. This example might sound absurd, but it is something that happens all the time in organisations.

Choosing ideas without understanding them

Group leaders may incorrectly think that their job is done if they manage to get a group to choose ideas. This normally happens at the end of a meeting or a workshop when people are asked to vote on their favourite ideas or choose what they want to commit to. Unfortunately, there is much more to just instructing people to pick their favourites—they will follow your instructions and complete the task, but they will probably stick to choosing their own ideas or commit to something without fully understanding it. If the person leading the group is inexperienced, he or she might see people respond to their instructions and think that it is a job well done when this may not be the case at all.

Even experts qualified to write books on effective leadership—myself included—have fallen into this trap. I was leading a creativity workshop for an urban recycling centre based in Estonia. The organisation bought up surplus building materials and then repurposed them. They asked for my help to create proposals for possible uses for excess plywood—they had just closed a large deal and now owned over a ton of it, so they wanted to brainstorm ways to market the stuff to get rid of it. I guided the group though an hour's worth of creativity exercises, and by the time the workshop was over, there were dozens of flipcharts filled with proposals, and a room full of tired people. They followed my instructions perfectly and thought up more than one hundred ideas, and they even chose a few of them to move forward with. But when it came time to call things to a close, I could tell that almost everyone was underwhelmed with the results. Out of the hundreds of possibilities, people ended up choosing their own ideas that they already understood, or ones that were like what they were already thinking. This was not their fault; I was to blame. I did not give them the time or opportunity for people to understand the other proposals that were created. Without understanding them, how could they be expected to commit to them?

My mistake was that I did not use tools that emphasised selecting the *best* ideas. Many group-level tools emphasise brainstorming much more than comprehension and selection of the best content. Some leaders just ask the group to read over the ideas and select their favourites. I don't think this is effective. To put people in the best position to succeed, they need to fully understand what they are selecting and committing to, and for this to happen they need to talk things over. My solution is to add more dialogue to the idea-selection process. This is an important aspect of breakthrough decision making, and since I have done this, I have not had groups leave a meeting unhappy with what was prioritised and committed to.

Many classic methods, like brainstorming, prohibit criticism and only give time to briefly present ideas. If Lena and I tried to use one of these methods when choosing what to eat, we would never get to the heart of the matter and talk about why our ideas are important. We would be stuck in a criticism-free zone uttering meaningless pleasantries to each other. What good would this do? The surface level of an idea is not what needs to be discussed—that is easily understood. It is the personal logic behind an idea that matters. *Why* did I want hot pot? Because it was a romantic food we could share together. *What* did Lena hope to get from the pizza she was craving? Cheese, a comfort food that reliably gives her energy. It sounds simple, but it can be difficult to stop and try to understand someone else's idea. When you come up with an idea on your own, it is your precious baby. You think it is unique and the prettiest little thing in the world. You see it through rose-coloured glasses and are excited to have discovered it. In this stage where you are in love with your idea, it is hard to focus on what other people are thinking and their suggestions. How can we force people to do this? By dedicating significant time to idea selection using dialogue.

Hasty decisions

One of the most well-known facilitation group methods today, the World Café, starts with many small groups simultaneously discussing topics, continues with participants rotating and cross-fertilising the discussions, and ends with small groups making a summary of their own topic. The World Café is a fantastic method for creating and understanding lots of ideas, but little time is spent finding out what the best ones are. Most likely, the participants will be happy after having a good discussion, but they will be far from aligning and choosing the ideas. In fact, they may be dealing with a bit of chaos after being exposed to so many different viewpoints and suggestions.

Most people I see leading groups are perfectly capable at guiding a group to create ideas. If they are particularly good, then they can get everyone to understand the ideas, too. But this is not good enough. Participants need a deeper understanding of why the ideas are important, and what their strengths and weaknesses are. This process of choosing and prioritising ideas is called *convergence*, and special tools and methods are used to help a group do this. While most of the focus is on the idea creation stage, convergence is just as important—when someone is asked to choose and defend an idea, new information is created, and passionate discussions come to life.

Unfortunately, most people try to breeze through this stage too quickly. Typically, the group leader simply asks the participants to choose and vote for the favourites. Or worse, they ask group members to first cluster the ideas, name the clusters and finally prioritises the vague group names covering multiple ideas. Prioritising helps you see individual preferences, but it is not the same as decision making.

My favourite topic is slowing down convergence. This means first using individual thinking to judge the logic behind ideas, discussing priorities in changing small groups, prioritising—not individually, but in small groups to force further discussion and prioritising again and again. As a result, there will be more alignment and better consensus. Even if one of the participants does not have his or her idea chosen, they have had the chance to explain why their idea is important and will understand the logic behind the selected ideas. Choosing the right ideas is just as important as creating and developing ideas. If you are dealing with complex topics, you might even consider using most of your time on convergence.

Being the centre of attention

Professional group leaders often feel the need to justify their presence (and their wages) by placing themselves in the centre of everything, leading every discussion, providing constant instructions and feedback to the group, and policing the whole process like a traffic warden. I am talking about trainers, coaches, project managers, innovation specialists, and team leads. These people need to talk, as their career is based in sharing their knowledge and leading. I love to talk too and understand the appeal of a good monologue, but you also need to know when to shut your mouth, sit back, and let the group do the heavy lifting.

Some years ago, our small team at my company was experiencing some internal challenges and we brought in a team coach to help. In facilitating a team development session for us, she talked about our challenges, gave each person a chance to share their story, and summarised all our thoughts. She supported all individuals, asked clever questions, and more—she was doing it all and doing it well. Despite her strong start, everyone was struggling to stay wake a mere 30 minutes into the session. Her problem was that she was overly involved. She was running the meeting process and telling us when to ask questions, who should be answering, making sure everyone had a chance to participate even if they had nothing to say, and even when we could take a break to get some coffee. Managing the process led to the coach speaking for most of the time, and long stretches passed when meeting participants were forced to listen passively. Naturally, people lost focus. It is crucial to give people time to talk with each other, instead of forcing them to idly sit and listen to one person run the show.

There are quite a few ways that you can go wrong when leading groups, but even with all the potential pitfalls, most people get some degree of positive results because when people are brought together to collaborate, good things happen. You can make great things happen and unleash stronger outcomes by eliminating these common mistakes from your leadership profile.

Breakthrough decision making

As you can see, I am quite capable at pointing out mistakes, but don't worry! This book much more than an opportunity for me to complain and identify errors. In *Handbook of Professional Facilitation: Theory, Tools, and Design*, I demonstrate how using dialogic tools and slowing down the decision-making process will help people make better decisions. In other words, I believe that if you get people talking, they will begin to understand each other and create fantastic ideas. Then give them time to decide together what the best ideas are. These are the keys to group decision making. This may sound simple, but in practice it can be difficult. My journey to becoming an expert in group leadership was rough and filled with many failures along the way. I was filled with a gung-ho enthusiasm to try everything and I rushed ahead without having all the tools and experience I needed to succeed. It is my hope that this book will illuminate a simple and direct path to optimal group decision making.

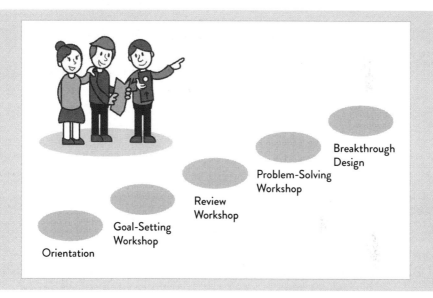

Handbook of Professional Facilitation: Theory, Tools, and Design Volume 1 begins with an orientation that covers the history of group decision making and the development of the most common group-level tools. To understand how breakthrough decision making works, it is important to visit its theoretical beginnings, which come from the field of social psychology. The orientation continues with an explanation of the three cornerstones of breakthrough decision making: emergent and convergent thinking modes, the CSA structure for workshop design, and a neutral leader to guide the group.

The following chapters showcase three different types of workshops: a goal-setting workshop, a review workshop, and a problem-solving workshop. Each chapter has an introduction explaining the content, tools presented, and why the material is helpful to you, the group leader. A scene from a meeting is presented first, and then dissected in the analysis section of the chapter. The chapters use actual examples from my career as a group leader and present them as case studies. At the end of each chapter I will share with you my process outline which shows how I executed each workshop. These process outlines can be copied and used as is, or you can modify them to your specific needs.

Finally, we will take a broader look at how to design workshops using the CSA structure. With CSA, a workshop is divided into three parts: clarifying, solutions, and action. You will learn how to choose the tools for each part, which is the key to success in group decision making.

Once you have finished Volume 1 and learned how to choose the right tools for the job, you are ready for the more advanced leadership techniques presented in *Handbook of Professional Facilitation: Theory, Tools, and Design Volume 2*. Volume 2 will show you the key competencies world-class leaders have. It also presents how to handle difficult leadership situations, like dealing with emotions and running effective virtual meetings.

Before we get started, I have an important disclaimer for you:
This book is for leaders, team coaches, trainers, organisational development practitioners, experts, enthusiasts, complete beginners, and anyone else who wants to help groups make better decisions. Since it provides you with everything you need to lead the group decision-making process, it is beneficial for both professionals planning week-long workshops and for someone who has volunteered to lead their first meeting at work.

I hope you do not get hung up on the terms. You will see the terms *facilitator* and *group leader* used interchangeably. We also use the term *leader*. This term does not refer to a traditional leader who runs a business or is in charge of finding the right answers, but a facilitative leader who helps groups develop the best solution. Not everyone who works with groups identifies as a facilitator, but everyone who guides groups through meetings and workshops is in a leadership position. Also, you will see some case studies talk about planning a workshop, while others mention meetings. The tools and methods presented here work for meetings and workshops, and are valuable to anyone who wants to work effectively with groups.

CHAPTER 1:
History of Group Decision Making

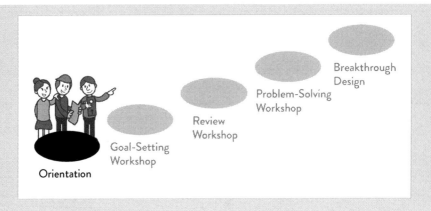

What's here
- The history and theory behind the most effective decision-making tools, including Kurt Lewin's model for change, Dynamic Facilitation, Sam Kaner's Groan Zone, and divergent and convergent thinking
- Current trends and the future of group decision making

How it helps
Once you learn the history and methodology behind group decision-making tools, you will be able to use them confidently and effectively.

War, bad meat, and Kurt Lewin: the beginning of modern group decision making

Most of the tools I use to help groups make decisions are not new. Some of them can be traced back almost 100 years to Kurt Lewin, a pioneer in the field of social psychology.

Lewin (1890–1947) was educated in both Europe and the United States and specialised in group dynamics. His work is so impactful that he was ranked as one of the most-cited psychologists of all time, according to a survey published in 2002 by *A Review of General Psychology*. Lewin is an important figure because of his research exploring group dynamics and behavioural change. Lewin's work intended to measure how everyone's skills, ideas, and potential connections within a group are utilised. He was truly ahead of his time, and his work gave birth to important tools and concepts like the 3-stage model for understanding organisational change, and Force Field Analysis, a diagnostic tool used for change implementation and to clarify problems.

One of Lewin's more famous studies took place in the United States during World War II. In his article "Group Decision and Social Change", published in 1947, Lewin presented the results of a series of trials which measured behavioural change in young mothers who were instructed to adopt habits beneficial to the war effort. The war put a tremendous strain on the economy and the U.S. government encouraged citizens to make sacrifices. One such sacrifice was for housewives to serve cheaper cuts of meat to their families. Sounds like a reasonable request, right? Well, it turns out that the pieces of meat that the government was trying to push were beef hearts, liver, and other organs that were strange and unappetising to most Americans. Lewin organised a trial where housewives were split into two groups. One group attended a lecture where a health professional recommended that they serve these cheaper cuts of meat. The other group of housewives attended a discussion where they were presented the same material, and then given time to discuss it with each other. After a few weeks, the housewives were surveyed and asked if they followed the suggestion to serve the cheaper cuts of meat. Less than 5 % of those that attended the lecture ended up adopting the new behaviour, while over 30 % that participated in the small group discussions served the cheaper meat to their families.

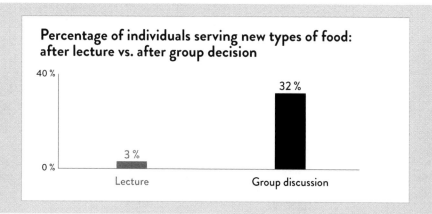

Percentage of individuals serving new types of food: after lecture vs. after group decision

*Lewin then decided to test how group discussion performed against personal meetings with an expert. He used a hospital in Iowa as the setting where mothers met privately with a nutritionist to receive nutritional advice and guidance about how to care for their baby. The nutritionist suggested giving cod liver oil and orange juice to the babies regularly to improve immune system health. Unfortunately, not very many mothers were taking the advice, so Lewin again set up study groups of 10 new mothers and a nutritionist. In both groups and in private meetings, the advice to give cod liver oil and orange juice was given. Follow-up interviews took place a few weeks later to see if the mothers were acting on the nutritional advice. Once again, group decision was superior, and the behavioural change was much higher than individual instruction with the nutritionist.

The results were undisputable—putting people into groups led to information being internalised and used! This was great news for the new-born babies that were healthy due to all the cod liver oil they were getting, although some people may not have been so keen on the new behaviour of eating beef liver instead of steak for dinner. But why were groups so effective in creating behavioural changes?

Lewin recognised that the decision-making process began with people naturally discussing the pros and cons of an idea. During the group discussions about using cheaper cuts of meat, Lewin observed wives voicing concerns to each other as they wondered if the meat would taste funny or if their husbands would like it.

These results illustrate a core principal of breakthrough decision making: lasting behavioural change will not happen without discussion and the interchange of ideas and personal rationale. Once people have had the chance to share with and learn from the group, their mindset can change. Lewin and his team of psychologists were working with groups to problem solve, create new ideas and connections, and build lasting change. These lofty goals and the methods they used to reach them made Lewin and his team pioneers in group decision making.

---

* Lewin, K. (1947) "Group Decision and Social Change." In: Newcomb, T. and Hartley, E., Eds., Readings in Social Psychology, Holt, Rinehart & Winston, New York, 197–211

Divergent and convergent thinking

J.P. Guilford succeeded Lewin as the next psychologist to make major theoretical contributions to group decision making in the early 1950s. Guilford spent a large part of his career mapping out the nature of creativity and problem solving. He devised a theory called the Structure of Intellect (SI) Theory, which outlines cognitive ability across different planes (visual, behavioural, etc). With this theory Guilford made the distinction between convergent and divergent production, which he presented in his book, *The Nature of Human Intelligence* (1967). Nowadays, we know these terms as divergent and convergent thinking.

Divergent and convergent thinking

Creative thinking can be divided into two very different modes: divergent and convergent thinking. Both are needed for effective creativity. Divergent thinking is essential for creating new ideas and convergent thinking is needed for analysing the practicality of an idea.

Divergent
thinking

creating
ideas

Convergent
thinking

choosing
the best ideas

Divergent thinking starts when content is created freely and without restraint. Convergent thinking can be thought of as logical thinking, when the content generated during the divergent phase is prioritised based on merit.

People tend to shoot down each other's suggestions. Therefore, when it comes to creating ideas, suggestions, an action plan, or anything else, the importance of separating convergent and divergent thinking was considered crucial. Instead of killing one idea at a time, we first withhold our judgement so that enough ideas are created before choosing the best ones.

Even before Guilford was developing his theories concerning the human intellect and origins of creativity, an advertising executive was pioneering methods to put these theories into practice. His name was Alex Osborn, and he invented something that I am sure you are familiar with—brainstorming. Osborn loved ideas, and he viewed them as important building blocks for life. He believed that brainstorming was for everyone, even the elderly! In his book, *How to Think Up!* Osborn stated that, "Even old folks can think up things when they try" (Osborn 3). As a facilitator who also happens to be an old person, I appreciate Osborn's commitment to ideas and his belief that anyone can create them. He was instrumental in helping people tap into their creativity.

While Guilford and Osborne solved the problem of prematurely shooting down ideas, they accidentally created a new one. In classical brainstorming there is no dedicated stage to criticise or challenge ideas. Without the opportunity to challenge someone else's ideas or the need to defend your own ideas, the logic behind an idea is not understood, and they are not strengthened and developed further. Thankfully, this weakness in classical brainstorming has led to the birth of better and more complete brainstorming tools.[*]

The rise of facilitated meetings

The importance of meetings and their function of bringing people together rose to prominence in the 1970s and 1980s. The book *How to Make Meetings Work*, by David Straus and Michael Doyle, proposed that modern society is built around group interaction, and without it, society would not be able to persevere. Straus and Doyle contributed enormously to modern facilitation by highlighting the importance of

---

[*] We will cover a few of these tools later on in this very book. If you are interested in taking a deep dive into a tool I find superior to brainstorming, try my book, *Idealogue: Beyond Brainstorming* (2016).

group memory and showcasing coming errors that are committed in meetings, such as one person dominating the floor by speaking too much.

To fix these errors, Straus and Doyle proposed to have a content-neutral person lead the meeting and only focus on the process while not worrying about the content of the meeting. This idea brought facilitation into meetings and was a big change from the traditional setup where a meeting was led by a chairman—usually the boss—who was focused on both the process of the meeting and the content.

People vs. task: Two competing focal points

The old saying "history is written by the victors" hints at the idea that there are competing narratives, and the winner decides which version is recorded in the annals of history as fact. Facilitation is similar in that there are competing schools of thought about where the primary focus of the facilitator should be. One side argues that the people are the primary focus, while the other side places greater emphasis on the methods and tasks that are used with the group. Lewin and his team adopted a very people-centric approach which used semi-structured group discussions to achieve results. Lewin believed that if you got people in a room together and gave them time to talk about a key topic, then alignment within the group and lasting change would follow. This approach focuses on interaction between people as the driver of alignment and agreement within the group.

On the other side are those who believe that aligning the goals and tasks creates productive interactions within the group. A prime example of this belief system is presented by Edgar H. Schein in his notable book, *Process Consultation: Its Role in Organizational Development*, published in 1969. Process consultation comes from the field of psychology. It stresses a common goal and a shared purpose within a group. Once this has been established, then roles are assigned. The theory here is that if everyone has a common purpose, they will be aligned and will interact effectively with each other. This idea introduced a small crisis into the field of organisational development. Should you focus on the task like Schein suggests? Or do you approach facilitation by being people-oriented, like Lewin outlined?

Schein popularised the task-centric approach, and as a result, many process consultants were active in the 1970s and 1980s. Today there is no clear distinction, and the group leader can choose the approach that they prefer. While it is natural to gravitate towards one of these approaches more than the other, I think it is essential to be familiar with both sides.

The Groan Zone

After brainstorming became popular, there was an abundance of ideas but no clear path about how to make sense of them. People were frustrated and needed a solution. From the 1960s through the 1980s it became popular to group ideas together when brainstorming. All around the world new tools categorising all ideas were being introduced to aid in decision making. This was the time when tools such as the Nominal Group Technique, Metaplan Pinpoint Facilitation Method, Affinity Diagram, Opera, and ICA Consensus Method were developed and widely used around the world. Many of these tools were built in the mould of classical brainstorming, which forbids the criticism of ideas during the creative process. As developing technology opened the door for collaborative projects on a larger scale, increasing complexity and offering a faster timeline, the tendency of these tools to simplify by grouping became more of a hinderance.

The shortcomings of these tools led facilitator Sam Kaner to invent a new framework called the Groan Zone. He proposed that the 2-part model of divergent and convergent thinking was incomplete and that there is a middle ground in between called the Groan Zone. According to Kaner, this is an unavoidable area where participants will feel a bit frustrated and uncomfortable. If a facilitator does not acknowledge this zone and help people work through it, then decision making will be poor.

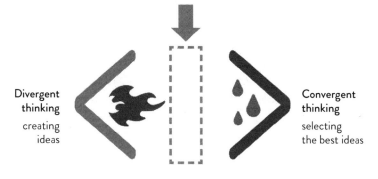

Kaner's Groan Zone

The Groan Zone lies between divergent and convergent thinking, and a group must pass through it for effective decision making to occur.

Divergent thinking

creating ideas

Convergent thinking

selecting the best ideas

According to Kaner, it is essential to understand the framework of an idea before making a decision. Kaner thought that this process was second nature to most, and that a group would engage in it automatically without being prompted. Kaner explained this phenomenon as the period that exists between divergent thinking and convergent thinking during which participants wrestle with the rationale and logic behind other people's ideas. He called it the Groan Zone because it is uncomfortable and can feel like a struggle when you are in it. This process may seem a bit inconsistent; first we forbid people from explaining their ideas during the divergent thinking phase, and then this is followed by the difficult process of explaining your thoughts in the Groan Zone. If this seems illogical or ill conceived, do not worry. In the pursuit of optimal decision making, understanding another person's reasoning is key, and Kaner's Groan Zone puts us firmly on the right path.

New approaches for dealing with complexity

Flash forward a bit to the last decades of the 20th century: Millions of professionals gained regular access to the internet, which was changing the face of business. The world was more interconnected, and projects that were once impossible now took place in real-time with teams scattered across the globe. Collaboration was happening in new and exciting ways and this led to tools like Open Space Technology, World Café and Dynamic Facilitation becoming popular. These tools specialise in dealing with complexity, albeit in different ways.

The Open Space Technology method is a bit different in that it helps groups deal with many small questions simultaneously. Harrison Owen published the method in 1993 in his book, *Open Space Technology: A User's Guide*. The method allows participants to propose any topic they want to talk about, and then chair a mini meeting about it. People can come and go as they please from mini-meeting to mini-meeting. The freedom to choose both the meeting topics and which meetings to attend allow participants to find and explore topics that are important to them. I must mention that in my experience, Open Space Technology succeeds in creating deep and passionate small-group discussions that other tools cannot match.

World Café is another method that can create multiple discussions that occur at the same time. David Isaacs and Juanita Brown noticed that the most important conversations took place in an informal atmosphere. They hypothesised that a method based around the relaxed atmosphere of a café would be both useful and popular, and they were right. World Café splits a larger group into several small groups and has multiple rounds of conversation.

Dynamic Facilitation is a group sense-making tool. When someone suggests the first solutions, instead of letting people shoot that idea down, Dynamic Facilitation helps the group explore related facts, concerns, problem statements, and new solutions aiding the group to define a common framework. A tool like Dynamic Facilitation is needed for creating shared understanding and it is an indispensable tool which I use frequently to help a group navigate the conflicts and complexity of modern times.

Group decision making today

After our trip through the history of group decision making, you may be asking yourself, What about today? Group decision-making tools and methods are being applied in new settings, an exciting development. One example is the introduction of participatory principles into Agile software development teams.[*] Normally, software teams analyse the success and challenges of a project after the fact in what is called a post-mortem. Now, they are abandoning this and using group-level tools to get continual feedback during a project.[**] This change towards participatory tools has been a huge success, as the tools add tremendous value to software development teams where individuals tend to be isolated in their work.

The most exciting change regarding facilitation today does not even come from the business world. Think back to when you were a student. Maybe a teacher guided you through exercises in a thick, dusty textbook. Or, if you are older like me, they wrote sentences on a chalkboard for you to repeat. The teacher was the centre of it all and the knowledge dispenser.

Do you think that model holds up and is being used today? It probably is in some places, but many countries are already looking to abandon it. With access to knowledge at an all-time high, and more and more people becoming highly trained and educated, the core question is no longer how to increase skills and know-how, but how to make sense of all of the readily available information. The challenge for organisations today is not access to information or a lack of expertise, but rather interpreting all this information and utilising it productively.

Recently I had a conversation with a director from the Finnish Ministry of Education about schooling systems. She told me that

---

[*] Agile teams refer to a small group that has the knowhow and skills to carry out a project from inception to completion. These teams are known for adapting quickly and being able to determine the needs of the project and how they should focus to meet these needs as they unfold. They can most commonly be found in software development.

[**] Diana Larsen, Esther Derby and Ken Schwaber cover the application of facilitative-like tools in the book, "Agile Retrospectives: Making Good Teams Great".

Finland is not looking to follow the mechanistic way of learning that has been used for years and years in other countries. Instead, she recognised that information is everywhere and that teachers of the future will need to focus on enabling people to make use of the knowledge and connect it with the realities of others. In other words, the teacher of the future will be leading their students in decision making. I like the sound of that!

Local governments and municipal organisations are now using participatory meetings to elicit feedback from residents in townhall-style meetings that are based around active dialogue from both sides. A prominent example is the group sessions held in Louisiana, USA, after Hurricane Katrina. The federal agency FEMA was widely criticised for their slow response to the disaster, which left many people home-less. In the months and years that followed, many sessions with local government and members of the community were held to ensure that everyone would be better prepared for the next devastating hurricane. To me, this is democracy at its finest, and I look for this trend to carry on as group decision-making methods continue to change the world.

CHAPTER 2:

Cornerstones of Breakthrough Decision Making

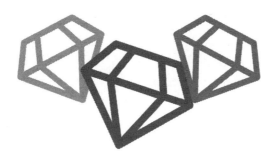

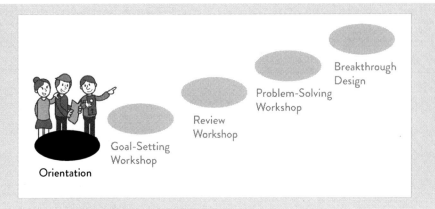

Orientation
Goal-Setting Workshop
Review Workshop
Problem-Solving Workshop
Breakthrough Design

What's here

Three cornerstones of breakthrough decision making

- The emergent and convergent thinking modes
- The Clarifying → Solutions → Action (CSA) workshop structure
- Content-neutral leader guiding the workshop/meeting process

How it helps

The thinking modes of the breakthrough decision-making process, along with the CSA workshop structure and the neutral role of the group leader, are the foundation for successful group decision making. These concepts not only illustrate how to lead productive workshops, they also shed light on what makes the decision-making tools we use effective. Learning the theory behind the methods will help you understand what to do and why you are doing it.

Breakthrough decision making defined

Before diving headfirst into the cornerstones that constitute breakthrough decision making, let's first establish a definition of what exactly it is. Individually, the words that form the term *breakthrough decision making* can be defined as:

breakthrough: a sudden discovery that usually has positive connotations

decision: a choice made after consideration

making: the action of creating or doing

When combined, these words define a dynamic process where a group of people discover new ideas before making a choice to commit to the best course of action. People make decisions individually and in groups all the time, so what is special about breakthrough decision making? The key difference is adding dialogue to the whole decision-making process. When ideas are created and then selected using communication tools that give people the chance to collaborate, ideas are better understood, and new discoveries happen which lead to even better ideas. Breakthrough decision making is a dialogic group decision-making process that gets everyone engaged and committed.

Breakthrough decision making =
A structured participatory dialogue process focused on creating understanding and making a choice.

The benefits of breakthrough decision making are:
- New discoveries
- Better decisions by combining group knowledge
- Acceptance and commitment to ideas
- Structured process leading to concrete action

You might be thinking that this is nothing new and asking why breakthrough decision making is necessary. After all, we all have come up with something important on our own, and people have individual breakthroughs all the time. You have surely had first or second-hand experience with this, too. If this is the case, then what is the need for breakthrough decision making? While it is true that people excel at creating ideas and making decisions on an individual level, the process gets muddied and much more difficult at the group level. In groups people become too focused on developing their own ideas and decisions, neglecting input from other group members. To get a picture of how this looks, simply think back to any lacklustre meeting that you have attended. Jack from Finance is talking about solutions, Ann is trying to micromanage specific actions, Joe is going on about his feelings, Billy just came up with a bright idea for a completely unrelated topic, and everyone else is either struggling to stay awake or updating their social media profiles. In other words, the group is fragmented and lacks cohesion. People are either working on different topics, or if by luck they are on the same topic, then they are focusing on different stages of it. Most large organisations are full of talented people with great ideas, but these ideas will not become influential unless people are aligned towards the same goals. In other words, for an idea to become a breakthrough idea, people need to be on the same page. A breakthrough idea is any idea that makes it through the resistance of people, gains acceptance and is agreed upon. It does not have to be unique. Perhaps the idea was always there, but it never gained enough popularity to be executed.

> **A breakthrough idea is any thought that:**
> 1. Makes it through any resistance other people have to it
> 2. Gains acceptance
> 3. Is agreed to on a group level

Breakthrough decision making is composed of three cornerstones:
1. Emergent and convergent thinking modes
2. The Clarifying → Solutions → Action (CSA) workshop structure
3. A neutral leader to guide the decision-making process

Cornerstone #1:
Emergent and convergent thinking modes

Breakthrough decision making is a process that guides participants through two modes of thinking; emergence, and convergence.[*] Emergence occurs when ideas are created, explored, understood, developed, merged, and rejected. The result of emergence is a common understanding of the best ideas and their logic—the ideas that survive people's resistance and scepticism become obvious options. Sometimes one breakthrough idea is so strong and overwhelming that it kills all other options, while sometimes there are several breakthroughs or simply potential ones. The convergence phase is when ideas are logically inspected, often keeping implementation and practicality in mind. Convergent thinking is for comparing ideas and deciding which are the best of the bunch. This creates a new type of discussion around the ideas—often deeper and sometimes longer than during emergence phase. The outcome of the convergence phase is a choice.

Emergence always comes before convergence. This order is always the same. The group leader can use their understanding of emergence and convergence to choose the right tools and to modify the workshop plan as needed. Creating the perfect plan for breakthrough decision making is all about balancing the two modes of thinking. Depending on the group's need, the leader may want to spend more time on emergence, or perhaps more time on convergence. They may decide that equal time for each mode is best. If the priority is creativity and understanding of ideas, then I give more time to emergence. If a strong commitment to ideas is most important, then I spend more time using convergent tools. It is important for the group leader to understand each of these phases and the purpose they serve for planning effective group decision making processes.

---

[*] The terms emergence and convergence are synonymous with emergent thinking and convergent thinking. You will see both terms used in this book.

Emergence

Let's look at the first thinking mode, emergence. Assume that you and I meet for lunch, and we both have an exciting business proposal to share. I want you to lend me £3,000, and you want me to contact a list of 50 business leads that you possess. When I ask you for the loan, you look at me as if I were crazy! Maybe you think I am headed off to the casino with that money. On the flip side, when you ask me to manage your business leads, I think to myself, "Why the heck should I do that? I don't know the ins and outs of the situation." We do not understand the logic behind these ideas, and I would call them cold ideas that will likely be rejected.

Now let's say that we have the chance to explain ourselves a bit more. I tell you that I need the loan to upgrade my workshop room and equipment in order to make it much more appealing for new clients. You hear this and excitedly respond that you want me to help with the business leads because you have a fantastic new product you are ready to launch, and you need all the help you can get in contacting as many people as you can. Now our ideas are getting warmer because we understand each other, but we can still take it a step further. If we are patient and continue discussing these ideas, we can have a breakthrough and realise that what we really want is one shared idea—to open a business training centre together. This way, I would have an upgraded meeting space, and you would have the support with your business leads that you want. Best of all, our breakthrough idea of opening a business together is more impactful than our two individual ideas.

Emergence is the phase where people begin to share their reasoning and interest in relation to the shared ideas. This begins the process of group members understanding each other. During emergence, ideas are shared, understood, and combined, which creates something new. Some ideas transform into new concepts, while others naturally die off and are discarded. A successful emergent phase involves people looking at the logic and reasoning that support or weaken an idea. Why was the idea suggested in the first place? What are the goals and beliefs tied to this idea? When someone explores and understands the pros and cons of an idea, they become connected to it and can make it their own by further developing it or using it as inspiration to create a new idea. As you lead a group through emergence, you might observe one major breakthrough, such as the creation of a new idea that everyone loves; or, there may be several smaller breakthroughs when people come to understand other frameworks and perspectives. People and organisations are full of ideas that have never been properly discussed.

I define emergence as the process where people share their ideas and begin to understand other people's ideas, logic, and assumptions. During emergence, a person may reject, accept, or accept part of an idea and create a new idea combining their own ideas and those of others.

> Emergence is the phase where people share their ideas, logic and assumptions with each other; ideas gain acceptance (or die) and ideas are combined to create breakthroughs.

The emergent mode of thought is crucial to any innovation process. It can create striking new ideas that can change the course of an organisation, and it also helps combat the tendency to shoot down ideas before they have the chance to be considered.

Emergence and *emergent thinking* are terms that have varying definitions and they have been used in multiple contexts since their introduction, often in the middle of a 3-stage decision making model. Bryan Rill and Matti Hämäläinen put forth a 3-stage model containing divergence, emergence, and convergence in their 2018 book, *The Art of Co-Creation: A Guidebook for Practitioners*. Rill and Hämäläinen state that their model was influenced by the work of German physiologist Herman von Helmholtz who is known for his 3-stage model of creativity (saturation, incubation, illumination).

The book *Gamestorming; a playbook for innovators, rulebreakers, and changemakers* (2010) defines emergence as a zone where old things are seen in new ways and where people have the chance to revisit and sort through ideas. They use the word in the context of games, and they claim every game has a period of divergence, emergence, and convergence.

As mentioned earlier, legendary facilitator Sam Kaner proposed that there is a middle phase between divergence and convergence which is a true challenge for participants, and aptly named it the Groan Zone.[*] Kaner states in his book *Facilitator's Guide to Participatory Decision-Making* that the Groan Zone can be so uncomfortable for some that it is perceived as an obstacle and a negative, and if mutual understanding between participants is not reached people will flee from the Groan Zone completely and the session will fail.[**] As Kaner tells it, the Groan Zone is a real battleground where people either fight through, or projects wither up and die.

I prefer to use a two-stage model that has two thinking modes: emergent thinking and divergent thinking. I think this is superior to a 3-stage model consisting of divergence, emergence, and convergence? Why? Purely for practical reasons. It is difficult to build understanding of lots of ideas after they have been created. People get anxious if they have to sit and listen to presentations for long periods of time. Or they can focus solely on their own ideas which they start furiously defending. It is better to get into sharing logic and frameworks as soon as possible. Instead of adding a stage of deep communication in the middle, we add dialogue both into beginning and ending stages. To start with, we need emergence for generating and comprehending ideas. You may think that once you have heard all the ideas you are then

---

[*] See Chapter 1: History of Group Decision Making for more on Sam Kaner and the Groan Zone.

[**] (Kaner 221)

ready to make a choice. If this is true, then perhaps one stage is enough, right? Well, not quite. My experience has taught me that understanding an idea and implementing it are two vastly different things. Before a group can decide what to do with an idea, they need a stage to compare the ideas and to chat about their practical implications.

Traditional divergent thinking tools hinder emergence. Classical brainstorming restricted the critique of ideas—a criminal offence that kills emergence! If an idea is not challenged or critiqued, then there is little or no understanding of the logic behind the idea, and it is nearly impossible to commit to an idea that you do not understand.

I remember seeing this unfortunate effect in action early in my facilitation career. I was facilitating a session for a large print house and they wanted to brainstorm ideas about what to do with an old historical printer that they affectionately called Big Barbara. Big Barbara was a bit sentimental to the company. She was purchased over 50 years ago and represented their expansion at the time into one of the larger print houses in Scandinavia. The creativity session was a success and hundreds of ideas were generated by the group of around 20. Classical brainstorming methods were used to create these ideas. The problem was that when we transitioned from divergent thinking to convergent thinking, people only prioritised their own ideas while lacking understanding of what their co-workers thought. Some of the ideas were good, and this made some group members quite pleased with themselves. I love to see people happy, but unfortunately this raised another challenge. When someone is happy with their own idea, it is hard for them to step back from it and consider other alternatives. Big Barbara ended up being donated to a local museum where she is still gathering dust to this day. The only reason that this was the outcome is because the company Vice President thought of it, and no one had the courage to disagree with him. Seeing how hard it was for people to pay attention to and understand other people's ideas led me to create my own emergence method called Idealogue—a tool based around stealing other people's ideas.*

---

* The motto of the Idealogue method is to *steal with pride*. Instructing someone to "steal only the good ideas" forces them to think about the frameworks and logic behind them. You can read much more about this method in my book, *Beyond Brainstorming: Idealogue*, which was published in 2016.

Why do we use the term emergence? The term emerge refers to the process of becoming visible or coming into existence. This fits my view of the decision-making process better than the term diverge which means branching off into different directions. When I am called to lead a workshop, my clients usually do not need too many different directions or options. They already know the answers themselves but cannot agree on the right solution. They already have diverged before I even got there, and what they need is for all the ideas to be made visible and understood so that they can make a choice. There are very experienced and intelligent professionals that would prefer the term divergence instead of emergence. If you decide to use the word divergence instead of emergence, I can accept that. I just hope you use lots dialogue-based tools to get participants talking and interacting with each other. Doing so will bring out the best results possible.

Facilitating emergence

Emergence is difficult. Do you remember the last time you came up with an idea that you were proud of? You probably felt a rush of enthusiasm and were keen on telling everyone all about it. The last thing you were interested in was putting your idea on pause to listen to someone else tell you about their idea, instead. Getting people to listen to each other enthusiastically while not becoming frustrated or impatient—this is the challenge during emergence. A facilitator can make this challenge much easier by giving time for individual thinking, discussion in small groups, and giving clear instructions and support throughout the entire process.

Effective emergence begins with connecting the individual with his or her own thinking. People need time to gather their thoughts and clarify their own thinking before they are ready to share it with other people. This is where many ideas are created at once. The most effective tactics are to give ample time for individual thinking and give plenty of encouragement to the group. Instruct the group to write down ideas and thoughts silently for a few minutes before continuing with the session. If anyone seems to be having a hard time, you can jump in with more instructions or some friendly motivational words to keep them on track and creating ideas. If you notice that some participants are stuck, do not push them. As long as some ideas have been produced, they are ready for the rest of the emergent-convergent process.

A major obstacle that stands in the way of ideas being accepted is the natural tendency for people to critique and kill ideas by thinking of reasons why they won't work. Thoughts and beliefs that limit or disallow an idea are called restraining forces. It is human nature to automatically gravitate towards restraining forces, and when one new idea is proposed, the drawbacks often come instantly to mind. How about two new ideas? Two surely must be more effective to consider than one, right? Well, this is also problematic because it creates competition between the two possibilities, and they are pitted against one another.

The steps that make up emergence:

1. Ideas are created individually

2. People are instructed to discuss their ideas and then come up with breakthrough ideas. These ideas are developed further in small groups and repeated rounds of dialogue.

3. Visualising the best ideas and making sure they are understood.

One key principle of emergence is to discuss multiple ideas simultaneously. Doing so leads to productive discussion and an exploration into the logic that drives the ideas. Many ideas at play creates confusion for participants as they internally try and make sense of the ideas and to connect them together. This results in people being more open to different idea than if they were only to assess them one or two at a time. The concept of starting with multiple ideas before choosing them is something that we have seen before—divergence and convergence.[*] In the 1950s, J.P. Guilford defined two different

---

[*] Refer to Chapter 1: History of Group Decision Making for more information on J.P. Guilford and the development of divergence and convergence.

thinking modes: divergent thinking and convergent thinking. This was an important development because introducing two modes of thought reduced the tendency to kill off ideas. By structuring separate times for creative thinking (divergence) and idea selection and prioritisation (convergence), Osborn and Guilford hoped to allow for more ideas to flourish and be considered, instead of engaging the restraining and supporting forces right away. How is our emergence different? We simply get the people to explain and to merge their ideas right in the beginning to create alignment and breakthroughs.

After creating ideas individually, emergence continues into small groups. Ideas do not get aligned when they are presented, rather emergence happens in small groups where people have a chance to discuss and explore ideas together. A key consideration is the size of small discussion groups. If you are leading a workshop, then most likely you will want to divide the entire group into smaller groups in order to have a more effective session. I have found that the best group size for creating understanding are three people per group. Pair work simply does not do the trick; perhaps there is not enough diversity in pairs to fully ignite the creative mind. Three is the magic number and an effective group size for emergence. Four or five works well too, but are large enough for some people to hide and not participate. I do not use groups larger than eight. The more you spend time mixing the small groups the more you will have alignment and understanding of the ideas. At the end of a successful emergent process, some options become naturally more viable than others and they might not even need to be presented. They have already been understood and accepted.

With groups you are likely to get what you ask for. If you ask the groups to share, they will be making presentations to each other, and listening to monologues gets boring in a little while. If you ask the group to come up with a breakthrough—the best ideas they can come up with—they are much more likely to truly discuss and align their thinking. It is important that everyone understands how emergence happens. Most people have not heard the term before, and it may seem daunting or a bit mystical if they do not grasp what is supposed to happen. I like explaining emergence by telling them a story that involves cold ideas (misunderstood or not understood at all and likely to fail), warm ideas (ideas that are partially understood) and breakthrough ideas (a shared discovery that is beneficial for everyone). You can draw from your own experience and give them a personal example or use the story of Big Barbara the printer, which I shared earlier in this chapter, as a template. Either way, once the group has heard an example of how emergence works, then they are more likely to achieve it themselves when it is their turn to share ideas.

Emergence and creativity

Is the emergence process creative? Not always. Sometimes participants choose practical ideas instead of new ones, but I do not see this as an obstacle. Even if the ideas chosen by the group are not original, I still consider them breakthroughs—they were successful enough to gain acceptance of the group.

Nevertheless, you may complement the emergence process with creativity tools especially during the individual stage. Edward de Bono, a psychologist from Malta, introduced a creativity method called Lateral Thinking. De Bono developed Lateral Thinking as an alternative to Vertical Thinking, which is a very structured process designed to pick a single solution based on logical merit. Lateral Thinking is an ability closely related to humour, insight, and creativity. It requires the thinker to force connections to create new—and sometimes curious—solutions. For example, let's suppose that I am hosting guests in my home, and these guests are visiting Finland for the first time, and I want to share with them some good Finnish food. A logical solution would be to smoke some salmon in my smokery. Salmon is a very popular food here in Finland, as it is in many parts of the world. Instead, I think laterally and imagine another popular animal, the bear. It roams the pristine Finnish forests and is respected by the animals and people that call Finland home. So, I end up smoking and serving my guests salmon, but I make sure that the magical and powerful bear is the star of the show. I fill the table with pine needles and forest berries, dress my visitors in traditional Finnish gowns and hats, and lead them in a sing-along of old folk songs that all pay tribute to the bear. By thinking laterally, I was able to give my guests a meal that they would never forget.

In the book *Lateral Thinking*, in which the term of the same name is introduced, De Bono stated that both types of thinking were crucial, but that the rigidness of vertical thinking needed to have creativity added to it to make it more adaptable. This was an important contribution to the creative process as it opened the doors for new and creative methods to be applied to the divergent thinking process.

De Bono used tools and objects to break our thinking patterns and to force connections. A few years ago, I was talking to an Innovation Director from 3M, a manufacturing company famous for their creative products. The director said, "Innovation never happens when the purchasing director talks to the sales director. They only discuss money. Innovation happens when two engineers with different expertise get together and start solving a concrete problem." New knowledge from other people forces us to connect ideas is a new way. Instead of using objects to stimulate our thinking, it is often more practical to have a good talk with someone who thinks differently! This is what we encourage people to do during the emergence phase.

Convergence: how people decide

Convergence is about making a choice. It is where ideas are compared, and their future impact and potential are explored. If there is one piece of wisdom that I want to impart again and again in this book, it is about the importance of spending adequate time on convergence. There are many people capable of leading a group to create ideas. Classical brainstorming is a great tool for this, and it is not a hard tool to use. The challenge is getting an entire group aligned and committed to the ideas.

> Convergence is the phase where people compare ideas and make a choice.

As the meeting shifts from emergence to convergence, the energy within the group also changes and the new question invigorates the participants. During emergence, the issue is to understand the idea. During convergence, the focus is to decide which idea to implement.

This transforms the ideas into competitors. It is one thing to understand an idea, but it is a different matter when people are explicitly instructed to choose *the best* idea. The ideas are now in competition with each other and this forces more discussion about the framework behind an idea.

Some group leaders may use fixed criteria here and give specific instructions or parameters to the group, but I usually do not. I believe that our mind and the environment is complex—people have different values, interests, and multiple goals. Trying to impose fixed criteria tends to be an oversimplification. Instead, I prefer to rely on group discussion when ideas need to be chosen, and simple voting tools when it comes time to visualising the priorities.

Facilitating convergence

When I facilitate convergence, I emphasise to the group that their job now is to decide which ideas to implement. This topic shift means that some people will want to take a moment and gather their thoughts, so I give a few more minutes to the group to work individually before continuing to discussion in small groups, preferably groups of three. By this point, the entire group has gone through emergence, and it is possible that everyone will be aligned and on the same page quite quickly. Next, I will lead everyone in a prioritisation activity in small groups. Once the ideas have been prioritised, I will end convergence by checking for commitment to the ideas.

The steps that make up convergence:
1. Reviewing and ranking ideas individually.
2. Considering ideas, preferences, and frameworks in small discussion groups.
3. Visualising group priorities for everyone (voting or polling tool).
4. Evaluating and deciding together as one large group.

Convergence is indispensable when it comes to group decision making and leading people to commit to an idea. Unfortunately, many facilitators and meeting leaders try to guide the group decision-making with a simple voting activity. Countless books on group voting and polling tools have been published, and there are quite a few well-known businesspeople who claim these tools as their calling card. One very popular tool is Dot Voting, which looks like this. You are handed three (or five or ten...) dots and instructed to place them next to your favourite ideas within a minute. It sounds like a reasonable way to poll a group, right? Well it can be, but only if the session had a dedicated and developed time for evaluating the options before. Simply polling will show us where the group is at a given moment but is not enough to create understanding about why the ideas should be chosen, or to create commitment to execute the ideas. The results of Dot Voting (or other similar polling tools) are incomplete without the time for discussing and understanding the content.

For clear and effective decision making, I propose giving equal weight to both processes: 50 % of the process as the emergent thinking and the remaining 50 % as convergent thinking. The time allocation is very different from traditional decision-making processes that emphasise creation of ideas but generates significantly better decisions. Sometimes the time allocation varies. In order to make a smart choice I once held a strategy workshop where we spent 15 % of the time creating ideas and 85 % of the time discussing and evaluation the numerous options. I also once held a creativity workshop where we spent 95 % on emergence and 5 % on convergence – simple because we did not want to make a final decision before the ideas were further developed.

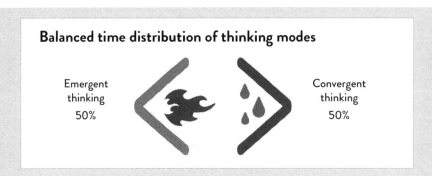

Balanced time distribution of thinking modes

Emergent thinking 50%

Convergent thinking 50%

Emergence and convergence—putting it all together

With his experiments on group decision making, father of social psychology Kurt Lewin demonstrated the power that group discussion has in creating commitment to an idea, suggestion, or course of action. Lewin stated that ideas and individual attitudes will always have driving and restraining forces. In other words, each idea will have reasoning for it (driving forces) and reasoning against it (restraining forces), and by changing these forces you can affect change. Furthermore, a decision does not happen merely because one choice seems more attractive than the other, but because through discussion one option is diminished so much that the alternative dominates the situation. In other words, some ideas get stronger and some ideas will be eliminated almost automatically as groups review them and restraining forces are identified. At the same time, supporting reasons will emerge, clarifying the stronger ideas as they become more attractive.[*] In other words, we need to have the chance to have a nice chat with each other before we can fully understand our options. Once this happens, we will be able to act intelligently and confidently.

You probably noticed similarities between the emergent and convergent phases; both began with individual thinking giving us time for connecting with our brain and for creating clarity. Next, we continued with small group discussion for creating maximum dialogue to understand each other's logic and frameworks. Unlike most current group decision-making models which group ideas and limit feedback and criticism, breakthrough decision making is based on profound dialogue. Cold thoughts that are initially not understood become warm when they are shared and discussed. People can ask questions and raise any doubts that they may have. When individual thinking and small group thinking are combined, some ideas are developed further and emerge as a clear choice. In breakthrough decision making group alignment becomes a natural outcome.

---

[*]   Lewin 1947

Cornerstone #2: The Clarifying → Solutions → Action (CSA) workshop structure

You may feel that you are armed and ready to lead groups to lofty goals using emergence and convergence, but there is a larger structure I use to guide these phases of thinking: the CSA structure, or Clarifying, Solutions, Action. CSA is a 3-stage process which organises the flow of ideas by giving the group a linear path to follow when they create ideas using the emergent and convergent thinking. The CSA workshop structure is versatile and can also be used to create new products, generate new strategies, build a vision for the future, plan a party, design a new office, decide what to cook for lunch, and countless other uses.

If we look at the breakthrough decision making process of emergence and convergence as a train, then CSA can be viewed as the tracks that steer the train as it speeds along. I remember one heated argument I had with my wife that showcases the importance of using CSA. Both of us were university students at the time, and between all our classes, extra activities, and time spent at the bar, we rarely had time to see each other. We thought that it would be a great idea to save money to take a vacation together, so we started thinking of as many ways that we could make this happen. She came up with the idea of looking for a part-time job, while I immediately began revising our monthly spending budget to try and save a little bit of cash here and there. The idea of a vacation together inspired us to immediately think of actions which we could begin doing immediately ("I can donate blood twice a month, I think it is safe!") and solutions which would help us reach our goal ("I think your family could lend us the money for a vacation, they are rich!"). But we were piling these solutions and actions on top of a foundation that was unstable. After a few hours of thinking, we began to second guess our ideas ("If you donate blood so frequently, you may feel weak and irritated all of the time!"). "Why do we want to even take a vacation together?" I asked her.

"So that we can spend time together," she replied.

A-ha. This was our true problem—we were not seeing each other as much as we wanted to. Instead of identifying this need as our primary problem from which all solutions and actions would be built around, we instead launched into ideas that could allow us to take a vacation, when in fact taking a vacation was only one possible solution to our main focus, not the main focus itself. While it was admirable for my wife and I to try and come up with ideas together, our endeavour was doomed from the start and it would have been much more successful with CSA structure to help us identify (clarify) our shared goal, and then create solutions and actions for it.

The clarifying stage also helps resolve conflicts, as people tend to argue about solutions without ever agreeing what the problem is. In organisations, a typical challenge is that someone has analysed the case in advance, but problems and goals are complex and come in different levels. The result is that when people come to a meeting or a workshop they have no idea what the problem is all about and actually have other problems in mind.

When leading workshops, I clarify the goal or problem together with the group. During the clarifying stage, a group will go through the process of emergence and convergence to align themselves about the context of the workshop and what is truly being discussed. This stage clearly defines the subject matter and ensures that everyone has a common understanding of the issue. Doing this allows for people to be more in synch and have more common ground in the later stages of a workshop. If you do this stage well, it tends to be easy to agree on solutions—they arise spontaneously.

After clarifying in CSA come the solutions and action stages, which also contain emergence → convergence structure. The key difference between these two stages is that solutions are broader, while actions are the specific tasks that a person will undertake to work towards a solution. It is common for some people to skip ahead to giving concrete and detailed actions while others give generic solutions. The solutions and action stages of the workshop may seem very similar to one another, and I have been asked if both are truly necessary. My answer is a definitive yes. Both the solutions and action stages of the workshop are needed, as they both serve crucial and distinct roles in effective workshops. In unstructured conversations, I have seen a common tendency for people to begin talking about solutions when asked about actions, and vice-versa. Separating the two and clearly defining what is expected during each stage ensures that everyone is thinking on the same level and yields better results.

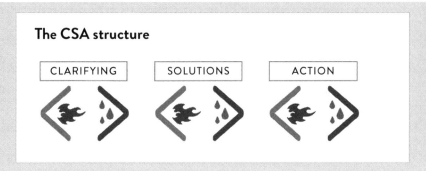

The CSA structure

CLARIFYING   SOLUTIONS   ACTION

Some professionals who are experts in leading groups add more stages to workshops than just CSA, but I do not recommend that. The stages may be logical and thoughtfully prepared, but the participants often have challenges following the logic and it is difficult to create alignment on each stage. I prefer to keep things simple by only using three stages in my workshops: clarifying, solutions, and action—the CSA structure.

If you jump from the clarifying stage directly to asking people for actions, the results will be undefined and even abstract when compared to the goal or the problem at hand. The CSA workshop process shapes and supports the following healthy decision-making process. First, you introduce a task—it could be sales process development, for example. Using CSA, first people clarify what the task is truly about: what is the concrete goal of sales process development? Or, does everyone have the same understanding of the problems at hand? Once clarified, then everyone creates solutions about how to solve it; broad ideas or initiatives that can be implemented to achieve the task. Finally, an action plan is created; specific things that can be done to enact the solutions.

The scope of the ideas becomes more defined as the group progresses through the stages of CSA, beginning with broad topics during clarifying, moving towards more specific solutions, and ending with concrete and defined actions that can be implemented without further refinement.

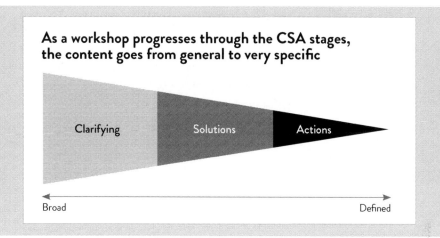

As a workshop progresses through the CSA stages, the content goes from general to very specific

Clarifying

Solutions

Actions

Broad

Defined

The two thinking modes, emergence and convergence, are repeated in each stage of CSA. This format, which uses the repetition of the emergent/convergent decision-making process within the CSA structure, is the foundation from which breakthrough decision making is built and is the blueprint for success. This format will serve you well to lead groups in almost any situation I can think of. There is only one cornerstone missing...

Cornerstone #3: A leader to guide the decision-making process

Lastly, breakthrough decision making requires a content-neutral group leader that guides the group through a meeting or workshop. The leader does this by introducing the ways of working, presenting the meeting goals and objectives, clarifying what is expected of the participants, monitoring progress, fielding questions, and more. All the responsibilities of the leader are related to the process of the meeting—tool selection, time allocation and so on—while the content of the meeting (ideas, decisions, breakthroughs, etc.) is left to the participants. They are not there to give any feedback or opinions about the content that is generated during the meeting. If they did, they would get caught up in the struggle to get their ideas heard and understood, like everyone else.

Sometimes it can be difficult to remain neutral. Imagine you are leading a meeting for the first time, that can be difficult enough. Now imagine that the results of this meeting directly affect your job. You may be hoping for a certain outcome, but with practice you will learn to focus on guiding the group using decision-making tools while putting your opinions temporarily on hold.

A great group leader...

- Is *neutral and impartial*. He or she does not share opinions or ideas. They do not criticise others' thoughts.

- *Focuses on the process*. The group leader is responsible for designing and leading the meeting process, defining the purpose of the meeting, and writing the agenda.

- *Enables everybody to participate* by selecting the best methods and tools to use.

- *Gets the group focused* on the same issue at the same time.

- *Helps with decision making.*

Imagine a beautiful red sports car, complete with chrome exhaust pipes and an engine more intricate than a swiss watch; these are our decision-making tools. It is something special sitting stationary in a parking lot, but you need a driver to unlock the car's true potential. The person leading the group is the driver capable of jamming into 5th gear while navigating hairpin turns and unlocking the benefits and value of our decision-making tools. The benefits provided by facilitation are often the missing ingredient that keep a team or organisation from achieving the results they want. Increasing collaboration, uncovering hidden competencies, and team alignment are some of the positives that come from having a group leader using the correct tools.

With a capable person overseeing group activity and making sure people are participating and focused on the same topic, the group members are able to devote all of their energy toward problem solving, goal setting, or whatever other meeting objective that there might be.

How to lead groups if you are the content owner

If you have been paying attention, then you know by now that it is important for the group leader to remain impartial and content neutral. But what should you do if you are the one holding the key information? Perhaps you are the team lead, and you have a direct stake in what is decided during a workshop. One option is to bring in someone else to lead the session. You eliminate this conflict of interest simply by assigning the role to someone else.

Another option is to use checkpoints throughout the workshop to link your ideas to the group. For instance, when the group has clarified the challenges, you may connect the group ideas with your own by adding your own challenges. When the group has created solutions, you connect group solutions with your own. After the group has made an action plan, you suggest necessary changes and add your own actions. Just make sure you appreciate the group work and explain why you cannot accept the group's suggestions. No matter which option you choose, the secret to success is having a content-neutral person to manage the meeting process.

Recapturing the cornerstones of breakthrough decision making

The cornerstones of effective decision making begins with two phases of decision making: emergence → convergence. Emergence is the phase where people share their ideas, logic and assumptions with each other; ideas gain acceptance (or die) and ideas are combined to create breakthroughs. Convergence is when the group compare ideas and their potential and make a choice.

These two phases of decision making are repeated in each stage of CSA structure: clarifying, solutions and action. CSA is a blueprint for meetings and workshops that guides the group together as they shift from different topics and narrow their focus. Clarifying is the first stage, and it is when the group defines a broad problem or goal that will become the focus of the rest of the session. During the solutions stage ideas of how to reach the goal or to solve the problem are created and chosen. Action is the final stage of CSA and where people think of concrete actionable steps that they can follow to reach the solutions that they outlined in the previous stage.

In addition, it is essential to have a person in place to lead the group through the breakthrough decision making process. This person makes sure that everyone understands the goals for the session. They focus on the process by giving clear instructions, allocating time for different activities to make sure that everything gets done while sticking to the schedule, and managing emotions and disagreements throughout the session.

Cornerstones of breakthrough decision making

1. The breakthrough decision thinking modes; emergence → convergence

2. The Clarifying → Solutions → Action (CSA) Workshop Structure

3. Content-neutral leader guiding the decision making process

Now that you are familiar with the cornerstones, you will need to make sure that they are all present in the group sessions that you lead. Now it's time to see how the cornerstones work in practice.

CHAPTER 3:

Goal Setting Workshop

3.1: Clarifying Goals with Me-We-Us and Dartboard

What's here

- **Case study**: The first stage of a 3-stage workshop. The objective in this stage is to clarify goals.

- **Tools**: Wishing, Dartboard, Dot Voting, Silent Moving, Me/We/Us

How it helps

The structure of Me/We/Us is found in many group-level tools, and for good reason. By familiarising yourself with Me/We/Us, you are not only adding a solid tool to your toolbox, but also indirectly familiarising yourself with other group decision-making tools and the principles behind them. In addition, you will learn a practical set of tools you can use for creating shared goals.

Meet Bill

Bill is the President of Upon the Sea Consulting Group, known as UTS Consulting, for short. While the names have been changed (the real Bill may not appreciate all the specifics being presented and dissected), the details presented here accurately portray a real workshop that I led and what I did to successfully guide the group through the decision-making process.

A team of experts with a growing problem

UTS Consulting President Bill Chen reached out to me through his secretary and asked me to help lead a workshop for a small group of employees that worked in the Technology Consulting branch of UTS. The company is one of the top 20 largest consulting firms in China, and while their Shanghai office is dwarfed by some of the neighbouring buildings, they are a significant player in the business consulting market. UTS is comprised of four branches: Economic Consulting, Analytics, Financial Consulting, and Technology Consulting.

As is common in many large companies, these four branches of UTS Consulting are self-sufficient and the operations of each sector do not tend to overlap. This segregation between branches runs vertically up through the company hierarchy all the way to the top. After giving me the background of UTS, Bill's secretary got straight to the point about why they were asking for my help.

"Unfortunately, the Technology Consulting branch is lagging behind the rest of the company in several key areas. There are fewer repeat customers, and customers rate the branch lower than other sectors of the company. Another area of concern is a high rate of employee turnover within the Technology Consulting branch. Our president would like to have a workshop with the several key members from the Technology Branch to create a development plan for the department that can be implemented to improve the situation."

This sounded straightforward enough, and I agreed to help.

A room with a view

It is always a bit surreal to me when I look out a window and see a landscape vastly different from the snow and green street cars I am used to when in my native Finland. Travel has been an important part of my career, and I have looked out of windows to see the dusty plains of Texas, palm trees in Indonesia, and brightly coloured orb towers of an orthodox church in Moscow. Now, in the global headquarters of Upon the Sea Consulting, I was enjoying the view from a 44th story window and looking out at the boats navigating the Huangpu River and the massive glass and steel skyscrapers that filled downtown Shanghai.

I glanced around the room and tried to match faces with a list of names provided to me. The meeting attendees were:

- Bill Chen—President of UTS Consulting
- Chi—Executive Assistant to Bill
- Sarah—Marketing Director
- Caitlyn—Head of Human Resources
- Paula—HR Team
- Josef—Hiring Director
- Yao—UTS Technology Division Lead Manager
- Phil—UTS Technology Division Assistant Manager
- Isabelle—Manager of Smart Contracts Team
- Sun—Manager of Emerging Technologies Team
- Donald—Manager of Blockchain Team
- Claire—Internal Accounting

As I waited to start the session, I noticed that Donald, Sun, and Isabelle seemed a bit uncomfortable. I guessed that they were probably used to reporting to the division manager Yao, and not to Bill or anyone else from the executive level. They were sticking with people that they were comfortable with, as the three managers practically had Yao cornered and were talking his ear off.

Apart from them, sitting in a clustered group of three were the two human resources employees, Paula and Caitlyn, and the man in charge of hiring new employees, Josef. Finally, sitting in the front of the room was the company president, Bill. His assistant Chi had two cell phones in front of her and was rapidly firing off texts. Bill was making polite conversation with Claire from Internal Accounting, while Donald and a few other latecomers settled into empty seats.

I looked at my watch and realised that it was time to begin. "Good morning, everyone! I'm thrilled to be here in Shanghai with all of you today. I know that we're not here to just enjoy the view, so can someone please tell me why we are meeting this morning?"

Bill Chen, the President of UTS took charge by replying, "Everyone should already know that I called this meeting to address Technology Consulting's lagging KPIs. We hope to find some ideas about how to change this."

Almost everyone in the room nodded in agreement. There were no surprises so far. However, I still decided to state the objective of the meeting and give an example of what we were going to be doing in the session.

"Today we are going to produce some shared goals, solutions and a concrete action plan together. The main objective is to improve the performance of Technology Consulting, and we have half the day to accomplish it. Before we go any further, let's make sure that we are all on the same page. Can someone remind me what a goal is?"

"A goal is a target that we aim to hit sometime in the future", said HR Director Caitlyn, smiling around the room at her co-workers.

Caitlyn was 100% correct in her definition, so I pressed onward. "Thanks, Caitlyn. Now, can someone tell me what a shared goal is?"

"A common goal. One that is held by multiple people." The respondent was Donald, one of the managers in attendance.

"Thank you, Donald. Today we are going to be creating shared goals. In addition to Donald's definition, I would add that a shared goal reflects what the group stands for, your collective values. For example, I want to lose weight and my wife wants to avoid processed foods by cooking more meals at home. These are our individual goals. Considering this, can someone give an example of what our shared goal would be?"

Isabelle jumped in with an answer. "I see that these two things can be captured by the shared goal of improving health, right?"

"Perfect, Isabelle. The two individual goals, our visions for the future, overlap under the broader goal of improving our health."

There were no questions from the group at this point, so I decided to move on to the next activity. I was about to put everyone into groups of two, but before the meeting I noticed that people were being a bit shy and grouping with people that they were already familiar with. Seeing this, I added another point to my instructions. "Now I want you to find a pleasant person to speak with. Please make sure to choose someone who you do not normally work with!"

Bemused, I watched as people came to terms with the fact that they would need to leave their comfort zones and speak with someone outside of their working teams.

Executive assistant Chi slowly stood up from her familiar spot at Bill's side and walked over to the HR Team. Others followed her example and soon everyone was seated in pairs.

"You have three minutes to chat about why you are here today and what your personal objectives are for the session. The time starts now!"

Conversations began as soon as the final instructions had left my mouth and I watched the six pairs chatter away.

"I'm here to talk about ways we can improve performance," said Bill. His assistant Chi had a similar take, which she shared with Josef. "We will make goals and strategies that UTS Consulting can use to reduce turnover among our new hires."

Participant objectives for the session

NEIL: Outline goals to improve personal performance as a manager and increase my team's morale
SUN: Team building and problem solving together
ISABELLE: Receive action points from management concerning short-term objectives and actions
JOSEF: Discuss weak points and brainstorm solutions
YAO: Make a plan to improve customer satisfaction levels and increase the percentage of repeat customers to levels found in the rest of UTS
CAITLYN: Get Technology Consulting caught up with the rest of the company
CHI: Create goals that will lead to improvement
BILL: Outline goals that will help create needed change
PHIL: No expectations, here with an open mind
SARAH: Create steps toward improvement
CLAIRE: Connect with teammates and form change
DONALD: Right the ship and take accountability to change

While some people like Chi and Bill focused on the broad objective of setting goals, other people were getting more specific. I heard Neil, the manager for the Data Security Team, mention that his objective for the session was to learn new managerial skills that would improve morale among his team. Yao was more specific with his goal which was to increase the percentage of repeat customers, and as I passed his desk, I heard him give a passionate summary of his objectives. He said, "The Technical Consulting division is not as well-reviewed by our clients as the rest of UTS is. We are falling behind, and we have fewer repeat customers than we should be having! My objective for today is to get to the bottom of this and create a plan with the rest of you to end it."

I was happy to see the group loosen up as they talked in pairs. I used this activity to open the workshop because I wanted to help people connect with each other and prepare for the work that lies ahead. I also wanted to make sure that their idea of the workshop was in line with the outlined objectives I had, so before moving on to the next part of the workshop, I asked for a few volunteers to share their objectives for the session. Josef said he hoped to identify areas of improvement for the Technology Division, and Caitlyn wanted to outline ways to get the Technology Branch caught up with the rest of UTS. Isabelle was finding it hard to adjust to the format of the workshop where everyone was responsible for the content. She kept looking for direction and ideas to come from her manager and other high-level employees. I explained to her that in a participatory workshop like this one, everyone worked together to come up with solutions and actions. After hearing feedback from the group, it was clear that their expectations were in line with the workshop's objective of improving the Technology Division's overall performance, so we were ready to continue.

Wishing for a Better Future

"Thank you for sharing your objectives today! First, we are going to clarify your goals for the next three years for the Technology Consulting division of UTS. I have come to understand that there are some improvements that need to be made. I think that striving for a more productive future is great, and in order to start the wonderful process of change, we need to imagine that better future now." As I explained this, I pointed to the phrase, *It would be great if...* which I had written on the flipchart displayed at the front of the room and said, "It would be great if I ate fewer hamburgers." I gave another personal example: "It would be great if I could spend more time with my family." Then I asked if anyone else in the room could complete that statement.

Yao offered a reply and said that it would be great if he could join a gym and stick to an exercise plan. Josef said that it would be great if he could cut out sugar from his diet, and Chi provided the final example and said, "It would be great if we could enjoy an unpolluted view of our beautiful city," as she gazed out the window at the buildings that were blanketed in a haze of smog.

"Great wishes everyone! I see we have a few personal examples of things that can be done better, and a very big wish from Chi. When we make wishes I do not want any of you to worry about being realistic or logical. A wish comes from the heart, and it can be as ambitious as you like."

I walked over to the flipchart and crossed out the statement *It would be great if....*

Below it I wrote a new wishing statement: *It would be great if UTS Consulting....*

"This is the new wishing statement that I want you to consider now. We are here to begin creating a better-performing Tech Division, so please keep your wishes within that topic. With that said, you can think as big and creatively as you like. In fact, it is encouraged! You have three minutes to do this, and the only rules are that you need to write your wishes down. This is an individual activity, so no talking. Go ahead!"

As everyone began wishing and writing, I walked around the room to see if there were any questions or concerns. Neil looked up and called me over. His pencil was a blur as he wrote furiously. "Pepe, I don't think you gave us enough time. I would need closer to an hour to write all of my wishes down!"

"Don't worry about that Neil. I'll make sure that everyone gets enough time to share their wishes today. Just write down what you can, and we will go from there."

Three minutes later I told everyone to stop writing. "Nice work. I imagine that you all have lots of wishes for the future judging by how quickly everyone was writing! But what good is a wish if we just keep it to ourselves? Now we are going to get into three groups of four."

I divided the twelve participants into three equal groups. Once the groups were formed, I explained just how they were going to share their thoughts with each other. "Your objective is to come up with the best wishes for the company. First, explore everyone's wishes. Ask *why* the wish is a good idea and try to understand the logic behind each wish. Together as a group you are more powerful and intelligent than you are alone, so take advantage of this time. Once you have explored the wishes, you are going to choose together as a group two to four key wishes for UTS's future. Any questions so far?" Not a single hand was raised, so I continued and explained the next stage.

"Your final objective in your groups is to write the two to four most important wishes on these large Post-it notes and then tape them to the wall on the front of the room. You have 10 minutes for this, get to it!"

Sharing wishes in groups

The three groups got right down to it, and wishes were bouncing off the walls. On the left side of the room, UTS president Bill was grouped with Caitlyn from H.R., and Sun and Neil, two managers from the Tech branch of UPS. Sun and Neil were not having any problem speaking candidly and directly to Bill. "We need to let people know that it is OK to take time off! I am not talking about a vacation, but the time that falls outside of a normal work week. The culture right now is so work-centric that it can cause a negative attitude to creep in and affect everything else."

Neil nodded at Sun's words, and continued, "As a manager, I know that I am being judged directly on the performance of my Team, so with this in mind, I will not be the one to tell an employee not to come in on Saturday, or work evenings to finish a project." Caitlyn said that this was news to her and shared a goal about improving communication channels between employees and H.R. so that these types of issues could be properly discussed.

On the other side of the room sat Chi, Yao, Josef, and Isabelle. When I approached them to see how things were going, I saw that everyone was listening intently to Chi.

"It would be great if everyone appreciated UTS consulting as much as I do! Working here is like a dream come true, and I never think about it as a steppingstone in my career."

Josef challenged her on this by mentioning that while he too appreciated his job, the UTS experience varied greatly from team to team. He pointed out that Chi's experience as executive assistant is much different from the employees that are contributing to high attrition rates.

When five minutes had passed, I let everyone know that they had five minutes remaining to choose the best two to four wishes as a group, write them down on a large piece of paper, and display it at the front of the room.

Reviewing the fruits of our labour

The discussion was finished, and the groups had posted their top wishes for everyone to see, so it was time to look at the results. I asked a representative from each group to read their top wishes they decided on in their groups.

Group #1 results:
Bill, Sun, Neil, Caitlyn

- It would be great if UTS Tech. had more repeat customers.
- It would be great if employees viewed UTS as a career, and not a steppingstone.
- It would be great if UTS Tech. was the industry leader in China.

Group #2 results:
Chi, Yao, Josef, Isabelle

- It would be great if a better work/life balance was achieved.
- It would be great if there was better communication between departments within UTS Tech.
- It would be great if UTS Tech. was the bright spot—a true positive example—of UTS.

Group #3 results:
Donald, Sarah, Claire, Phil

- It would be great if UTS Tech. was the most productive departmᵉ
- It would be great if we always stayed ahead of our competitors.

Everyone looked over the wishes and seemed satisfied with the final eight that were chosen. Bill declared, "These wishes don't seem to be complete fantasy. I see some tangible things we can work towards." I followed his logic and added, "You are right, Bill. In fact, these wishes look a lot like goals to me."

In fact, that is exactly what we wanted to create. Goals were being discussed and produced during the Wishing activity, and now the group was left with eight goals for the future that UTS could work towards. "Does anyone have any comments or questions about these wishes?"

Sun chimed in, "It looks like all the small groups were thinking along the same lines, even though we were separated. Look at the third wishes of both groups, being the bright spot and industry leader—they are basically the same."

Sun was right; both wishes related to making the UTS Technology Division more respected. I asked, "If the wishes are the same, could we remove one of them?"

Bill did not agree at all with this thinking. "The wish of being the industry leader is related to market position and being the bright spot within the company refers to being better than other departments of our own company. It is about quality and process development, so I do not see these two as being the same."

Everyone considered what Bill had to say, and in the end the two wishes were both kept.

Chi was feeling very motivated and ready to get on with conquering these wishes, and said, "On behalf of everyone here, we want to thank you for a great session, Pepe. You have guided us in forming these wishes, and we have what we need to take it from here."

"Thanks for that," I laughed. "But our work here is not done. We are only halfway through the first stage. You all did great in creating these wishes for the future, and our next step is to choose the best goals for the next 3–5 years…and play some darts while we are at it!"

Some shot me a funny look, curious as to what I meant by playing darts, but they would not have to wait long to find out.

Bringing everything together

"Let's get right back to it. Individually, take two minutes to think about the wishes. Choose your personal favourites that would be the best goals for the next three to five years."

A few people began writing immediately, while others looked at the large Post-its that displayed the wishes. While people were reflecting on the wishes and picking their favourites, I began setting up the next part of the meeting by drawing a large dartboard on a jumbo-size flipchart located at the front of the room. I stopped drawing for a moment and gave the next set of instructions.

"Now it is time for some spirited discussion. I want you to get into groups of three. Try and find new people to chat with this time, so don't get into your old groups from before. In these new groups I want you to explain why the goals you chose are the best. Convince the others on your reasoning. Sell them on it! You surely have different ideas here, so get to it and begin convincing everyone else why you have the answers!"

Once again, the group snapped into action. I saw Yao immediately begin to explain why it was most important to improve communication between all levels of employees, while on the other side of the room Josef was arguing that the biggest goal should be revamping the hiring standards to find candidates that will spend most of their career with UTS. "We need to go after new candidates and vet them better. Looking more carefully for long-term fits is the key!"

While everyone was lost in discussion, I continued to draw the dartboard and set up for the next step of the meeting. As I was doing this, I was pleasantly surprised by how everyone was so actively and passionately discussing their goals. Once the time was up and the discussions had died down, I called for everyone's attention.

"I have asked you all to do quite a bit of discussing and persuading today, and I imagine that you might be a bit tired of talking for now. I think we should switch things up and try something different. Can someone tell me what we have here?" As I asked this, I gestured to the dartboard which was now fully drawn on the flipchart.

"It looks like an amateur drawing of a bunch of circles...perhaps planetary orbital paths?", guessed Yao.

There is always a jokester in every group, I thought to myself.

"I think it's a dartboard," guessed Bill.

"You guessed right, Bill! Has anyone played darts before? I have facilitated in places like Ireland where darts are an after-work must, but I am not sure if that is the case here in China."

"We play darts here, too," replied Caitlyn. There are some clubhouses and bars that cater to expats like me."

"Great, I am happy to hear that you are familiar with the game. Now I want you to forget everything you know about darts. We are playing a much different version of the game today." I pointed to the dartboard that I had drawn. There were three different circles, each with a different level of prioritisation for the wishes. "On the outer-most circle are wishes that are *nice to have*. Place good goals here that you may view as a nice bonus to have, but not essential. The next circle inward is labelled *important*. And right in the middle is the bullseye which is labelled *crucial*. The indispensable and absolute must-have wishes go here."

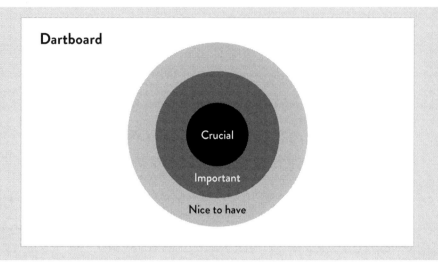

Dartboard

Crucial

Important

Nice to have

Next to the dartboard were the eight large sticky notes which had the wishes written on them. "To play this game, you will need to follow a few rules. First, there is no talking. The game is played in absolute silence. And you do not need to throw anything," I added while smiling. "You simply pick up a sticky note that has one of the wishes written on it and place it on the dartboard. You decide where it goes, and there are no wrong answers."

"Wait, Pepe," said Josef. "I doubt all of us agree on the placement of the goals. And if there is no talking, how can we agree on what goes where?"

"Great question. Now you do not need to talk. Simply place the goals where you think they should go. And if someone has already placed them in a different spot, just move them again to match your viewpoint. One person moves the goals at a time, but you can keep moving them as much as you like until an agreement is reached. Any questions?"

"How much time do we have for this?", asked Chi.

"You have maximum five minutes, but the game stops when the Post-its stop moving. You can begin now!"

A few sets of eyes glanced towards the president, Bill, but he deferred and motioned for someone else to go first. Chi began by arranging the Post-its. Most of the eight wishes were scattered in the *important* circle, and she had placed the wish 'It would be great a better life-work balance was achieved" in the middle of the dartboard. Sun went next and arranged the dartboard to fit his beliefs. People approached one-by-one, and after a few rounds, fewer and fewer Post-its were being shuffled. There was one hiccup when Neil and Isabelle had a stretch of shifting one Post-it in and out of the *important* circle, but they eventually resolved this non-verbally by placing it right on the border between *important* and *crucial*. Once the Post-it notes came to a rest, there were three wishes that were placed in the *crucial* section of the dartboard:

1. Improve communication between departments and teams
2. Reduce employee turnover
3. Have more repeat and long-term customers

These were the three goals that were prioritised as crucial from the original pool of eight when the Dartboard activity began.

Revisiting the objectives

It was time to bring the session to a close. "I see that the papers are not shuffling anymore, so everyone can take a seat. You all have been quiet for a while, so I want to end the session with some more chatter. Find a partner and take about three minutes to chat about if we met our objectives today."

After allowing three minutes for discussion in pairs, I decided to end the session with my standard question; "Is everyone happy with the results of today?"

Nods around the room confirmed that everyone was pleased, and that the session was a success. Bill did have something to say, though.

"I am having trouble moving past the game of darts. You made us do it in silence. How can we know that people are committed to the results? Maybe everyone stopped moving the sticky notes because they wanted to go for a smoke."

Bill brought up a great point, and I decided we needed to solidify the prioritisation of the goals a bit more.

"Thank you for the feedback, Bill. As everyone stands up to take a break, please take these three stickers that I am handing you now and place them on your three favourite goals as you walk past the dartboard. You do not need to do anything more than that. Wait by the door before leaving so we can check the results."

I handed each person three small dot stickers as they walked by. Following my instructions, they placed them on the goals as they walked past the dartboard, and after all twelve had passed we stood back to check the results. Most of the stickers were placed on the three goals that were placed as *crucial*. This confirmed that the group agreed on prioritising the goals. Seeing this was a great conclusion to the session, and a great start for UTS Technical Consulting towards their long-term goals.

"Take a quick fifteen-minute break to stretch and grab some coffee if you like, and we will reconvene and continue."

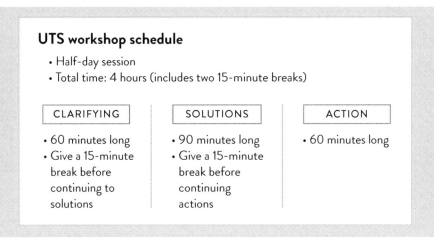

UTS workshop schedule
- Half-day session
- Total time: 4 hours (includes two 15-minute breaks)

CLARIFYING	SOLUTIONS	ACTION
• 60 minutes long • Give a 15-minute break before continuing to solutions	• 90 minutes long • Give a 15-minute break before continuing actions	• 60 minutes long

Analysis

The aim of the first stage of the workshop with UTS was to create goals related to improving performance of the Technology Consulting division. All three stages of the workshop (clarifying, solutions, action) took place on one day in a single session, but they are presented here in separate sections for the sake of clarity. This section covers the *clarifying* stage, which was 60 minutes long. The following sections will cover the *solutions* and *action* stages of the workshop.

Check-in

Before the clarifying stage of a workshop can begin, it is imperative to make sure that all the participants are on the same page and have the same objectives for the session. After all, how can a group work together towards a common goal if they are pointed in different directions? I begin by immediately dividing the group into pairs to discuss their expectations for the day. Discussion in pairs focuses people as they begin the session by being accountable and having to share their thoughts about the day. Pair discussion is also effective because it creates a sense of psychological safety. How? When a person has a conversation with someone else, they create a bond as they share and listen to each other. This reduces feelings of nervousness and anxiety. People that find themselves leading groups in decision making are generally people-oriented and social. Meeting new people and public speaking is probably easy for them. It can be a mistake to assume the same traits exist within the group they are leading. Some people are simply not comfortable with public speaking, and the tasks or exercises that require conversation and other things that are outside the norm of a standard workday can be hard for some. During the allocated time for pair discussion I was walking around the room monitoring the conversations. People were continuing to bounce ideas off each other, and most of the objectives were in line with what Bill and the session organisers had in mind. Isabelle, the manager of the Smart Contracts Team, voiced that her expectations were to receive action points directly from upper management. This was a bit different from how the session was planned, but it was no problem. The activities planned would get her in a creative mindset to produce her own action points. It was OK that her objective was a bit different than the rest of the group so long as she was talking and prepared to actively participate.

When I first met the group from UTS Consulting I assumed that everyone worked closely with one another, but this was not the case. Many of them were from different divisions within the large company and they did not have any reason to meet and collaborate normally. Moreover, several distinct hierarchical levels were represented within the participant group, ranging from a team manager to H.R. directors all the way up to the company president. This can create a type of tension within the room, a nervousness felt by some employees that relates to speaking with new people, or direct superiors or high-ranking employees that they do not often encounter. Asking them to be candid in this type of situation can be stressful, which makes it even more important to aid the process by properly warming up the group and creating a relaxed and friendly atmosphere.

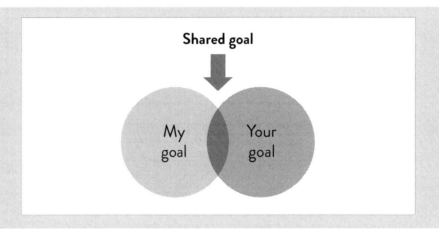

I also defined the term *shared goal* to the group. Not all goals are shared goals, which is OK. However, in this workshop we were looking specifically for goals that multiple people had in common. Common goals bring people together and boost cooperation. They often reflect the larger values and standards that exist within an organisation. Shared goals are broad, and the actions that people take to achieve them are specific.

Emergence

The tools used during the emergent phase of the workshop were Wishing and Me/We/Us.

Wishing

The Wishing activity requires participants to dream big by imagining a better version of their company. What wishes did they have and how could UTS be improved?

Wishing

Wishing helps expand thinking and connects ideas with the heart.
Wishing is used in visioning or to create goals.

I wish I...
Wouldn't it be nice if our team...
Within the next 10 years, it would be fantastic if our company...

For most, a wish is associated with childhood and dreaming with your heart for an item, outcome, or reality that you desire. The result of the activity is to elicit the wishes of a group, but they are often the same as goals. As we saw in the case study, many of the wishes the group came up with were goals in disguise, for example, *reducing employee turnover*. But imagine the difference in results if the instructions were to list three mid to long-term goals that you and your department can implement to that will positively affect lagging key performance indicators. That does not have the same ring to it as a wish does, and I guarantee that the outcome of the activity would not be the same because people would naturally limit themselves.

Me/We/Us

During this session, the various activities followed a specific pattern which made up the foundation of the workshop. First, I would ask the group a question and give them time for individual thought. After that, I would have them discuss in pairs or small groups, and finally everyone was brought back together for total group discussion. This structure that progresses from the individual, to small groups and finally to the entire group, is called Me/We/Us. It forms the backbone of breakthrough decision making.

Me/We/Us: A tool for getting everyone involved

1. **Me**
   - Writing down ideas individually

2. **We**
   - Ideas are refined in pairs or small groups
   - Choosing the best ideas

3. **Us**
   - Sharing the ideas with the whole group
   - Collect and display the ideas so everyone can see them and review together

All three stages of Me/We/Us create a group atmosphere in which everyone is comfortable participating. Me allows time for introverts to gather their thoughts and formulate ideas. We is the platform to share these ideas. It helps people get deeper into their own ideas and provides psychological safety for sharing their thoughts with others. People explain the reasoning behind their ideas as they discuss in small groups. The amount of ideas decreases as people begin to merge ideas together or create new breakthroughs that are built off the content created during the individual (Me) stage. Finally comes Us, a platform for informing others. During the Us section, ideas are shared, but usually not developed further.

All three parts are important, but at this point you may be thinking about the case study with UTS Consulting where I allocated about 80 % of the time to the We portion, and only 10% each to Me and Us. Perhaps you are yelling, "Pepe, if all three parts are important, then why was much more time devoted to We?" I devoted the most time to the We part because for one, it is the most efficient. There are many simultaneous conversations happening at once, and it is effective in helping people understand ideas and create new ones. On top of it all, people enjoy working in small groups.

Me/We/Us is not limited to only creating strategic goals for a team. It can be applied anytime you want to get everyone involved. The magic of the process is to get everyone comfortable, thinking creatively, getting people to discuss ideas and most importantly, thinking critically about other people's ideas. If these things sound beneficial to you, then Me/We/Us is a sound choice.

I have had a lot of fun using Me/We/Us over the years. It is a tool that has different strengths and reacts differently when used in different countries and working cultures.

I first learned about the Me/We/Us in Finland, where I am from. We Finns are generally introverted...unless there are a few beers and some karaoke involved. For us timid Finnish folk, the Me part is key because it gives time for people to gather their thoughts and prepare for speaking with others.

In China, We is most important. Culturally, individualism, at least within working environments, has not been highlighted or encouraged. Because of this, a person may feel a bit timid when it comes to speaking candidly. Sharing your true opinion in public is not the most natural thing to do. This makes the We portion key; people gain courage in group settings. When they share an idea with a partner or small group during We, they gain courage. An idea is modified as it is shared and picks up pieces of other ideas, making it both stronger and transforming it into shared property. Ideas become accepted and validated, which gives people courage to share them more freely.

Me/We/Us is a key tool for a few different reasons. It is also an extremely effective group energiser. Having to constantly switch the mode from individual thinking to small groups and to big groups activates people and essentially eliminates the possibility of someone tuning out.

Convergence

Dartboard, Silent Moving and Me/We/Us made up convergence in this session.

A game of darts...but no talking!

The Dartboard activity is simple and has only one objective—place your goal on the board in relation to its importance. Is the goal crucial, important, or just nice to have? People can do this quickly and almost automatically when prioritising their own ideas because their choices make sense, and they understand the reasons and logic behind each choice.

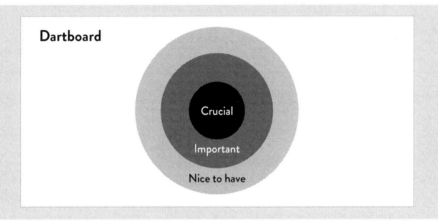

But what about other people's ideas? This is where the no-talking rule becomes important. I told the group to play the game in complete silence because they had already spoken a lot during the day, but this was not the real reason for my choice.

I chose to have the activity be conducted silently because although people are not talking, they are going through a critical thinking process as they see ideas being moved around on the dartboard and as they prepare to move the ideas themselves. Silently observing others during the game of darts required that the participants think about the logic of the ideas. When someone watches another person place an idea on the board, they read it and at the same time consider its placement on the dartboard. *Why was it placed there? Does it make sense? Do I want to move it?* As they ask themselves these questions, they reflect on the underlying logic behind the goal without talking about it. Their own goals are also reconsidered if someone else moves it to a different place on the dartboard.

Silent Moving

1. Small groups write down ideas onto large Post-its and display them on the wall.

2. Review ideas together, reading and checking that everybody understands them. Activate the conversation at this point.

3. The group leader asks everyone to arrange ideas based on priority (using an activity like Line or Dartboard). Speaking is forbidden, because it easily leads to disagreement and longer meetings.

4. Review the result together.

Now imagine if I said that people could discuss and argue during the game of darts. It could take ten times as long and it probably would get a bit combative. How would you react if you lay out the ideas to the best of your ability, only to see them be moved by someone else? You move them back again and begin to explain only to see someone else move them. This would be frustrating, to say the least, and most likely, some arguing would ensue and the activity would drag on and take too much time. The trade-off is that people sometimes have a hard time believing the results because there is no verbal commitment to the ideas. That is the reason why we often use Dot Voting to confirm the results.

Me/We/Us

The backbone of the convergence phase was Me/We/Us. We first had an individual stage letting the participants choose their favourite wishes, next the logic was shared in small groups, finally we shared our opinions with everyone in silence by moving ideas on dartboard.

Check-out and evaluation

Normally the evaluation stage is simple and brief, but it serves a very important purpose. It is the group leader's last chance to make sure that the group is satisfied with the results and that the objectives were met. After a stage of the workshop is complete, I usually check by asking, "Is everyone happy with the results here?" This is to make sure that no one leaves disappointed or confused.

There are many different tools or ways to end a meeting, and entire books have been devoted to various check-out tools. Discussion in pairs is simple and effective, and it is what I used in this session. I simply asked people to find a partner and discuss if the objectives for the stage were met.

After discussion in pairs I wanted to check the results, so I asked for a few people to share their thoughts. I also adapted when I saw that Bill was not satisfied with the results of the darts activity, so I had an additional prioritisation tool ready to use, Dot Voting.

Dot Voting

- A tool used to visualise group priorities
- A convergence tool
- Quick to set up and use

Dot Voting was a good tool to combine with the darts activity because it brought everyone back together to confirm that the results of the non-verbal game of darts were correct and that the group was aligned. After Dot Voting was complete, everyone had additional visual evidence that they were all on the same page because most of the dots fell on the three goals that were prioritised as crucial.

Dot Voting is straightforward, but I see it being misused far too often. This is because group leaders mistake the activity as a decision-making tool. They see people place dots during the activity and think that this represents decisions being made, when in fact this is not the case at all. In this case, Dot Voting was a success because it followed a long process where the group was able to discuss their wishes and the decisions that they made earlier. Dot Voting served as the final piece of the decision-making process, not the main part of the process. If I used Dot Voting without a long period of discussion, then people would still place dots on the board. Consider Dot Voting a tool to confirm results, not create results.

The tools used and their purpose

- **Me/We/Us** – A basic tool for getting everyone involved
- **Wishing** – To help goal setting
- **Silent Moving** – Prioritising
- **Dartboard** – Visualising priorities
- **Dot Voting** – Visualising Priorities

Workshop process: Clarifying goals

Objective: To find the key elements of a common goal
Time: 60 minutes
Intro (5 minutes)
Presenting the objective and what a common goal looks like

Check-in tool: Pair discussion (5minutes)

1. Find a pleasant person and discuss why you are here today.
2. Now I would like three of you to comment, whether the objective is right.

Emergence tools: Me/We/Us and Wishing (20 minutes)

1. Write down wishes, it would be great if we....
2. In groups of four participants create 2–4 key wishes.
3. Write your ideas on jumbo Post-it notes with big letters.
4. Post and check if ideas are understood.

Convergence tools: Me/We/Us, Dartboard, and Dot Voting
(20 minutes)

1. Think on your own and choose your favorite goals (3–5 years perspective).
2. In new groups of three, influence each other.
3. In silence move the Post-it notes on the right place on the dartboard... Everyone can move the Post-it notes whenever they feel like. When the Post-it notes do not move anymore, we are ready.
4. Take three stickers and place them on key goals

Check-out: Pair discussion (8 minutes)

1. Find a pleasant person next to you and discuss whether we reached the objective.
2. Now I would like three of you to comment.

Final Check-out: "Is everyone happy?" (2 minutes)

3.2: Goal-Setting Workshop: Finding solutions with Café

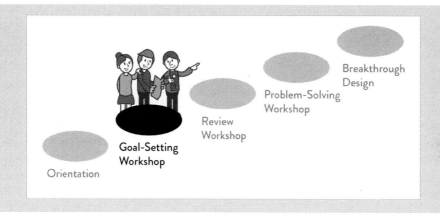

What's here

- **Case study**: The second stage of a 3-stage workshop. The objective in this stage is to find solutions to current challenges.
- **Tools**: Café, Investment Activity, Silent Moving, Group Ranking

How it helps

Café lets a group discuss multiple topics at once and is an ideal tool for emergence. This section shows you an example of a successful Café method and teaches you how to incorporate it into your meetings and workshops.

The workshop continues

After a short break following the clarifying stage, I continued the workshop with the group of UTS employees to build on the work done earlier in the day. It was time for them to take the next step in turning their goals and visions for the future into a reality; I was about to lead them into the solutions stage of the workshop.

Check-in

I gave a friendly wave as Yao, Bill, Chi, Donald, and everyone else filed back into the room. I pulled out the dartboard from the previous stage which still had the Post-it notes placed all around it. In the centre of the dartboard, there were three Post-it notes that had been placed in the zone marked *crucial*. I pointed to them and said, "These are the specific goals that you all decided were the most important." I pointed to each note one by one and read the goals aloud; "Improve communication between departments"; "reduce employee turnover"; and "increase the number of repeat customers."

No one had any questions so far, so I continued and explained to them that the objective for this afternoon session is to figure out solutions for the goals. "Your job now is to look at the goals and decide what would allow UTS to reach them."

Paula stopped me and jumped in with a question. "So, by solutions you mean how we are to solve the problem ourselves? Actions we take?"

"Not quite Paula. By solutions I am referring to more general trends or factors that would help UTS achieve a goal. One good way to distinguish between the two is to think of a solution as something larger than one person, and an action is something you can specifically participate in yourself to help reach a solution. Take your goal of having longer customer relationships. A solution for this goal could perhaps be to provide unmatched service that is so good, customers will have to come back. Creating solutions to our goals is serious business. We will need something out of the ordinary to make sure that we are up for it. Luckily, I have just the thing in mind."

"What now? Should we prepare ourselves for a game of billiards or to go skiing?", asked Sarah.

"That is not a bad idea, but no more sports. Instead we are going to partake in a classic Finnish pastime; We are going to a beautiful café to chat amongst friends. Look around the room now! We are already there!"

Sun was already looking around and he seemed a bit disappointed. "Pepe, we know this room. It is conference room #4. We had the morning session here, remember? I don't see any donuts or coffee. There are just some groups of chairs and flipcharts scattered about."

Sun was right, and I hoped that he did not mind the lack of coffee and donuts too much. To make things clear, I continued with the instructions and emphasised that a bit of imagination would be required to bring the café to life.

"Think again, Sun," I said. "Most of you probably think that you are seated in a large conference room in UTS headquarters, but don't be so sure! We have left the boring confines of conference room #4 and moved to a wonderful café. Look around. There are different tables around the café."

I pointed to the three separate groups of chairs, each with a large flipchart at the centre of it and with a few markers on the table.

"Those are not menus on the flipchart. If you look a bit closer, you will see that each flipchart has one of your goals written on it. Can someone read out loud what the three flipcharts say?"

Donald nodded and said, "This flipchart says, 'reduce employee turnover'. Over here on this other table the flipchart says, 'improve internal communication'. And on the table in the back the flipchart says, 'increase the amount of repeat customers'."

"Thanks, Donald. These are the goals from earlier today. First walk around the room and take a few moments to think about solutions for each of the goals. Write down your own ideas for each topic, and once you are ready, choose a seat at one of the tables. This will be your discussion group. Do not worry about which table you choose, because you will rotate through all of the tables before the activity ends."

Everyone stood, and around the room they went, silently considering each goal and occasionally pausing to write down their thoughts. After about five minutes, everyone was seated at a table, so I continued by giving the next set of instructions.

"Just like in a real café, we are going to have some great conversations with friends listening to each other and connecting diverse perspectives. Look at the people seated at your table. This is your discussion group, and together you will rotate from table to table writing down your discoveries so that you have the chance to discuss each topic...well most of you that is.

Each table will have a host overseeing each table in the café. The host has an important job which is to stay and write down the solutions that the group comes up with. The hosts also help develop the conversation with new groups as they rotate by explaining the solutions that have already been written down."

I continued, "I need one volunteer for each table to be the host and help newcomers to catch up with the conversation and to also record solutions on the flipchart as you think of them. The host needs to stay at the same table for the entire 30 minutes, so this person should be very enthusiastic about the goal that they volunteer to host. Let's start with the goal to improve internal communication in UTS. Would anyone like to..." Before I could even finish, Caitlyn, the head of Human Resources, shot her hand up to volunteer. Hiring Director Josef volunteered to host the conversation about reducing employee turnover, and Donald volunteered himself to host the meeting about increasing the number of repeat customers.

"Thank you, hosts, for volunteering. I will be here to help if needed, so let me know if I can assist in any way. I will not keep you from your café time any longer, get to it!"

Conversation flowed freely at all three tables and people rotated easily from table to table when I asked them to. Josef was hosting the discussion about reducing employee turnover, and he was doing a good job by leading the discussion, asking people to expand on their thoughts, and taking notes the entire time. I could tell he was quite passionate about the topic, considering that he was responsible for all hiring practices at UTS. One table over, Caitlyn was already beginning to write down solutions on the flipchart for her hosted topic of improving communication between teams and departments. Considering her role in human resources, this topic was an important one for her, too. In the other corner of the room was Donald who was loudly leading his group in a discussion about the obstacles that are keeping UTS from having more repeat customers.

About every twelve to fifteen minutes I would call for everyone to rotate groups and announce how much time was remaining.

"26 minutes left, time to move to the next table!"

"13 minutes remaining, so rotate to the next table."

"Just 2 more minutes, so make sure you have time to finish your thoughts and do not leave any business unfinished!"

And finally, "OK everyone! Your time in the café has concluded, it is time to come back to conference room #4."

"That was a quick 40 minutes. I feel like I could go for another 40 minutes or so," said Chi. A few others agreed, and more remarks were made about how quickly the time had passed. I said, "Time flies when you are having fun. Speaking of fun, we are going to now transition from our nice café to another favourite thing of mine, money!"

Put your money where your mouth is

"First things first. Can each host make sure that their flipchart with the solutions is set up so it is easily visible for people walking past?"

Seeing that this was the case, I gave the instructions for the next stage. "Everyone please take out a piece of paper and something to write with. Around the room are three tables with the solutions for each goal written on them. Your job now is to walk around and read all of the solutions that are written on each flipchart. Take a few moments to think about them, and then choose only your favourite solutions that you want to be implemented for each goal. Some goals might have several favourite solutions, and others might not have any. I know that this may be hard as there are so many good solutions, but not everything can be your favourite. This is a silent and individual ativity, so there is no need to talk to anyone, but if you have any questions, please ask me."

Solutions for reducing employee turnover

- Hire right (now the skills match and people perform on a high level, but perhaps change the slant of the hiring process slightly to include long-term motivation and fit as well
- More support systems in place—reduce isolation and silos
- Outbid competitors to retain talent—competitive salary and ages and compensation packages
- Sustainable workload for employees to avoid burnout
- Review old talent pipelines and establish new talent pipelines
- Develop a deeper orientation for new hires
- Push HR as an available resource that should be actively used
- Find out why employees are leaving and analyse the data

Solutions for improving internal communication

- Avoid silos and isolated working practices—(within UTS tech division)
- More collaboration and discussion beyond small talk and exchanging pleasantries
- Unified team vision and KPI's that go beyond a singular person or project team
- Common targets
- Sharing more time together during normal working days
- Spend time together outside of work
- Better email communication
- Higher participation using internal tools
- Expand mindset to include more people (not "I work for the Blockchain Team" but "I work for in the Tech Division of UTS, one of the best consulting firms out there!")

Solutions for increasing the amount of repeat customers

- Follow up post-service with customers to check exprience
- Offer level of service that stands out
- Package services in a way that lends itself for repeat business
- Solicit reviews to identify strengths and areas to improve
- Find out why customers switch from us to a competitor
- Create personal relationships with valued customers
- Offer competitive pricing to keep current customers
- Market towards existing customers and not only to find new customers

The group did as they were told and circulated the room silently and wrote down their favourite solutions. They had half an hour in the café to discuss and debate, so for this I only gave them a few moments.

"It looks like you are finished choosing your favourite ideas. Now it is time to put your money where your mouth is. Please find a partner for this activity. I am going to give each pair $15 to invest in the best solutions. Decide with your partner where you want the money to go. If one solution is by far the best, you may want to invest all your money into that. Or you can decide to split the cash up between a few different solutions. If all the solutions seem bad simply keep the money for yourselves."

The six pairs got to it. Most groups were deciding quietly among themselves where to invest, but I could hear Isabelle and Phil from across the room.

"Thirteen dollars? That is almost all our money! How can we put that much into just one idea?"

"Well it is easy if it is the best, and I think that this is the key for better communication among employees!"

They carried on their spirited discussion, which I liked seeing. *At least they care*, I thought.

Finally, people began to quiet down and turn to me once their money had been invested. Even Isabelle and Phil had reached an agreement and found peace with one another and were ready for the next stage.

I walked around the room distributing markers and pieces of A4 paper, and said, "The last part of this activity is to count up the amount of money spent for each solution. If a solution has $3 or more invested into it, write it down here on this piece of paper in large letters. One solution per paper, please. When writing down your solutions, also write down the goal that it corresponds to. It may seem obvious, but this will help keep everything clear later."

The group decides

Among the six pairs, there were nine total solutions that had $3 or more invested into it. I took the pieces of paper from each pair and shuffled then together to mix them up.

"Alright, please get back into three even groups that match the original topics. I have here a stack of the ideas which you invested in. I mixed them all together because I want each group to have the chance to see and compare solutions from all three topics. I will distribute the ideas randomly to all of you. Your job is a simple one; read them and decide together what the best ones are, and no ties allowed! You are going to rank them from best to worst. Once you have decided what the best solution is, take that piece of paper and write a #1 on it. Do the same for the rest of them. The second best is #2, and so on. You have 5 minutes."

Once five minutes had passed, I collected the papers and rotated them to new groups so they could be ranked again. I did this a 3rd time to give each group the chance to review and rank all the solutions.

"Now that all the solutions have been ranked by each group, let's tally the results! Please add up the ranking scores for every idea now."

I walked to a large wall and explained how to organise the solutions. "Since we have three groups of solutions, the best possible rank is three. Who has a three? Please use some tape and place the solution on this wall. Who has a four? We will organise them by rank; the solutions with the highest rank go towards the top of the wall, and the solutions that were ranked lower can go towards the floor. Tape them on the wall so we can read the solutions. Who has a five?"

Everyone followed instructions (what a great group!) and soon the solutions were taped to the wall.

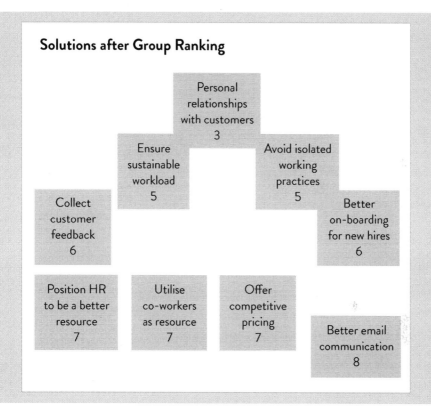

Once the jumbo Post-its had settled, everyone stood back and admired their work. "Nice work, everyone. What we have here are the pathways towards the goals we were wishing for this morning. And better yet, you all have organised them together, and we can clearly see what the best ones are. But we are not quite done yet. We need to take things a bit further. The last step for today is to commit to our solutions. Read them all, and if you see a solution that you are willing to commit to, take it off this wall and walk over and place it on the wall behind you. Once you have done this you can sit down. If someone takes a solution off the wall that you want to commit to, that is OK. The important thing now is to make sure at least one person is committed to making the solution a reality. No need to chat here, either. You can read the solutions quietly and move any of them that you are committed to."

Bill started things off by pulling a piece of paper off the wall almost immediately and moving it to the other wall. Others followed his lead, and soon almost all solutions were on the other wall. Only the lowest-ranked idea related to better email communication remained. I was feeling proud. We began the day only a few hours earlier by wishing for an abstract better future for UTS, and now the entire group from different departments and levels within the company had agreed on the solutions to get these goals, ranked them, and committed to them.

I closed the session by asking everyone how we did in achieving the objectives for the day, and by calling on three volunteers to give feedback. Everyone was content, so I was able to end things there.

Analysis

This section covers the *solutions* stage of my workshop with UTS, which was the longest stage of this workshop, clocking in at 90 minutes.

UTS workshop schedule

- Half-day session
- Total time: 4 hours (includes two 15-minute breaks)

CLARIFYING	SOLUTIONS	ACTION
• 60 minutes long • Give a 15-minute break before continuing to solutions	• 90 minutes long • Give a 15-minute break before continuing actions	• 60 minutes long

---

Check-in

This stage of the workshop took place with the same participants and was a direct continuation of the work done that morning, so I did not need to use any icebreaker activities. This check-in could be quick and simple, and I used it to focus the group after their short break and to present the objectives for what was coming next.

I presented the objectives, which were to outline solutions and find the elements needed to achieve the goals that the group created in the morning. It was worthwhile distinguishing *solutions* from *actions*. The task of this stage was to think of solutions for their goals, which are broader and more general than an action is. It can be common for participants to mix up terms, so clarifying with examples is a reliable way to avoid confusion and misunderstandings.

Emergence

I gave everyone time to walk around the room and think individually about the three goals that were posted on flipcharts. The aim of this section of the workshop was to break down the broader goals into solutions towards realising the goals. I gave the following instructions to guide participants: "Look around the room and think about the key elements of these goals. What are the solutions that you can work towards to make these goals happen? You can write down your ideas if you wish."

I used a method called Café to help UTS find the solutions to their goals. It was an obvious choice, really. In the solutions stage of a workshop you typically have several topics. The Café method allows the group to work on several topics at the same time. And—most importantly—the group size is always small; people can have a good talk, ideas become clear, and new ideas emerge. Café also creates a relaxed atmosphere within the group, making at a perfect tool for emergence.

Café process

1. Choosing a topic
- Can be done before the event
- Normally around 3–5 topics

2. Group work
- Grouping based on own interest and knowhow
- Each group should be the same size
- Participants take notes using a flipchart

3. Rotation
- One of the group members stays behind to present the notes to the new group (host)
- Other group members rotate to a new flipchart
- New groups add ideas after hearing the presentation

4. Summaries
- Original work groups will make and present a summary of best solutions

The Café method has four steps. The first step of choosing topics was completed in the morning workshop when the three goals were created and prioritised by everyone. The three goals were the topics to be discussed during the 30-minute Café. The second phase of the Café calls for discussion in groups. Each group has one dedicated host to the topic, and the host's job is to take the meeting notes and to fill in gaps in the conversation and bring newcomers up to speed. This brings us to the third phase of the Café method, rotation. This creates many simultaneous conversations at once. And we end things with the final step, conclusion. This is where the convergent tools are added, and the group comes to an agreement and understanding of the results. Depending on the type of Café tool, sometimes groups summarise the content by talking about it, and sometimes they prioritise the content using a polling tool, like Dot Voting, for example.

My Café, the World's Café, Finnish Café... many different cafés

In my opinion, one of the biggest advantages of Café is creating a relaxed atmosphere where people are completely comfortable talking and exploring ideas at their own pace. This atmosphere is where the method derives its name—people communicate in a way that resembles how friends talk with each other in a real café. The Café method allows participants to explore complex questions and gain new insights by listening to and encouraging one another. These principle benefits make Café an outstanding tool for dealing with multiple, complex topics, like we had in this session with UTS, making it a perfect emergence tool. While the benefits of Café are consistent, the method itself goes by many names and can be applied in a variety of ways.

In addition to Café, the method is also known as, Learning Café, Knowledge Café, Group Expo, Poster Method, and its most famous version, World Café, which is perhaps the most well-known facilitation method there is, along with classical brainstorming.

A world of Cafés

The World Café method was originally developed by David Isaacs and Juanita Brown in California in the mid-1990s, and as they tell it, it was a bit of a happy accident. David and Juanita were hosting a reunion of leaders and academics. It was a rainy morning and traffic was terrible. People living close to the venue arrived early and sat in a café waiting for others and spontaneous conversations broke out. People were exploring ideas and as the discussion topics got more complex some people started keeping a written record on tablecloths. When everyone had arrived the quality of discussion was so deep that Isaacs and Brown decided to continue the event at the café, but there was a challenge; how to connect the conversation groups? This was their a-ha moment—let's leave a host or hostess to explain and have the others rotate! The Café method was born. They realised that this was magic in a bottle, and they explored the format further, and later gave birth to the World Café method.[*] While the World Café method is widely adapted and very famous, its principles were being used long before David and Juanita stumbled upon it. The World Café method is a dialogue method. This means that it prioritises relaxed and authentic conversations above anything else.

I have heard of similar methods being used already in the 70s, though it is difficult to identify the original founder of the idea since there are many variations on the World Café method. There is even a Finnish version called *Group Expo*, which was developed by Veikko Mantere, a well-known and successful consultant. His method has many principles in common with the World Café. In true Finnish fashion, Veikko developed a practical method that did not have any added frills to it. He did not focus so much on creating a "café" atmosphere, and he did not leave any cookies or drinks on the tables. Instead he had flipcharts placed around the room where people could formally write down key conversational points.

The version of Café that I used follows Mantere's practical version more closely than the World Café method. I do not have cookies on the table either, and I think that the average group will have no problem creating spontaneous conversation without the prompting of cookies or coffee. With my business groups I do not see the need to try and develop this aspect of the method too much. I am working in offices and sometimes very formal working situations, which means that the increased formality is more appropriate and better received than a plate of cookies would be. Instead of cookies, I have shared flipcharts (large pieces of paper) where the topic notes are recorded during the session.

Convergence

Café methods work wonderfully for emergence, but the most important thing I can say about Café methods is that they are incomplete without convergent methods. Most experienced group leaders and facilitators can create a perfect Café with great conversations and have groups create lots of interesting ideas. Yet, the Café method is the source of a lot

---

[*] You can read more about the history at the official World Café webpage: http://www.theworldcafe.com/about-us/history/

of bad facilitation because many group leaders will end a session after the conversations during Café but will not use the correct tools to bring everyone back together and align them. Remember, during Café, people are talking in small groups and rotating from topic to topic at regular intervals. They will understand the framework and logic of the other Café groups, but they have never talked about which solutions should really be implemented. As a result, they will leave the workshop with an incomplete picture. "What did we decide?", "What next?", "What's my role now?" These are the questions that remain for confused participants after a Café session without the proper convergent tools being used.

In the solutions stage of the goal-setting workshop with UTS, multiple topics were discussed at once. Moreover, each topic was detailed and carried with it its own set of complexities. To make sure that things were clear, and everyone was on the same page at the meeting's conclusion, I used several rounds of prioritisation.

The tools used during the conclusion part of the session were the Investment Activity where I gave USD $15 to each pair, and Group Ranking. I began with the Investment Activity (also known as USD $15). This is a prioritisation tool that forces people to rank the content they produced. Money is a great tool to use with groups; it is important to everyone and it makes the prioritisation process seem more real. People tend to be good at voting with their wallets, and the act of spending is a great way to see what is important. The Investment Activity followed the Me/We/Us format. I began the activity in the Me portion of Me/We/Us by asking people to think of their favourite solutions on their own. After this, I separated them into pairs and gave them $15 which they could invest into their favourite ideas however they pleased. Once their money was invested, they were asked to write down the solutions which had more than $3 invested in it. The Investment Activity can be adjusted depending on group size and the amount of material that needs to be reviewed. Here, I gave $15 to each pair, but I can choose to give more money or less money as needed.

It was time to rank the ideas in small groups. The ideas with a minimum of $3 invested were considered the best and written down on separate pieces of A4 paper. Now the papers were rotated to different groups and each group added their own scores—first, second and third—to them. Rotation was repeated until every group had ranked all the ideas and the scores were added up.

Group Ranking

- Group Ranking is a communication tool that creates better understanding and priorities by discussing, evaluating, and ranking content.
- Small groups rank ideas/solutions/actions.
- Ideas rotate from group to group until everything has passed through all of the small groups.
- The results are then posted for all to see, and at the end of Group Ranking there will be a clear hierarchy of importance.

Finally, I moved the Investment Activity to the Us section. The ideas with the highest scores were posted on the top of the wall, and those with the lower scores were placed closer to the floor. This gave a great visualization to the group, and with this setup one can see at a glance where things stand. But hey, I could have visualised the ideas on the wall immediately after the Investment Activity! Why did we have to do the ranking, too? Because it is extremely effective at creating understanding of ideas. When someone asks you to rank something, you automatically begin weighing their pros and cons and pit the ideas against each other. You can't help but think why one idea is superior to another, which requires you to understand the logic behind it.

If I lead a workshop, the minimum quality requirement is that people understand what was decided and why. Group Ranking is the right knowledge sharing tool in situations when you have had many simultaneous meetings or if multiple solutions or complex topics are involved.

The sound of silence

Convergence continued after the best ideas were posted on the wall. The tool I used here was Silent Moving. People were asked to look at the solutions, and if they found one that they were committed to, then they could take it off the wall and move it to the other side of the wall.

You may think that the higher-ranked ideas would be the first to be taken off the wall and committed to, but this is not always the case. Sometimes an idea is very highly prioritised, but no one wants to do it. This could be because the task is difficult, or it slips through the cracks and no one thinks that completing it is their responsibility. On the other hand, sometimes the lowest-prioritised ideas are the first to be taken off the wall. This is because they may be a needed step to achieve a larger idea or to take a step forward.

Now stop and imagine if the session ended with the Group Ranking tool. We would be left with the ideas ranked (which is a great start!) but without anyone committing to them. I like to use Silent Moving to check commitment. It is fast, easy to do, and straight to the point. There is no need for discussion at this point, and I do not want any further debate or for people to begin arguing over who does what. I just want to make sure that there is a clear commitment to each idea we take to the next stage, action.

Check-out

An effective check-out can be done by bringing everyone back to the objective. "How did we do today in reaching our meeting goals?" A prompt like that works well, especially if the convergent phase of the session was detailed and ended with clear commitment. After posing this question to the group, I ask for three volunteers to share their comments. This is a simple stage, but an important one as it provides a final opportunity for anyone to share concerns or doubts. I have facilitated sessions where things go wonderfully smooth, and after the meeting I receive an email, or someone pulls me aside to ask for clarification or express confusion about the results. I ask for three different people to comment in order to briefly take the room's temperature and give a fair chance for people to share what they need to. If there are more than three people that wish to comment, then I try to keep the session going until no one has anything else left to share.

The tools used

- **Café** – Tool for getting everyone involved and for creating understanding when there are many simultaneous questions

- **Investment Activity** – Uncovering priorities ($15 was given to pairs but you can choose to give more or less money to invest depending on group size and the scope of the content)

- **Me/We/Us** – Getting everyone involved and creating an understanding of thinking frameworks

- **Group Ranking** – For discovering and creating understanding of priorities

- **Silent Moving** – More of a component of an activity rather than a tool itself, Silent Moving quickly checks for commitment by placing ideas or content into a shared space

Workshop process: Solutions

Objective: To find the right solutions for the key elements of a common goal.

Time: 90 minutes

Presenting the objective

Check-in tool: Asking whether the objective of the next stage is clear and presenting the main stages of the process (5 minutes).

Emergence tool: Café (40 minutes)
1. "Look around the room and think about the solutions for the key elements of a common goal. You may write them down if you like."
2. "Next go to your favorite topic (max 4 participants/topic) and listen, explore, and write down solutions on the flipchart with a marker."
3. "Choose a host or a hostess who will stay to explain the topic to future participants. Others will move to the next topic, listen to the presentation and add ideas."
4. Repeat until all topics are discussed by everyone.

Convergence tools: Investment Activity, Group Ranking, and Silent Moving (40 minutes)

Investment Activity

1. "Think on your own and choose your favorite solutions."

2. "With a pair invest $15 into best solutions. You may put all money on one solution, or you may split the money on best ideas on different solutions under different topics (5+2+3+4+1=). Remember that the total should be $15 per pair.

Group Ranking

1. "Get back to your favorite topic and write down all solutions that have more than $3 invested into them. One idea per A4 paper and with a big marker" (if there is a danger that the initial topic and context can be lost, it is a good practice to write down a topic number or name, too).

2. The group leader shuffles the solutions and gives each group an even number of solutions (as even as you can, do not worry if one group gets one solution less, there will be a final round of prioritising to make sure the statistical errors will be corrected).

3. "Please rank the solutions. For the best solution write number one on the back of the paper, for the second-best solution number two and so on..."

4. Rotate papers.

5. Now that you have ranked all solutions, count the total and write the score on the front with a marker."

6. Start counting and posting ideas: "Since we have three groups of solutions, the best possible rank is three. Who has a three, four, five, six...." Post the solutions on the wall, the highest-ranking ones the highest.

Silent Moving

1. "Here are the results and the rank of each solution. Now let's check for commitment. If there is a solution that you are personally committed to implementing, please move it on the other wall in silence."

Check-out tool: Evaluation (5 minutes)
1. "Did we reach the objective?" Solicit three responses.

3.3: Goal-Setting Workshop: Creating actions with Me/We/Us and Blossom

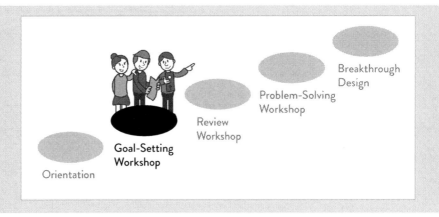

Orientation — Goal-Setting Workshop — Review Workshop — Problem-Solving Workshop — Breakthrough Design

What's here

- **Case study**: The action stage of the 3-stage goal-setting workshop. The objective of this stage is for the group to create steps to follow to reach their larger goals.
- **Tools**: Me/We/Us, Blossom, One Breath

How it helps

You will learn to facilitate an action planning session that creates concrete results and outlines the who, what, and when for each action. These actions are also related back to the content created in earlier stages of the workshop to create a unified plan that spans from the broad goals all the way to the specific actions that will achieve them.

The home stretch

After the break I was back to complete the final stage of the workshop with UTS. The now-familiar group was gathered in conference room 4 after enjoying a cup of tea.

"I hope everyone enjoyed the break as much as I did! If I worked here regularly and had access to your company's fantastic biscuits and cakes, my diet would be in serious trouble!"

"The struggle is real, Pepe!" said Paula in a show of support.

I continued, "We have come a long way so far; we began by wishing for a better future for your company. Then we found solutions which can make those wishes a reality. Now we will take things a step further in our final session together. We are going to find out which actions each of you will take in order to put the solutions into place. You will break down the solutions into actionable steps, and then decide which ones you are going to complete."

Josef raised his hand and asked, "Are we only thinking of individual actions? Some of the solutions involve more cross-team collaboration, so I hope that we can make these as a group."

"Great point. You will have the opportunity to involve others in the actions you create, so no need to worry about that." I drew everyone's attention to a wall with eight large sticky notes placed on it. "Remember these? They are the top solutions that you guys created and committed to during the last session. Now we are going to map out the actions needed to attain these solutions, which in turn will help you reach the goals that you wished for earlier. That is our objective. Any questions?"

The solutions prioritised during the previous session:

- Create personal relationships with valued customers
- Avoid silos and isolated working practices
- Ensure a sustainable workload
- Follow up with customers post-service for feedback and review
- Develop a more detailed orientation process for new hires
- HR as a more available and regular resource
- Showcase co-workers as an available and helpful resource
- Offer competitive pricing to maintain customers

Growing actions from solutions

No one had any questions for me, so it was time to start. "Please begin by looking at the chosen solutions that are posted on the wall and write down action points for yourself. You do not have to commit to anything now, but you will need to think about what your next actions are. You have around five minutes to do this, so please begin."

Everyone stood up and walked over to the wall to read the solutions. It took a few moments for the group to read and familiarise themselves with them before pen hit paper and they began writing. After a few moments it was time to change gears and move on.

"Does everyone have at least three actions written down?" A chorus of nods was the reply. "Fantastic, now please find the person who is standing closest to you, turn to them and smile. This is your partner for the next stage. Once you have a partner, go find a place to sit with them." A moment later the group was divided into six pairs.

"Now I want you to discuss your actions with your partner. Take a few moments to ask each other questions about them, align, and improve actions together. Take about ten minutes for this. Go!"

Twelve voices filled the room, and as I walked from pair to pair, I heard people describing a wide range of actions. Company President Bill was talking to Chi about lobbying to increase personal vacation days, Josef was telling Yao about how he was going to create an orientation packet to help new hires get used to their roles, and Donald was loudly stating that he was going to call an old client of his that had not been heard from in some time; "I don't know if they have simply quit using us or if they found another provider, but you can be sure that they will be hearing from me one way or another!"

I was happy that the conversation was flowing so easily, and equally as important, I was glad to see that most everyone was writing down new actions, too. *This is exactly what emergence should look like* I thought to myself. As the pairs finished up their discussions, I walked to the wall where the solutions were posted and adjusted the eight Post-it notes so that they were evenly spaced apart. It was important that there was plenty of room around each one for what was coming next.

I gathered everyone's attention. "You all make my job too easy! I will miss you guys and how wonderfully you follow instructions. I have gone ahead and passed out a stack of jumbo Post-it notes to each pair. Together with your partner I want you to write down your actions in the following format: who, what, and when. Only one action per Post-it note. Once you have written down all the actions on the Post-it notes, please place them around the corresponding solution on this wall." As I said this, I pointed to the wall with the solutions behind me.

"Pepe, what if an action could apply to more than one solution?", asked Paula.

"In that case you can write it down twice and place it around both of the related solutions. The idea here is to surround each solution with the actions. See if you can make it look like a flower! Take a few moments to do this now."

All twelve participants each had a few actions to place on the wall. Once everyone had finished, each solution was surrounded by concrete actions. And while the result did not look too much like flowers, it was beautiful, nonetheless.

A blossom

GOAL: Increase amount of repeat customers

SOLUTION: Create personal relationships with valued customers

Who: Bill
What: Create budget and allocate funds for new customer initiatives
When: Within 1 month

Who: Sarah and Yao
What: Managers and team leads make customer calls between projects
When: New way of working running within 3 months

Who: Chi
What: Organise golf tournament with top customers
When: Spring

Who: Sarah and Donald
What: Managers and team leads build customer profiles for marketing (likes, wants, needs, etc.)
When: New database with all customers ready in 6 months

Who: Yao
What: All employees with customer-facing roles create social media accounts for new communication channel between UTS and customers
When: Within 2 months

Who: Chi and Bill
What: Invite loyal customers for quarterly dinner
When: Beginning of Q3 (September)

"Very impressive", I said. "If you squint your eyes just so, they almost look like flowers! More importantly, you all have plenty of actions that relate to each solution. Please take a moment to read all of them silently. If you have a question or if anything is unclear, please ask!"

Choosing the best actions

Everyone was quietly focused on the blossoms on the wall. "We can take these blossoms a step further", I said. "Think critically about what is missing or what should be changed to improve these actions. Look at the actions and the names and times associated with them. Is anything missing? Do any actions need to be added? You can also adjust the timeframe of the actions as you see fit." This is still an individual activity, so no talking for now."

After a few moments I gathered everyone's attention once again. "If you need to add a new person to one of the actions or you want to change someone else's actions, please make sure you talk to that person and let them know you are doing so. Now find a new pair and take five minutes to share your ideas with them. If you need to change some actions, you are welcome to do so!"

New pairs were formed, and more discussion took place. The actions were becoming more and more detailed and refined. The discussions were becoming more focused as well; earlier they dealt with broad points and now everyone was diving into the minutia of each action. The group was ready for the final step.

"You all are doing a wonderful job. Now we are going to come back together as a group. Look at the blossoms once again. Is there anything that you still need to change?"

After a few moments and some revisions, I instructed everyone to read the actions once again in silence. I stood back with the group and admired their work. Detailed, concrete actions surrounded each solution. Some blossoms were larger than others as the solution had more actions related to it, but all eight of the solutions had a few or more actions surrounding it. I took a look at one of the larger blossoms which had the solution *ensure a sustainable workload* at the centre of it. The actions that surrounded it involved employees at all levels. *WHO: Yao, Isabelle, Donald, Sun WHEN: Next week WHAT: Revise the performance review process.* I was glad to see that the managers were going to review their practices to find a better and more sustainable way to assess how well their team members are performing. Bill Chen, UTS's President, wrote down that he was going to discuss expanding the number of employees to lighten the workload. He was going to bring this up with the board of directors during their next meeting;

WHO: Bill Chen, the Board WHEN: Q3 board meeting WHAT: Discuss the possibility of expanding the hiring quota to ensure proper division of work.

No solution was left without actions blossoming from it.

One Breath to say goodbye

I was pleased to see the results, but my opinion was not the one that mattered.

"Can I have everyone's attention here please? You all can take a seat," I said. "It looks like our work here is done. You all have developed detailed, concise actions for each solution. Just this morning we began by making broad wishes about how to improve your company, and now you have identified what is needed and how to do it to make these wishes come true. We are going to bring things to a close by sharing our thoughts about the workshop. Anything that comes to mind is fine, but due to limited time, you only have one breath to share your thoughts, so chose your words carefully! Who starts?"

A few people began inhaling their one breath sharply in preparation to share, but Caitlyn was the quickest. "It was a great workshop and I liked chatting and working with everyone and I hope to take some of these tools with me back to my role in human resources!"

Josef was next. "It was great to see our dreams and wishes become more and more realistic as we outlined them and how to achieve them. I enjoyed it."

The group was satisfied and more importantly, the workshop produced the results they wanted. I thanked everyone for a great workshop and left to enjoy my remaining time in Shanghai.

Analysis

This 60-minute long session concluded the workshop with UTS, and it was the final part of the CSA workshop structure—the *action* stage. The objective of this session was for the group to create specific action points to be completed in the coming days, weeks, and months. By this point in the day, we had already been working together for hours, so I did not need to provide much of a check-in activity. I opened the *action* stage of the workshop by simply presenting the objective and asking if it was clear, or if there were any questions.

UTS workshop schedule

- Half-day session
- Total time: 4 hours (includes two 15-minute breaks)

CLARIFYING	SOLUTIONS	ACTION
• 60 minutes long • Give a 15-minute break before continuing to solutions	• 90 minutes long • Give a 15-minute break before continuing actions	• 60 minutes long

Emergence

I began by having everyone look at the top solutions that the group ranked the highest during the Investment Activity from the previous session. These solutions were posted on the wall for everyone to see. I used jumbo Post-it notes for this session, but you can also tape a piece of copy paper to the wall; the important thing is that everyone is able to view the solutions. The instructions I gave the group at this point were to "look at the solutions on the wall and write down action points for yourself." I emphasised individual commitment; we start with our own actions and thinking about what we personally can do. People are very capable of thinking of actions for other people to do—creating action points for other people does not require a high degree of commitment. This can become problematic later when it is time to commit to the actions. It is better to have people think about their own actions from the beginning.

As seen in the previous stages of the workshop, the Me/We/Us structure was used. Participants were first asked to think about actions individually (ME), then develop actions with a partner (WE), and finally review the actions together as a group (US).

Me/We/Us was used for both emergence and convergence in this session. One trick I learned through the years is to have people work in pairs for a good portion of the session, instead of working in a structure where people can give lengthy monologues with only one person talking at a time, and everyone else stuck listening. People tend to work very constructively together in pairs or small groups, whereas in one big group people end to take positions and argue. In addition, pairs or small groups are the best format to create thoroughly new emergent ideas.

Blossom

Blossom provides a visual reminder of how actions relate directly to a solution (and goal). The actions surrounded the relevant solutions, and each solution was marked with the broad goal it pertained to, which meant that everything tied together—all the way from the bold and broad wishes that were made in the morning, to the specific actionable steps produced in the afternoon. Blossom is designed to allow the exploration of multiple topics at once, and it was a great choice for this session because there were eight different solutions that the group created actions for. Blossom requires that all actions link to a specific solution. If each solution has 5 actions created for it, then there are 40 actions. Imagine a wall filled with 40 sticky notes. It would be a bit chaotic without some organisation, right? With Blossom, actions are placed around the solution that they are linked to which clearly illustrates how everything fits together when looking at the big picture. There are also different timeframes for executing the actions. These important details are accounted for by labelling each action with a defined *who* and *when*.

After the workshop ended and I had left Shanghai, UTS still had the finished action plan with the top solutions surrounded by clear actions that defined the *who, what,* and *when* to refer to and to review.

Blossom

- Collect specific action points around each solution: *who, what, when*
- This allows you to visualise the actions and to make sure that each solution has the correct actions surrounding it.

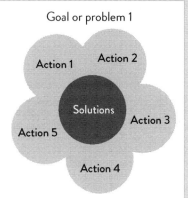

Goal or problem 1

Action 1
Action 2
Solutions
Action 3
Action 5
Action 4

Convergence

All parts of Me/We/Us were present during convergence. First, I had people look at the actions and think individually about how they could be further developed. Second, we worked in small groups to give participants time to share and talk about how to develop the actions. Finally, we looked at the results together as one large group.

I concluded the convergence phase by asking everyone how well we did in achieving the workshop objectives. To evaluate, I usually take comments from at least three participants. The evaluation went smoothly in this workshop with UTS. People were satisfied and they understood the results. But what if this is not the case? One thing to look for is if there are solutions that do not have people clearly committed to them, or if the group seems to be having difficulty getting the right people matched up with the right actions. If there is confusion about the actions, disagreement, or a lack of alignment, I circle back to more convergence. As the group leader, you can decide which part of Me/We/Us you want to circle back to. You can return to individual thinking, discussion in pairs or small groups, or you can have the entire group discuss together.

One Breath

- Participants form a circle
- Ask participants to comment on the workshop or meeting
- Prompts: I enjoyed..., I did not like...., I liked....I learned.....I had....

Rules: You have only one breath to use when sharing.

After everyone has shared, it is time to applaud. The workshop/meeting is over.

One Breath

I ended the workshop with a feedback activity called One Breath. It gives everyone the chance to share their thoughts about the session with the catch that they only have one breath to do so. This activity may seem like just a silly game, but when you give someone a limited amount of time, they will be more careful in gathering their thoughts and give feedback with a greater sense of purpose. Different prompts to begin such as "I learned...", "I enjoyed...", or "I didn't like..." can be given to help encourage people to begin.

What tools were used and why

- Me/We/Us—Basic tool for getting everyone involved and for creating understanding
- Blossom—For visualising actions
- One Breath—Used to collect candid feedback during check-out

Workshop process: Action

Objective: To create concrete actions that actualise the solutions outlined by UTS.

Time: 60 minutes

Presenting the objective

Check-in tool: Asking whether the objective of the next stage is clear and presenting the main stages of the process (5 minutes).

Emergence tool: Individual thinking—Me/We/Us and Blossom (25 minutes)

1. "Look at the chosen solutions on the wall and write down action points for yourself. You do not have decide to do anything, but you will have to think about actions for a few minutes!" (**ME**)
2. "Share and develop actions with the nice person next to you." (**WE**)
3. "Write down your actions in the format what, who, when on jumbo Post-it notes and post them next to the corresponding solutions. Let's see if we can form flowers by adding leaves."
4. "Read the actions in silence. If you have a question about one of the actions, please ask!" (**US**)

Convergence tools: Me/We/Us (25 minutes)

1. "Have a critical look at the actions in silence and think about what is missing or needs to be changed." (**ME**)
2. "Pair up with someone you need to talk to and share your ideas." (**WE**)
3. "Make the necessary changes on the blossoming flower field. If you need to add someone's name, feel free to connect with them and ask their permission."
4. "Let's read the actions again in silence. If you have a question about one of the actions, feel free to ask!" (If there is still disagreement after this step, you can repeat convergence from the beginning). (**US**)
5. Evaluation: "Did we reach the objective?" Ask for three comments from the group.

Check-out (5 minutes)

1. "Now that we have the actions ready, it is time to finish the workshop. I would like each one of you to share your thoughts about how the workshop went. To keep things moving, you only have one breath to share your thoughts. Who starts?"

3.4: Goal-Setting Workshop Review

Goal-setting workshop

UTS workshop schedule

- Half-day session
- Total time: 4 hours (includes two 15-minute breaks)

CLARIFYING	SOLUTIONS	ACTION
• 60 minutes long • Give a 15-minute break before continuing to solutions	• 90 minutes long • Give a 15-minute break before continuing actions	• 60 minutes long

Chapter 3 presented a 3-stage goal-setting workshop which I facilitated with the company UTS. The workshop was 8 hours long including a one-hour lunch break and two fifteen-minute breaks. The objective of the workshop was to clarify goals for UTS, find solutions to reach those goals, and then create specific actions to follow that would implement the solutions. You should pay close attention to the tools you decide to use, but the same is true for the workshop structure, too. One of the main ways group leaders provide value is by implementing an effective workshop structure. I used the CSA workshop structure, which dictates that workshop stages are presented in the following order: *clarifying, solutions, action*. The structure was backed by methodology; all workshop stages have a clear beginning, emergence, convergence, and end. The leader decides which tools to use in each stage.

UTS workshop tools

CLARIFYING	SOLUTIONS	ACTION
Tools	Tools	Tools
• Me/We/Us	• Tools	• Me/We/Us
• Wishing	• Me/We/Us	• Blossom
• Silent Moving	• Café	• One Breath
• Dartboard	• Investment Activity	
• Silent Moving	• Group Ranking	
	• Silent Moving	

Clarifying the goal

Time: 60 minutes

Objective: Produce shared goals

During the clarifying part of the workshop, the topic is still general and needs to be *clarified* (it is no secret where the name of this stage comes from). Before any clarification took place, I needed to start the workshop by **presenting the objectives**. By explaining the expectations for the day, what we were going to do and why, I made sure that everyone in the group started the workshop with a shared understanding of what we were trying to accomplish. Then I began by using emergent tools to create goals, followed by convergent tools to select them. The session concluded with a check-out activity where participants discussed if the objectives (which were presented at the very beginning) were met, and if everyone was happy with the results.

Me/We/Us was the foundation that covered both emergence and convergent phases of this workshop stage.

A variation: Sometimes you may have a predetermined goal that you want to introduce to a group. If this is the case, then it would not make sense to lead the group in activities to create and clarify goals, as we did in this workshop with UTS. Instead, you would lead them in a goal implementation workshop. Goal implementation workshops also follow the CSA structure and are similar, but instead of creating and choosing goals as a group, the leader introduces the predetermined goal or goals and then continues with the solutions and action stages of the workshop.

Solutions

Time: 90 minutes
Objective: Find the right solutions to reach the goals

The aim here was to break down the broad goals into achievable components. By the end of the solutions stage the group had identified their top solutions and prioritised them by importance.

The process and tools I used for the solutions stage is typical when there are a few topics to cover. In this workshop we had three goals that needed to be discussed. Our main objective was to align priorities and create a shared understanding for all three so that solutions could be created, prioritised, and committed to. Café was the perfect tool to use because it is time efficient. Café is structured in a way that allows for multiple topics to be discussed at the same time. This meant that the group could create solutions for the three goals at the same time as people rotated around the room when they wanted to talk about a different goal and its solutions.

Creating solutions for the three goals was the primary objective of this part of the workshop. Breakthrough decision making also requires that people are aligned together towards the same solutions. For this to happen, I needed a detailed convergence phase complete with multiple rounds of prioritisation. I led the group through 4 rounds of prioritisation. First, I asked participants to think about the solutions individually and choose which were their favourites. Then I grouped everyone into pairs and had them rank the solutions using the Investment Activity. Next, I used Group Ranking to have small groups review and rank the best solutions for each goal. Finally, once the top solutions were chosen and posted on the wall, I used Silent Moving, which required individuals to commit to specific solutions.

You might think that I am showing off or using an overly complex workshop structure, but I assure you that it is necessary. Most group leaders only use one round of prioritisation, which does not create the level of understanding and alignment that breakthrough decision making requires. In this workshop, we were finding solutions for three important goals all at the same time—that is no small feat! When we are dealing with complex topics or more than one topic at the same time, I make sure to use multiple convergent rounds, as this crucial for clear decision-making where everyone understands what is taking place and why. My record is seven rounds of prioritisation in a complex strategy workshop, and in that case, each round was required! I challenge you to try to use convergence too much. It is such a common mistake to not converge and prioritise enough that I would love to attend a session where there is too much convergence.

Action

Time: 90 minutes
Objective: Create concrete actions to reach the goals

At the beginning of the workshop the participants had a series of big problems that they wanted to fix. Employee turnover was too high, there was a lack of repeat customers, and employees were feeling burnt out. The clarifying stage opened things up with thinking about wishes on a broad level, and the next stage was a middle ground spent outlining solutions that would contribute to making these wishes come true. The actioning stage of the workshop fills in all the details that need to be decided in order to fulfil the solutions and reach the group's goals. The action stage is all about specifics, and in this stage the *who, what,* and *when* were answered.

This actioning session concluded my workshop in Shanghai with UTS Consulting. I think it provides a great example of what properly executed group leadership can do. By the end of it all there was an action plan that showed the way to making the wishes come true. That is pretty cool if I do say so myself. Normally it's hard to commit to something, especially if it is someone else's idea that you had no hand in creating. Me/We/Us and the other facilitation methods used here help people become invested in ideas and commit to them. The contrast in effectiveness is stark when compared to traditional methods like delegation, or management simply deciding for everyone and then assigning tasks and roles to their teams.

When to use a goal-setting workshop

Goal-setting workshops are versatile, and they can be applied in a variety of different situations. UTS first contacted me to lead a workshop to help create new ideas and goals to fix the lagging performance of their Technology Division. The first part of the workshop was devoted to thinking of broad goals for UTS, the second part of the workshop was more specific and focused on finding solutions to reach these goals, and the final part of the workshop was spent creating and committing to specific actions that could be followed to execute the solutions. For UTS, the result of this 3-stage workshop was a new strategy for UTS's Technology Division to follow.

A goal-setting workshop can be used when something new needs to be created. This could be a new strategy, new ideas relating to existing workflows, project planning, and much more.

Common situations for a goal-setting workshop
- Strategic planning
- Product development
- Office design
- Team development
- Project planning
- Service design
- And much more... It is a good fit whenever you are creating something new

CHAPTER 4:
Review Workshop

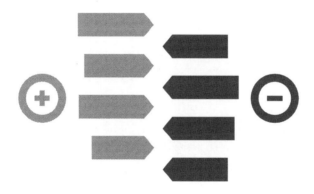

4.1: Review Workshop: Clarifying Current Challenges with Force Field Analysis

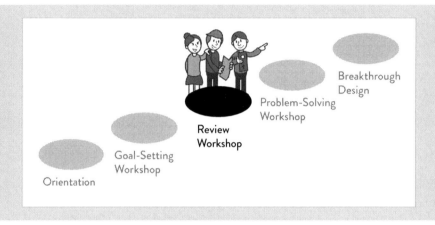

What's here

- **Case study**: The clarifying part of a review workshop with UTS that took place a month after the goal-setting workshop

- **Tools**: Force Field Analysis, Silent Moving, urgency-importance matrix, Dot Voting

How it helps

Force Field Analysis is the tool I use for in-depth review.
It identifies the key underlying factors behind any strategy, process, service, or project, and it also can be used to assess team health.

Dealing with emotions

The last time I was in Shanghai was a month earlier when I was leading the goal-setting workshop with UTS consulting. The team performed well, participated enthusiastically in during the workshop, and worked together to produce breakthroughs and relevant solutions for their original problems. The result was a detailed action plan comprised of concrete tasks and actions, all marked with *who, what* and *when*.

Although the action plan clearly outlined what needed to be done, new challenges often arise once a workshop ends. An action plan, no matter how detailed or precise, cannot help you with obstacles that arise once the action plan is being followed, so a follow-up meeting is required. Let's review the follow-up session I had with UTS after the actioning workshop to see just how a follow-up meeting should look.

A month had passed, and I was back in Shanghai to work with Bill, Chi, Yao and the rest of the group of twelve that attended the goal-setting workshop. I was back within the familiar walls of UTS's conference room #4 and I was pleased to see that the results from our last session were still displayed. The goals and solutions agreed by the group were posted on a wall in the conference room. Each solution had a cluster of Post-it notes surrounding it that detailed the specific actions that were to be taken and also linked the actions and solutions with the broader goals that were created in the beginning of the workshop.* Believe it or not, quite a few groups go through a workshop and work hard to create an action plan, only to have it taken down or tossed into the recycling bin a few days later. Thankfully, UTS did not make this mistake.

Once everyone had taken a seat and morning greetings were exchanged, I began the day's workshop by sharing the objective for the day.

"Today our objective is to discover the current challenges that you are facing in relation to the implementation of the plan that we created in the last workshop."

---

* This is a description of the Blossom activity that was demonstrated in Chapter 3.2. The result posted on the wall is an action plan—a visual guide that shows the next steps that need to be taken to work towards a goal and implement solutions.

"*Discover* the current challenges? That should be easy," said Phil.

A few people nodded in agreement, while Chi replied, "Challenges *and* successes. There has been plenty of success if you are capable of seeing it."

There was a palpable tension that I could feel in the room. It may not have been serious, but Phil, Chi, and perhaps some others were a bit more charged up now than they were the last time I saw them. I wanted to find out more about how people felt, and I knew just the tool to use.

"Thanks for the comments, Chi and Phil. We all have plenty to discuss today, and it is great to see that you are ready to go. But before we do that, can everyone please stand up?"

Once everyone was standing by their desks, I directed their attention to the front of the room.

"Look at this," I said as I pointed to the ground.

"It's our carpet," deadpanned Isabelle.

"That's right, Isabelle, but I am not referring to the carpet. Look closer! There is an imaginary line on the floor that runs from one side of the room to the other." I illustrated my point (and the line) by pointing to the floor as I walked from one side of the room to the other. "Each spot on the line has a specific meaning. This side of the line means that 'I feel terrible today'. Stand over here if it is one of the worst days of your life."

I walked to the other side and continued, "And this side of the line means that it is an absolutely fantastic day; a combination of Christmas and your birthday mixed in with payday on a Friday. Stand here if this represents your mood more accurately. Of course, if you feel somewhat between these two extremes, stand somewhere in between. Find your spots now!"

Everyone chose a spot to stand on the line without too much thought. Over half of the group was standing on the *happy* side of the line, and there were a few people in the middle, too. Towards the *worst day ever* side was Phil, who began the session with a negative comment.

"Now turn to the person next to you and let them know why you chose that spot. You have one minute!"

I listened to bits of conversation along the line. On one side Josef was smiling to Caitlyn as he described how he was going to take next week off to go visit old friends in Australia. In the middle of the line I heard some comments about 'decent coffee' and heavy traffic on the morning commute. On the far side of the line was Phil, who wore a large frown on his face as he explained to a tired-looking Sarah that he was in the middle of a rough morning. He punctuated his complaints with, "And the cherry on top is spending hours today working to fix actions that are stuck and beyond repair!"

I took this as my cue to step in. "Great work everyone, thank you. Can I hear from three people about why they chose their spot in line? Let's start on the happy end."

Bill raised a hand and said, "I slept very well last night, and tonight I am going to spend some time with my grandchildren."

On the far side of the line was Phil, who made it clear that he was not having a very good day. "All these different forms of stress have been piling up and turning into something more. Small things at home, bills, appointments, bad weather, annoying songs you hear in the elevator...everything is just coming one after another and that makes today not very good. The same goes for my state of mind; the actions I have been trying to work on feel like I am running into a wall."

"The only way is up from here, Phil. Chin up!" said Sun. Phil thanked him for the words of encouragement.

I pointed to the middle of the line and Yao commented that so far, the day has been very plain. The subway was crowded, but not too bad. The coffee was not hot, but warm enough, and the week ahead seemed long, but also manageable.

Celebrating success and embracing new challenges

I moved the group to the next activity. "Let's review the work that we did together in the previous workshop. Everyone can stand up and look at the plan which we created last time. It has all the goals, solutions and actions that we created. Take a few moments to review all of these. Which solutions and actions have been implemented and are working well? Write these down as successes. Also write down the solutions and actions that just don't seem to work, or the ones that you can't seem to make progress towards. Mark these down as your challenges. You have around five minutes to do this individually."

After five minutes, I had the group of twelve split into smaller groups of three.

"Share with each other the challenges and successes that you wrote down. Once everyone in your group has had the chance to share, select two challenges and two successes, and write each one down on a large Post-it. Your criteria for choosing the successes and actions is important. What are the most pressing challenges that need to be fixed? On the other side, what have been the biggest and best successes that you have accomplished so far? You have 15 minutes."

As people chatted in groups, I could see smiles words of encouragement when successes were shared. But despite this optimism, I could see that groups were spending most of the 15 minutes discussing the challenges and difficulties that they had encountered.

"Once you have selected and written down two-three challenges and two-three successes as a group, please post them on this wall so we all can see."

Everyone followed the instructions perfectly, and after a few moments the challenges and successes were written down and posted on the wall.

"Let's start with the successes. Please take a few moments to read the success in silence."

Successes

- H.R proactively offering support and info via email
- Showcased co-workers as resource for knowledge and help
- Improved personal relationships with clients
- Contacted customers proactively to follow up and collect feedback
- Improved work balance

After a few moments had passed, I began clapping loudly and told everyone to give themselves a round of applause. "You have achieved a lot and you need to take some time to give the respect and gratitude that you deserve!"

The sound of applause filled the room, and I could see that people were enjoying patting their own backs for a bit. I told everyone to take a few moments to read the challenges silently, and once they had done so, I asked if everything was clear. No questions so far, so I told everyone to review the challenges and remove any duplicates. Some groups had independently arrived at the same challenges, so a few duplicates needed to be taken down from the wall. Once that step was completed, there were six challenges remaining.

Challenges

- Improve personal relationships with clients
- Building internal knowledgebase
- Cold calling clients and/or emailing clients in a way that feels organic and not like a sales call
- Implementing collaboration tool for cross-team communication
- Establishing contact with former customers via email at > 5 % response rate
- Identifying competitor pricing and product lines

"Which challenges do you prioritise as both urgent and important? In other words, what challenges do we need to solve today? Take a few moments to think about it. Then find a partner to talk to. Sell them on your choices about which challenges are urgent and important."

A few moments later, everyone was ready and sharing with a partner. Sarah, the director of marketing, was telling Chi that reviewing the price points so far had been an utter failure. Next to her was Bill who was stating that his biggest challenge as company president was to work with team leads to help revise the amount of expected workload that an individual has to take on—something that he had not made progress towards so far.

Next, I changed the dynamic a bit and instructed each pair to find another pair and continue the discussion in groups of four. While they chatted away in their groups, I drew two lines on a piece of flipchart paper so that they formed a large L shape.

"OK, all of you can stop talking and focus your attention up here,", I said while pointing to the piece of paper. "In front of you is a matrix which we are going to use to prioritise the challenges that you just finished discussing. Can someone read the words written under each line?"

"Urgency and importance," said Bill.

"Thank you. In silence I would like everyone to place their Post-it notes on the matrix so that they properly match the level of urgency and importance for each challenge. The top right is for the most important and urgent challenges, while the bottom left is for the least important and urgent challenges. Everyone can move the Post-it notes whenever they feel like. When the Post-it notes do not move anymore, we are ready. As an added challenge, let's try to reach consensus without speaking a word."

Some people considered for a moment where to place their challenges, while others got right down to it. There were only six challenges to prioritise and placing them on the board initially was quick work. The activity really got going when the challenges were placed and then moved by someone else. Earlier when the group was writing down challenges and successes, both Neil and Sun had mentioned improving relationships with clients. That is not a big coincidence, but it is worth mentioning here because Neil had listed it as a success while Sun prioritised it as a top challenge. Now they were both in front of the matrix trying to find a place for the Post-it note that represented *improving relationships with clients*. They were not talking because this was a silent activity, but no words needed to be said. They both wore tense looks occasionally glared at each other as they moved the Post-it from one corner of the matrix to the other. Eventually a compromise was silently agreed to and the Post-it stopped bouncing from one side of the matrix to the other and settled right in the middle.

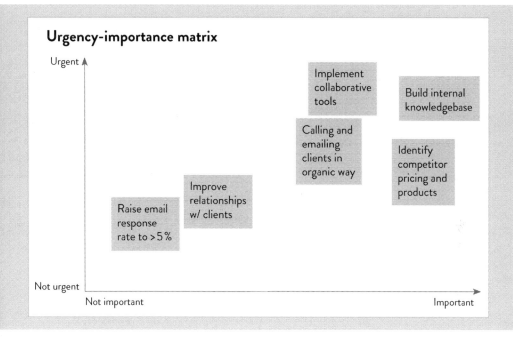

Urgency-importance matrix

Urgent

- Implement collaborative tools
- Build internal knowledgebase
- Calling and emailing clients in organic way
- Identify competitor pricing and products
- Improve relationships w/ clients
- Raise email response rate to >5%

Not urgent

Not important — Important

Wrapping up the session

"Great job, everyone. Our work for the day is just about done. In front of us we have the key challenges, which you now all agree on regarding their urgency and importance. But before we go, someone please remind everyone what our objective was for the first stage.

Bill did the honours by replying, "We had the objective of discovering the challenges that we are facing in implementing the plan."

"Thanks, Bill. Now everyone can find an intelligent person to partner up with and have a quick discussion about how we did in reaching that objective."

After some discussion, I asked for three final comments from the group about the objective. All the comments indicated that the objective was clear, and there was no evident confusion about the results, so I thanked everyone for their hard work and drew the session to a close.

Analysis

UTS review workshop schedule

- Half-day session
- Total time: 4 hours (includes two 15-minute breaks)

CLARIFYING	SOLUTIONS	ACTION
• 60 minutes long • Give a 15-minute break before continuing to solutions	• 90 minutes long • Give a 15-minute break before continuing actions	• 60 minutes long

The review workshop is a follow-up to the *goal-setting workshop* that was covered in Chapter 3. The objective of this follow up session was to discover the current challenges that have risen when the solutions and actions from the previous workshop were put into practice. In this case with UTS, the time between the two workshops was around one month, which is within the normal 4 to 6-week range of time that separates a workshop from a follow up session. However, fast-moving teams like software developers may elect to have a follow-up session only one or a few days later.

Check-in

To start things off, I presented the objective to the group. By now you have probably noticed that this is how I have started each stage of the workshop, and for good reason! I believe in explicitly stating the objective to everyone so that no assumptions are made, and to give people a chance to react with any questions they may have. In this session, a participant made a comment indicating that he was feeling frustrated by how difficult it has been to implement some of his actions. I could see that there was some tension in the room, so I decided right then to use a check-in activity called Line to warm the group up. Line is a classic group tool that can measure almost anything. It is often used to measure work experience, attitudes, or to form groups based on age, hair colour, place of birth, or anything else that you could possibly think of.

In this case I asked everyone to take a place on the line based on mood, and to chat with the person next to them about why they chose to stand where they did. This was no accident-I asked people to discuss their feelings as a direct response to the tension that I observed earlier. This is a rule which I try to follow whenever possible: I ask people to share emotions when I sense trouble. Self-disclosure builds trust, and talking about emotions is therapeutic.

Line
Bad feeling   God feeling

- Line is an active way to measure something.
- It is particularly useful to measure the temperature in the room in the beginning of a meeting or workshop.
- Mark clearly on the floor the line, e.g., by using sticky tape. Walk through the line explaining what different spots on the line signify. Clarify the ends and the middle of the line.
- Ask participants to find a spot on the line that signifies their feeling/ position at that given moment.
- When everyone has found their spot, ask participants to chat with the person right next to them and to explain why they are standing just on that given spot. After a short while, ask a few participants to share their explanations with the whole group.

To this point, a good friend of mine who happens to be a psychologist told me that people are typically not present when they enter a room. Instead, they are preoccupied with their own thoughts and emotions. One way to help people become present is to ask them to talk about their emotions. This works because when we talk about our current feelings, we become more aware and focused on our thoughts, which brings us to the present moment.

Emergence

I used the familiar Me/We/Us structure once again to oversee when people work individually, with a partner, and together as one large group. This time Me/We/Us was matched with Force Field Analysis.

Force Field Analysis

Force Field Analysis is a tool used mostly in change implementation. It is a natural fit with workshops where the objective is to identify challenges that stand in the way of implementing a goal.

I often use Force Field Analysis when facilitating a session dedicated to change management or change resistance. It is common for group leaders and facilitators to work with these topics when organisations implement large-scale changes or some radical new protocol.

The steps of Force Field Analysis

1. Introducing the topic
2. Listing pros and cons
3. Prioritising the cons that need to be solved

In relation to UTS and their actions, we wanted to review the status of their plan. I first asked them to think about the successes (+) and challenges (–) individually, and then discuss and prioritise challenges in pairs, and finally again as one large group, as Me/We/Us dictates.

Remember the brilliant and influential psychologist Kurt Lewin who was introduced in the first chapter of this book? Through his work he developed Force Field Analysis. Think back to Lewin's discussion groups and the housewives complaining about the negatives of cooking the strange new meat. This was a negative force keeping them from adopting a desired change. On the other side are opposing forces, or positives, such as *it will cost less money*, and *it will help the war effort*.

Lewin calls the negative forces "restraining forces" and the positives "driving forces". The restraining forces keep things the same and restrict change; they are the thoughts that pop into your head and voice doubt when a change is suggested. The driving forces push towards change. And stuck between these opposing forces is the present state/desired state. An interesting phenomenon exists when companies try to focus too much on the positive side of change (which is a common tactic, I might add.) If the positives are introduced first, and with too much focus placed on them, it actually causes people to think more about the negatives! When there is resistance to change, it is best to first discover the restraining forces that are holding you back. Once these forces are identified, you can introduce the positive forces that will help bring about the desired change.

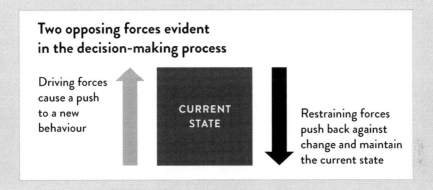

Two opposing forces evident in the decision-making process

Driving forces cause a push to a new behaviour

CURRENT STATE

Restraining forces push back against change and maintain the current state

The goal of this stage was to identify the challenges so that they could be addressed and eliminated, but Force Field Analysis suggests that the plusses are to be discussed, too. But why? If we only really care about the challenges, why even bother discussing the successes at all?

Let me give you several reasons:

1. We want to gain a whole picture and understanding of what works and what does not work

2. Listing only the negatives could make an entire project seemed doomed

3. We want to highlight the successes, so they carry forward and can be built upon

The application of Force Field Analysis is broad, and I use it to facilitate such topics as strategy review, process development, team health, product development, budget refinement, and more. Once I had a group use Force Field Analysis to review the practice of eating cookies and other high-sugar treats during coffee breaks.

Convergence

To structure the convergent portion of the workshop, I used a familiar structure: Me/We/We/Us. Yes, you read that correctly; there are two *We* sections here. Think back to the workshop process. After the individual stage I asked for people to find a partner for discussion—this is the first *We* section. Next, I had each pair find a new pair to combine with, creating groups of four—this is the second *We* section. I did this to slow down the decision-making process and create deeper understanding of the challenges.

You can decide to slow down thinking or decision-making by extending the *We* section, which can be done by creating new pairs or larger discussion groups.

Prioritising with Field of Two Criteria

I dedicated more time to convergence by using the urgency-importance matrix combined with Silent Moving. I have seen many workshops end after ideas are selected in groups and posted for everyone to see; this is a good start, but the convergent work is not done. A lack of time dedicated to convergence is a critical error that I see again and again.

The urgent-important matrix is like the Dartboard activity, yet it provides a different way of visualising the results. The end results will be similar, but it is important to vary the activities to keep people tuned in and willing to participate. The urgent-important matrix comes from a broader tool called Field of Two Criteria. There are two lines on the matrix, each representing degrees of the two chosen pieces of criteria.

Field of Two Criteria

Choose the two most important pieces of criteria. Make a matrix on the wall. Place ideas on the matrix. Those that fulfill both criteria are located in the upper right corner.

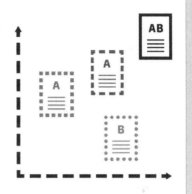

Common criteria for example:

- Urgency
- Importance
- Impact
- How easy it is to implement
- Newness
- Quick wins / long term goal
- Estimated costs
- How much can we influence ourselves

Participants place their content on the matrix. Content that fulfil both pieces of criteria go on the upper-right of the matrix. The lower left of the matrix is for content that does not fulfil either piece of criteria. One piece of criteria will be assigned to the left axis of the matrix. The stronger content fulfils this criterion, the higher on the matrix it goes. The other criterion is assigned to the bottom line of the matrix. Content that weakly fulfils this goes to the left, while content that strongly fulfils this criterion is placed on the right of the matrix.

The criteria I used in this instance were *urgency* and *importance*, a combination that worked very well. I would love to take credit for thinking of this combination on my own, but I can't; it was made famous by a tool called the Eisenhower Matrix, which was created originally for prioritising tasks. While it is true that you can use many different criteria with the Field of Two Criteria tool, I find that importance and urgency work great together. Importance makes us question our deeper beliefs and question why some things are more important to us than other things. Urgency also stresses prioritisation, but in terms of how time is allocated. As a group leader, it is easy to go wrong by choosing criteria that is too specific. When we enter the world of criteria, there are always complexities and always multiple criteria to choose from; individual preferences, value for business, resources, feasibility, management support, budgetary constraints... the list can go on and on.

Check-out

Once again, this stage of a workshop ended by returning the conversation back to the main objective of the day. I had people discuss in pairs how successful we were at reaching the review workshop's objective, which was to discover the current challenges that were standing in the way of completing the actions and reaching the goals outlined in the goal-setting workshop from a month earlier. This is an important habit to get into because if the objectives were not met, then the group leader would know that more work needs to be done. In this case, if the feedback I received from the group was lukewarm, then I could further develop the ideas or make sure that the content was clearly prioritised by using further rounds of discussion in small groups, or a convergent tool designed to prioritise ideas like the Investment Activity or Dot Voting.

What tools were used and why

- **Me/We/Us**—Basic tools for getting everyone involved
- **Force Field Analysis**—To reveal a status, to find a challenge, to deal with change resistance
- **Me/We/We/Us**—Basic tools for getting everyone involved. You can extend the We section by forming new groups or larger groups
- **Silent Moving**—Prioritising
- **Urgency-importance Matrix**—Visualising priorities

Workshop process: Clarifying the challenges

Objective: To discover the current challenges
Time: 60 minutes

Presenting the objective of the workshop
Check-in tool: Line (10 minutes)

1. "There is an imaginary line on the floor and each spot on the line has a meaning. This end means that I feel terrible today. The spot in the middle of the line means that I am ok. And the other end means that I am feeling super happy. Please find your spot!"

2. "Find a pleasant person next to you and discuss why you chose that spot!"

3. "Now I would like have three participants share what they discussed. Let's hear from each part of the line. Let's have the happy people comment first."

4. "Thank you. Please sit down!"

Emergence tools: Me/We/Us and Force Field Analysis (20 minutes)

1. "Look at the goals, solutions and actions from the previous meeting. Individually write down successes—what we have already accomplished—and current challenges with implementation."

2. "In groups of three—discuss and find two to three key successes and two to three challenges!"

3. "Write your key successes and challenges on jumbo Post-it notes with big letters."

4. "Post successes and challenges."

5. "Eliminate the duplicates (but do not group ideas)."

Convergence tools: Me/We/We/Us, Field of Two Criteria, and Silent Moving (20 minutes)

1. "Let's look at and read the successes in silence. Everything clear? We have done a great job. Let's give ourselves a hand!"

2. "Now, lets look at and read the challenges in silence. Everything clear?"

3. "Think on your own and choose the challenges we need to solve today."

4. "In pairs, influence each other."

5. "Now join with another pair and influence each other."

6. "On the wall in front of you is a matrix with two lines drawn on it. The line running from the bottom to the top is marked *urgent*. The higher the urgency, the higher on the line. The line running from left to right is marked *important*. The degree of importance on the line increases the farther left you go. Place the challenges on this matrix based on how they match this criteria, with the most urgent and important challenges ending on the upper left of the matrix."

Check-out: Pair discussion (10 minutes)

1. "Find an intelligent person next to you and discuss weather we reached the objective."

2. "Now I would like three of you to comment."

3. "Thank you, we did a great job!"

Note: You can always check the results of Silent Moving with Dot Voting.

4.2: Review Workshop: Finding Solutions with Bus Stop

What's here

- **Case Study**: The solutions part of the review workshop
- **Tools**: Bus Stop (for both emergence and convergence), Dragons, Earth Energy

How it helps

Bus Stop is a fast-paced tool that can be used to create ideas at the beginning of a workshop, or to select the best ideas at the end of a workshop. In this section I show how to use Bus Stop as both an emergent and convergent tool.

Get energised

Life is pretty good, I thought to myself as I sat sipping an herbal tea in UTS Consulting's employee cafeteria. I was enjoying my time in Shanghai with UTS, and I hoped that the feeling was reciprocated by my workshop attendees. A good amount of time earlier in the day had been spent working with challenges. This required a lot of time focusing on things that needed to be changed and that currently stood in the way of their long-term goals. I was excited for what the afternoon had in store—solving the challenges. I did not have too much time left to daydream however, as Chi, the executive assistant, politely tapped me on the shoulder and informed me that everyone was ready to proceed. I followed her to the now familiar conference room #4 to begin.

Walking into the room, I wasted no time. "Good afternoon, everybody! I hope that you enjoyed the break and had time for some coffee."

Nods greeted me in return and a few half-hearted affirmative murmurs answered my question.

"We spent the morning identifying the current challenges that you are facing in relation to your goals, and now we continue our work in solving them. Our objective for this afternoon is to find solutions to these present challenges, and we have about 90 minutes booked to do so."

Upon hearing the objective, no reply was given by the group, but onward I went.

"Solving challenges is no small task, and to help us do this I have an activity planned which will require some fast-paced writing and rotation. If previous results are any indication, I am sure you all are up for it. Is everyone ready?"

Again, more polite nodding, and a courteous reply from company president Bill; "We are ready, Pepe."

Always well mannered, I thought. *But apart from being polite, half of them seem to be asleep in their chairs.* As I was considering this, Yao yawned loudly right on cue. I decided that before anything else could be done, the group needed an interjection of energy.

"I can see that all of you must have spent so much energy before the break that there is not much left over. I have an idea that can help us change that. I learned an old martial arts technique which helps us utilise the energy that is in the physical space all around us. I must warn you though, it requires focus, some movement, and a bit of shouting. Does this sound appropriate?"

I could see that this perked some interest from the group. "Let's give it a try," said Donald.

"Fantastic. This is an activity that I learned from an old friend of mine who spent a lot of time traveling and studying martial arts. He had a sensei that taught him how to harness the energy that is always circulating in the earth. It is a little-known fact, but we too can harness this energy, and I will show you how. Everyone, please stand up, and watch carefully."

Once they stood, I spread my feet shoulder-width apart, and rotated my feet as if I were digging them into sand.

"The energy of the earth is extremely powerful, so you need to start by first establishing a very strong base. Spread your feet apart like this and bend your knees slightly as if you were bracing for an impact."

I could hear all twelve pairs of shoes of the participants swooshing on the carpet as they matched my movements.

"Good, now that we are good and strong, getting the energy out of the earth is quite simple. You can...simply...pick it up!"

While saying this, I bent down and with two hands motioned as if I was scooping handfuls of something heavy from under the carpet. "As you can see, I have the energy here in my hands. It is a bit heavy, but all in all, it is not too hard to get. Give it a try, yourself!"

A few people began laughing as they followed my lead.

"Now that we all have harnessed some energy from the earth, the most important step is to push it to everyone else...*hi-YAAAAAAA!*"

The final step, and by far the loudest step of giving the energy to everyone else I punctuated with a loud yell and a thrust of my palms forward to shoot the energy across the room towards everyone. I was happy to hear each one yell back and give the energy to me, too.

I could see that everyone was participating, and most importantly awake. They were ready to continue.

"Now that we have our energy levels back up to where they need to be, lets focus on the challenges that you identified this morning. As mentioned before, our objective now is to find solutions to the current challenges. Are there any questions about the objective?"

Solving the challenges

"Take a look around the room. I have posted the challenges from the last meeting on the wall around the room. Each flipchart paper you see represents one challenge that was identified this morning. Now you may notice that I did not use all of the challenges. Instead, I selected the four that were labelled as the most urgent and important, according to the matrix we made this morning. Does this seem okay, or should we review all of them?"

Bill glanced at the matrix and said, "I probably speak for all of us in saying that focusing on the top four is fine."

Around the room heads nodded in agreement, so I continued, "I would like everyone to begin by walking around the room and individually writing down solutions for each challenge on your own piece of paper. After this, go stand by the piece of paper that has your favourite challenge written on it. Form a group with the other people who chose the same challenge as you, and together write down solutions for that challenge."

"One question," said Josef. "What if we all choose the same challenge? Is this OK?"

"I am glad you asked. Out of the six challenges you identified earlier and placed on the matric, four of these were grouped tightly together as both urgent and important. I have taken these four challenges and posted them on flipcharts on the wall. There are twelve of you, so please keep the group size at three. You will have a chance to discuss everything, so no need to worry. If everything is clear, feel free to begin, and find your spot!"

Everyone began circulating the room, and after a bit, settled by a flipchart paper. Each challenge had three people discussing it, so I was pleased.

Challenges

- Building internal knowledgebase
- Cold calling clients and/or emailing clients in a way that feels organic and not like a sales call
- Implementing collaboration tool for cross-team communication
- Identifying competitor pricing and product lines

"Now that we have our groups formed, you have seven minutes to have a good talk and to write down solutions for your favourite challenge. Then we are going to rotate the flipchart papers around the room while the groups remain the same. As the papers rotate you will continue to write down solutions in your groups. You will be developing the solutions other groups came up with as their papers rotate to your group, and other groups will be building off what you write, so it is important to write clearly and in complete sentences."

I kept track of the time during the group discussion, and every seven minutes I would announce "switch!" and help rotate the flipchart papers from group to group. By the end of the 28-minute discussion period, each flipchart was filled with at least four different types of distinct handwriting, and lots of solutions.

"Great job, everyone. You must have produced at least 50 different solutions here, very impressive! Now that we have an abundance of solutions, we need to see which ones are good. Look around the room and spot two other people who are not in your group and form new groups of three with them." Everyone took a moment to shuffle around and form new groups.

"Pick a challenge and review the solutions in your new groups and decide which ones you like the best. You will mark your selections by drawing a dragon—the most powerful of all animals—next to solutions that you think must be implemented. Solutions that are just ok or not worth implementing do not get any dragons."

"How many dragons do we have?" asked Isabelle.

"You have an unlimited number of dragons to give, so if all of the solutions you see are absolute must-haves, then give a dragon to every solution. But remember that in practice you may not have time to implement everything. So, if you do not prioritise the solutions now, you still might be forced to when trying to execute them. You have seven minutes to discuss in your groups, and then I will rotate the flipchart paper again so that every group has the chance to vote on every solution. Any questions?"

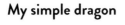

My simple dragon

"How do you draw a dragon?" asked curious Isabelle.

I showed the group my simple way of drawing a dragon. Isabelle claimed she can draw a better one and I encouraged the group to begin.

Dragons were drawn as the discussions carried on. Every seven minutes I would rotate the papers from group to group, and at the end of the activity I posted the flipchart papers at the front of the room.

"These are some well-drawn dragons! And so many of them, too. Let's count the dragons and see which solutions have the most dragons. Each group, please write down all solutions with two or more dragons on a piece of computer paper. And just one idea per paper!"

Once the groups were done, I thanked everyone, and asked them to back down. "Here we have the top ten solutions that received two or more dragons. Are you happy to implement these ten?"

Top ten solutions

Identifying competitor pricing and product lines
- Get feedback from customers about pricing and product offerings of UTS competitors
- Call competitors directly to get pricing and product information/ conduct market research

Building internal knowledgebase
- Create content and draft internal knowledge base
- Identify external software options for knowledge base to avoid having to build it in-house

Cold calling clients and/or emailing clients in a way that feels organic and not like a sales call
- Find reasons to cold call customers
- Record customer calls
- Research examples of successful customer outreach initiatives
- Share learnings and tips from good and bad customer calls

Implementing collaboration tool for cross-team communication
- Test different collaboration tools to be used for cross team communication
- Test alternatives to use in place of new collaboration tool

"Right off the bat I think we can implement testing collaboration tools and researching software to use for the internal knowledge base. I think that we spent too much time trying to find the perfect solution, instead of just going ahead and trying new things and then reviewing in hindsight," said Yao.

Sarah agreed, and added, "He's right. The same goes for drafting content for the internal knowledge base. Once it is built, we can add content and then revise it later as needed. It does not need to be in a state of perfection."

The discussion continued, and more solutions were agreed upon. Recording customer calls was put on the back burner when Josef correctly pointed out that a lot of calls are made from cell phones or from a personal line, which made recording them an exceedingly difficult prospect. But apart from that, the group decided that the other nine solutions could easily be implemented with a little better time management and less concern about getting it perfect the first time around.

A job well done

"Thank you everyone for a great session today. At least I thought it was great, but my opinion does not matter. I want to hear from you guys. At least three comments, please."

"I enjoyed rotating the papers and keeping the groups the same," said Sun.

Yao added, "I entered the room half asleep, but after you had us grab the sky energy in the beginning, I was wide awake."

Earth energy, not sky energy! I thought silently as Yao misremembered the name of the activity. And finally, Bill concluded, "I am happy that we have some results we can build on."

Analysis

UTS review workshop schedule
- Half-day session
- Total time: 4 hours (includes two 15-minute breaks)

CLARIFYING	SOLUTIONS	ACTION
• 60 minutes long • Give a 15-minute break before continuing to solutions	• 90 minutes long • Give a 15-minute break before continuing to action	• 60 minutes long

This case study showed the second stage of a review workshop where the objective was to create and choose solutions for challenges that arose when following the previous workshop results.

Check-in

When you continue a workshop, you do not need to devote much time to do a long check-in. Just make sure that everyone understands the goal and the ways of working. I began the session by clearly stating the objective for the workshop stage and I made sure that everyone had the chance to ask any questions or seek clarification if they needed to. I also explained how we would be achieving the objective by introducing the ways of working. I mentioned that the main portion of the workshop would require discussion and was fast-paced, and when I introduced the energiser activity, I asked the group if they wished to try it, instead of just launching into the instructions.

When I begin with a group I try to be as transparent as possible. This means that I want people to feel comfortable with me and understand my motives. I am there to help the group as they create ideas and solutions, and I do not have any hidden agenda. Being transparent builds trust and makes people feel like they have more of an active role in the workshop process, instead of just being herded from one activity to the next. While it is important to introduce the ways of working to a group, I usually do not tell them the specific names of the methods or tools that I will be using. Doing this can cause people to react poorly, become bored and tune out. Tool names sound a bit clinical, and I rarely see workshop participants get motivated when they hear a tool name like *Force Field Analysis* or *Bus Stop*. Instead, I just give them the big picture by generally explaining how they will be working and what I need them to do. For example, rather than saying Bus Stop, I would introduce the tool as fast-paced activity where you write down your ideas and rotate around the room.

When I noticed that energy levels were quite low, I decided to use an energiser. I chose Earth Energy. I first learned about the Earth Energy activity from a fellow facilitator when I was working in South Korea. I added it into my own collection of energisers, and it was an instant success. When I went to use it when facilitating in China, however, I was informed that the principles of the activity are based on old Chinese martial art traditions. In doing my own research into this activity, I found that some martial arts hold the belief that someone can utilise the energy from the earth to become stronger, and therefore I would not link this activity to a specific country, rather to martial arts and the idea of Chi energy.

Earth Energy

- Earth Energy is an active energiser which is based on a belief found in many martial arts: we can harness and use the energy of the earth in our own bodies to do great things.

Steps

1. Have everyone stand up and place their feet shoulder-width apart.
2. Plant your feet firmly to the ground and make sure you have a strong stance.
3. Bend down, and scoop up the invisible, yet powerful energy from the earth using both hands.
4. As you hold the energy in your hands, look forward.
5. Push the energy to everyone else by stepping forward, thrusting your hands and giving a powerful shout.
6. Once the energy has been harnessed and shared, sit back down and enjoy the positive feeling from the earth's energy.

Emergence

I used Bus Stop for the emergent section of the workshop. In England I have heard this technique referred to as Round Robin, while my American colleagues tend to call it Rotating Flipcharts. When leading groups in Moscow, a participant told me that she knew it as Bus Stop. I like this name and I prefer to call it Bus Stop. The simple guiding principle is to have small groups discuss and write down their ideas related to a topic onto a piece of flipchart paper, and then rotate the papers. Depending on the dynamics of the situation or group size, you can rotate people instead of the flipcharts. I can change the amount of time given depending on group size or the complexity of the topics, but I always want to rotate the papers at a quick pace. This quick pace is one key difference that Bus Stop has from Café. In Café, each meeting has a host assigned to it to make sure that everyone understands the topic and that ideas are explained. With Bus Stop, you are rotating the papers quickly, and people are producing ideas in a rapid-fire fashion, instead of leisurely exploring a singular topic. There are time restrictions for each round of discussions before the group leader rotates the papers on to the next group, and I sometimes see people writing as fast as they can before the papers are rotated as they try to get all their ideas down in time.

Rotating papers is simple and nothing new. Bus Stop is an old brainstorming tool which was created in the 1960s by Berndt Rohrbach, a German businessman. He created Bus Stop in response to classical brainstorming methods, which were new at the time. The purpose of Bus Stop is to quickly produce a lot of ideas about various topics at once. Berndt's method was originally called 6-3-5 Brainwriting. This name comes from all the rules that he initially had for the tool; there were to be exactly six questions and six participants, each of which had to write down three ideas in five minutes after which the questions were rotated (6 participants creating 3 ideas in 5 minutes = 6-3-5 Brainwriting). Under the 6-3-5 Brainwriting method, 108 ideas would be created within half an hour. Pretty impressive if you ask me. I have never seen the original version of 6-3-5 Brainwriting being used, and I have never used it myself—I find it a bit too structured—but I have seen numerous variations. Brainwriting was done in silence and individually, while Bus Stop requires people to talk in small groups. I find the method works fantastically as an emergent group activity helping participants connect with each other and connect their thinking.

Bus Stop

This is a tool for quickly producing a large amount of ideas for various topics at once.

1. Topics are introduced to the group (posted on the wall on large flipchart pieces of paper).
2. Everyone silently walks around the room and writes down their ideas on a piece of paper.
3. Smaller groups are formed when people are instructed to stand by their favorite topic.
4. The small groups discuss and write their ideas down onto the flipcharts.
5. The flipcharts are quickly rotated from group to group.
6. As they rotate, everyone contributes to each topic and builds off each other's ideas.

Convergence

I continued with Bus Stop for the convergent portion of the workshop. At this point, each challenge had dozens of solutions written down for it on the flipchart. Would it be a good idea here to have the solutions presented to the group for discussion? No. That would take hours and be very tedious. Even if everyone would be able to sit through the presentations, the comprehension of the presented content would be low, and not good enough for decision making. Instead, I formed new groups. In these newly mixed groups, participants could clarify the solutions to each other, if needed.

I asked the groups to rank the ideas they wanted to implement by drawing dragons next to them. Why dragons? Well, I was in China, and dragons are associated with luck and prosperity. In practice you can have groups mark their preferred ideas with anything; a smiley face, an X, whatever you like. Some groups like to draw their company logo next to what they wish to implement.

The important takeaway is not how they mark them, but the process that marking them requires. Making a choice is not easy and forces people to look at the solutions from a new perspective. As people begin to decide how to mark the ideas, they begin to naturally evaluate them and talk about why they should mark them with dragons (or smiley faces, logos, X, etc.). This brings up the type of authentic and important conversations where the logic and reasoning behind an idea is explored. A lot of facilitators will quickly prioritise ideas once they have completed the emergent phase, but this would completely skip the deeper understanding that occurs when in convergence. That is why the convergent round of Bus Stop was as long as the divergent one. I am a convergent believer through and through, and I hope that you will be, too.

Check-out

To end the session, I find that the best practice is to revisit the objective to see if it was reached. If it were not, I would demand more from the group and lead them through more rounds of emergence or convergence until everyone was happy with the result.

What tools were used and why

- **Earth Energy**—A fun energising tool
- **Bus Stop**—Basic tool when there are many simultaneous questions
- **Bus Stop**—Basic tool when there are many questions and solutions to choose from
- **Dragons**—Prioritising

Workshop process: Solutions

Objective: To find solutions for current challenges
Time: 90 minutes

Check-in (5minutes):

1. Energiser: Earth Energy (5 minutes) Connecting with the energy hiding in the earth.
2. Presenting the objective of the stage and the workshop process.
3. "Is the objective of the next stage and way of working clear?"—short discussion

Emergence tool: Individual thinking and Bus Stop (40 minutes)

1. "I have posted the key challenges around the room with an empty flipchart paper. Look at the challenges we chose and individually write down solutions on your piece of paper."
2. "Choose your favorite topic and write down solutions with the other participants. Remember to write full clear sentences because no-one will be presenting the solutions and max 5 participants per topic (make equal size groups). You have 6 minutes to discuss and write down your ideas. After, we will rotate the flipchart papers. Find your spot!"
3. Rotate flipcharts until all groups have red all flipcharts and have given their solutions to all challenges.

Convergence tools; Bus Stop, Dragons (40 minutes)

1. "Think on your own and choose your favorite solutions."

2. Form new groups. Try to mix the groups in such a manner that each new team has one member from each one of the previous teams. If you succeed, there will always be someone to explain the ideas that were not understood, and you do not need lengthy presentations.

3. "Now let's choose the solutions we want to implement. Draw a dragon next to the solutions that must be implemented. You may give a dragon to all solutions if you have to, but remember, your resources are limited!"

4. Rotate flipcharts until all groups have rated all solutions.

5. "Document and post the solutions with most dragons."

6. "Look at the solutions with most dragons. Are you happy to implement these?"

Check-out (5 minutes):

1. "Now I would like three of you to say what you think about the workshop results."

2. "Thank you, we did a great job!"

4.3: Review Workshop: Creating Actions with Kanban

Orientation — Goal-Setting Workshop — Review Workshop — Problem-Solving Workshop — Breakthrough Design

What's here

- **Case Study**: Using Kanban and Me/We/Us to develop and choose actions in the final part of the review workshop with UTS.
- **Tools**: Me/We/Us, Kanban, One Step

How it helps

Kanban lets you visualise the status of multiple actions. You can update Kanban in real-time to reflect the exact status of multi-team projects.

What's on the wall?

The writing was on the wall as my workshop participants filed back into conference room #4 for the final stage of the review workshop. In fact, I could see people scanning the large board behind my shoulder trying to get ahead and read its contents as I called everyone together.

"I hope that today has been a good one for you all, and I am looking forward to bringing everything to a close, together. I can see that some of you have already began reading what's behind me, and you may already have an idea of what is coming. Our final objective for this workshop is to create concrete actions for the solutions that we have just made. And as some of you have already noticed, I have arranged some help for us. Does anyone care to guess what is behind me?"

"It is a blossom—similar to the one that we made during our first workshop about a month ago," said Donald. Others nodded in agreement as they looked at the large 4-columned board that hung behind me on the wall.

"Good guess, Donald. But this is not quite a beautiful flower. The blossom listed future actions and who was going to complete them and when. Look behind me—this is a bit different. Can I have a volunteer to read the three columns that are on the board?"

"Solutions, to do, in progress, and done," read Chi.

"Thank you. This is a special tool that is often used by software development teams when they need to keep track of complex projects. And we are going to use this fast-paced tool to keep track of our actions and their statuses. Does this sound like a good plan to all of you?"

I knew that my friendly group would go along with the idea, and sure enough, everyone nodded yes.

Kanban			
Solutions	To do	In progress	Done

"The first column is labelled Solutions. As you might have guessed, it contains all the solutions that you committed to implement earlier today. You will have the chance to review them by yourself for a few moments, and then think of some actions that can be taken to achieve these solutions. Then, you will have time to discuss the actions in small groups. By the end of the day we will have the entire chart filled out. Does this sound like a plan?"

More nods of agreement—everyone was excited to begin.

Creating ideas

Chi, Bill, and everyone else stood up and approached the board to read and begin to write down the actions that came to mind.

Top solutions posted in Kanban solutions column

- Get feedback from customers about pricing and product offerings of UTS competitors
- Call competitors directly to get pricing and product information/conduct market research

- Create content and draft internal knowledge base
- Identify external software options for knowledge base to avoid having to build it in-house

- Find reasons to cold call customers
- Research examples of successful customer outreach initiatives
- Share learnings and tips from good and bad customer calls

- Test different collaboration tools to be used for cross team communication
- Test alternatives to use in place of new collaboration tool

---

Only fifteen minutes had passed since the group thought of these solutions, so they were fresh in mind and most everyone was writing down actions quickly.

"Amazing work! Now that you have some of your own actions written down, find two other people to chat with and form groups of three."

Bill found Donald and Chi, Isabell paired up with Sun and Caitlyn, and everyone else also found places in their own groups.

I continued, "I am going to give each group a set of jumbo Post-its for you to write on. Share with each other the actions you have written down, and together as a group decide which ones you like the best. When you agree on an action that you all like, write them down on a jumbo Post-it and place the Post-it on to the board under the column *to do*. There is no limit to how many you can choose, but please use your discretion and choose the most important actions. You have fifteen minutes or so for this, so get to it!"

As the minutes ticked by, actions appeared in the *to do* column one by one. By the end of the fifteen minutes, everyone was just about ready and well over a dozen actions had been placed on the Kanban.

Kanban

Solutions	To do	In progress	Done
Get feedback from customers about pricing and product offerings of UTS competitors	Conduct survey of current competitors and their pricing		
	Propose new pricing policy		
Test different collaboration tools to be used for cross team communication	Try new collaboration tools and adopt the best ones		
	Launch new collaboration tools company-wide		
	Provide training and IT support		

"Take a moment to read these actions silently to yourself. If any questions arise, feel free to ask me or one of your colleagues."

"I have a question," said Sun. "I feel that my name is missing from these actions. Other people should have their names by specific action, but they don't. Do I add myself now, or…?"

"Great question. You will have a chance to add your name as you see fit in a little while. Are there any other questions? If not, let's continue."

Developing the action plan together

"Now we are going to shift back to individual work for a little while. Take a few minutes to think about the actions we have on the board now. Sun mentioned changing one of them to add himself to it. Now is your chance to write down any changes to the actions that you want to make. This can mean taking out some of the actions that are unrealistic, outside of our control, too vague, off topic, or are duplicates of other actions. Write down any changes that you want to make and think about which actions you want to start first."

I gave everyone around five minutes to do this before I ended the individual time. "Now find one partner to share your actions with. Develop the actions as needed. Also, when you find an action that you want to begin, write your name on it and move the Post-it to the *in progress* column. If it is a shared action and you need to agree with someone else about it, you are welcome to do that now!"

People began conversing in pairs and modifying the actions. If a pair decided to change an action, a new Post-it was written and placed in the *to do* column to replace the old action. People also began leaving their pairs to discuss shared actions with others. Once the time drew to a close, a good portion of the actions had been modified and many were underway as people had taken ownership of actions and removed them from the *to do* column into the *in progress* column.

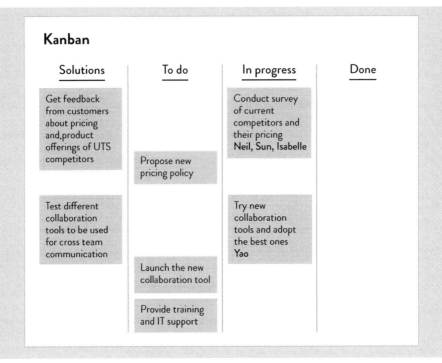

Once everyone was finished, I gave time for people to read the actions silently and ask questions if needed. It seemed like all the questions had been answered during the conversations and when collaborating with others about shared actions.

Stepping out of the workshop

"We are just about done. I want to thank each and every one of you for another great workshop here in Shanghai. When we began, you all were facing some real challenges that were impeding your goals. Now take a look," I said as I pointed to the Kanban behind me. "We have specific actions to combat these challenges, and some of them are already underway! But the work does not end here! This Kanban is not simply to look at. You need to use it and update it! Stopping here would be like cooking a 3-course meal and then throwing it away instead of eating it. The real utility of Kanban comes in the days and weeks ahead as you use it to track the progress of these actions."

I was happy and looking around the room I could see that Bill and the rest of the UTS employees were happy, too. But I could not end things just by trusting their smiles. I needed to make sure. "Please indulge me by standing up and participating in one last activity before we go. Please arrange yourselves so that we are all standing in one large circle. We are going to share our final thoughts together about the workshop. Each person has one opportunity to share. When you wish to share, take a big step forward towards the centre of the circle and comment. Once all of us have shared, the workshop is over and we all can give ourselves a big round of applause. I will go first." I started things off by taking a large step forward and saying, "I will definitely miss this stunning view of Shanghai," I said as I looked out of their floor-to-ceiling office window.

Chi was next to share. She stepped forward and said, "I really appreciate the energy that I got from these activities."

Donald stepped forward and said, "I liked having the chance to work with a lot of you who I normally don't talk with at all. I hope that continues."

The steps forward and the comments continued, until the only person left to take a step and share was UTS President Bill. He stepped forward and said, "These actions make me optimistic for what we can achieve, and even more so I am impressed with this group and the amount of talent that already exists within our team."

At Bill's kind words we began giving ourselves a round of applause—a great note to end the workshop on.

Analysis

UTS review workshop schedule

- Half-day session
- Total time: 4 hours (includes two 15-minute breaks)

CLARIFYING	SOLUTIONS	ACTION
• 60 minutes long • Give 15-minute break before continuing to solutions	• 90 minutes long • Give 15-minute break before continuing to action	• 60 minutes long

This session was a direct continuation from the earlier session when Bus Stop was used to identify solutions. The goal of this workshop stage was to create commitment and accountability to actions that people would take to employ the solutions.

Check-in

Since such a small amount of time had passed between the two sessions, I did not need to give an extensive check-in stage to the group. My only mission here was to share the objective of this stage with everyone and to explain how we were going to work to achieve this objective.

Emergence

First, individual thinking was used. This was time given for people to review the solutions posted on the Kanban and decide which ones they wanted to create actions for. Next, I used small group discussion before reviewing the actions together as one large group. Discussion in small groups helps crystalise what really needs to be done, and new ideas emerge. The tool I used for visualising actions is called Kanban. It is a template which helps visualise the status and progress of actions. It is like the Blossom tool in that it lists multiple actions, but the primary difference is that actions can be moved to different columns to reflect their status. This creates an awareness of the progress that has been made and who is doing what in a specific moment. The four columns I used were:

1. solutions
2. to do
3. in progress
4. done

As actions are completed, people move them from one column to the next. I have seen other group leaders use formats that are slightly different; perhaps three columns instead of four, or different words to title each column. Sometimes the group leader will use a digital Kanban instead of the old-fashioned pen and paper. I find that these differences are trivial. The main feature of the Kanban is it is a tool which gives a fluid representation of multiple tasks and their status. And for this to work it needs to be updated constantly. I repeat: a group can make and fill out a Kanban, but it is especially important to stress that it requires constant updating for a group to unlock its benefits.

Kanban was originally developed to improve production efficiency. Instead of making various parts to a machine at the same rate, the idea was to make only what was needed when it was needed. Japanese car maker Toyota was the first company I know of that used this tool, and the name Kanban means *see-cards* (*kan = see, ban = card*) in Japanese. Nowadays Kanban is a popular method for software developers to map and track their work. For them, it is normal for projects of varying lengths to always be stopping and starting. One person may need to deploy a new script which takes a few hours, while another tests the new product over the span of a few days. A third person is monitoring the whole ecosystem to ensure that nothing breaks during the transition to the new program. A tool is needed for these guys to keep track of everything and this is where Kanban comes in. In fact, I use it every chance I get when I am facilitating groups of developers; the tool is so familiar to them that it is always a popular choice and a natural fit.

My group in this workshop was not made up of software developers, but Kanban was a good fit anyway—there were many different actions to track that were all working towards larger solutions which the Kanban can help visualise.

One participant mentioned that the Kanban looked a lot like Blossom, which was used in a previous workshop. They were correct in that there are some similarities between the two; mainly that they list future actions which will be taken. How can you decide between the two? The key difference is that Blossom required a specific person to commit to an action, and Kanban does not. With Kanban, the actions are interdependent and can be executed by more than one person. It is not so important who does what, what is important is the status of the tasks shown on Kanban because the status of one may affect the other. For example, let's suppose that we are throwing a party. We need to book a room and we need to decorate it. These two things can be executed by more than one person, but we cannot start decorating until we have the venue booked. Kanban shows the status of booking a venue, and when it is completed, we can then proceed with the decorations.

Now can you see the difference between Blossom and Kanban? Kanban is dynamic and helps avoid bottlenecks in workflow, while Blossom is static.

Convergence

Me/We/Us was used for both emergence and convergence. It is important to give everyone a chance to modify and strengthen the actions via convergence, and after this period the actions were modified by participants; they made them more specific, matched the right people to the right actions, and decided which actions to begin immediately, which were then moved to the *In Progress* column of the Kanban.

People have the tendency to create unrealistic actions for others. A common way for this to manifest itself is a group creating broad actions for Human Resource Teams that fall outside of their responsibilities or placing too much responsibility on upper management to execute the needed actions. The convergent phase aimed to get rid of actions that were not realistic, and instead develop actions that could be executed by the entire UTS Team. Also, when the actions were first posted on the Kanban, they had not been discussed as a group, so there was some fine tuning that needed to be done.

One Step

Participants form a circle. Ask participants to take a step when they are ready to comment on the workshop: I enjoyed.., I did not like..., I learned..., I had....

Rules:
- Everyone only shares one sentence each.
- Look around and try not to step at the same time as others.

When everyone has taken a step it is time to applaud. The workshop is over.

Check-out

It is a great habit to check with the group if the objective was reached before you end a workshop. There are thousands of ways you can collect comments from participants, and I decided to use a method which required one comment from every person and then a group round of applause to close the workshop. This tool requires that everyone stand in a circle and take a step forward when they comment. Once everyone has stepped forward, the whole group must give itself a round of applause. Sometimes I have ended other parts of the workshop by just asking for comments from three people or so, but as this was the very end of the workshop, I wanted to hear from everyone and also end things on a fun and positive note, so One Step was a tool that achieved both of those things.

What tools were used and why

- **Me/We/Us**—Basic tool to get everyone involved when there is one key question
- **Kanban**—Used to visualise actions tha are collaborative and constantly updating
- **One Step**—Used to end the workshop and collect comments from the group

Workshop process: Action

Objective: To create concrete actions for chosen solutions
Time: 60 minutes

Check-in (5minutes):

1. Presenting the objective of the stage and the workshop process.
2. "Is the objective of the next stage and way of working clear?"
   —short discussion

Divergence tool: Me/We/Us and Kanban (25 minutes)

1. "I have posted the key solutions on the backlog of the Kanban, a visualization tool. Look at the solutions you want to implement and individually write down actions for yourself on your piece of paper."
2. "Discuss the actions in groups of three and write down best ideas on jumbo Post-it notes."
3. "Post your ideas on the Kanban under the column labeled *To do.*"
4. "Read the action points in silence. Do you have questions about the actions?"

Convergence tool: Me/We/Us (20 minutes)

1. "On your own, take a critical look on the actions. Is something missing or duplicated or overlapping? Also, choose the actions you want to take first."
2. "Discuss the possible changes with a partner."
3. "Now develop the action points if needed. Also, choose your actions, write your name next to your action point and move it in the column In progress. If you need to agree on shared actions with someone, you are welcome to do it now!"
4. "Read the action points in silence. Everything clear?"

Check-out (10 minutes):

1. "Let's form a circle of everyone standing in the middle of the room. I would like everyone to make a short comment on our review workshop. When you are ready to take talk, take a step forward. When everyone has taken a step forward, the workshop is over, and we will give ourselves a round of applause to the great work we did."
2. "Thank you!"

4.4: Review Workshop Review

Review workshop

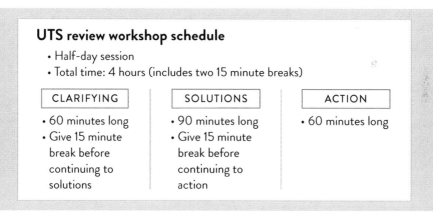

Chapter 4 covered the review workshop I had with UTS. The purpose of this workshop was to revisit the results from the goal-setting workshop. You may already be familiar with a review workshop and even participated in one. The review workshop is so popular and widely used that it goes by many different names. Some of the other terms used to refer to review workshops include retrospective, status meeting, progress meeting, or action learning.

We first clarified the challenges that UTS encountered when implementing the goals that they created during the goal-setting workshop. Then we created solutions to those challenges, and finally specific actions were created with people taking ownership of the actions by placing their name by the actions they want to complete.

The workshop lasted about 4 hours. I know some group leaders that work almost exclusively in the corporate world, and they find that the businesspeople who attend their sessions have trouble attending long meetings. How could we possibly combat this? We could divide a session into separate stages that are about 60 to 90 minutes long. This helps keep participants fresh without sacrificing the time devoted to each session. This sounds like a logical idea, but in some fast-pace companies it is a bit difficult to execute. If you spread 4 hours of workshop time over 3 consecutive days, you would find that it is highly unlikely to have the same people attend throughout the duration of the workshop. It is hard enough to get a group together for one afternoon, let alone 3 days in a row. It is worth noting that there are some advantages to having a workshop divided into smaller sections that take place over a few days; people would be less tired, and new perspectives may come to the surface as new participants show up on day 2 or day 3 and provide their opinions.

Like the first workshop with UTS, this workshop also followed the CSA structure; clarifying challenges, identifying solutions, and creating actions.

The tools used during the review workshop with UTS

CLARIFYING	SOLUTIONS	ACTION
Tools	Tools	Tools
• Force Field Analysis	• Dragons	• Me/We/Us
• Dot Voting	• Earth Energy	• Kanban
• Silent Moving	• Bus Stop	• One Step
• Field of Two Criteria		

Clarifying

Time: 60 minutes
Objective: Discover current challenges

The workshop took place about one month after the initial session where the original set of actions were created. This one-month gap gave time for UTS to try to implement the solutions. In that time, they would be able to have an idea of what is working, and what is not. The aim of the clarifying stage was to identify the challenges that they were facing.

Solutions

Time: 90 minutes
Objective: Find solutions to current challenges

In the solutions stage, the objective shifted to solving the current challenges—what strategies could the UTS employees adopt to work past the challenges? The topic here became more complex—creating different solutions for each challenge—so I decided to use the tool Bus Stop which is great at dealing with many simultaneous questions.

Actions

Time: 60 minutes
Objective: To make concrete actions for chosen solutions

I used a Me/We/Us again as the main tool for the action stage and Kanban for visualising actions. With Kanban, many tasks can be listed at once and the status of the task can be updated as frequently as needed. By the end of the workshop the group was left with a series of actions that were assigned to specific owners. UTS would continue to use the Kanban board to update the status of the actions until everything was completed.

The power of reviewing

The review workshop is widely used because it is a powerful tool. The purpose of a review workshop is to check in on progress made in a previous workshop. If a company ran a strategy workshop to deploy new sales techniques, then a review workshop would take place a few months later to give people the chance to discuss how implementing the new sales techniques had gone. The review workshop gives people the chance to celebrate the success that they have had while also reviewing the challenges and figuring out what needs to be done in response to these challenges.

An effective leader uses the review workshop in many different situations. If the current situation could be improved upon by discussing challenges and any doubts or problems that the group is experiencing, then the review workshop would be a good fit. If major changes were made a few months prior, then it can give people the chance to discuss their doubts, which then frees them to move forward confidently. If you want to give your team's health a check-up, then the review workshop provides the forum for team members to clear the air and resolve any lingering problems that may exist. Or, if you want to see how a new strategy, process, or goals are coming along, then it is a good fit yet again.

The review workshop strengthens the effectiveness of a workshop that took place months before by revisiting a topic and helping people troubleshoot issues, pat themselves on the back for their successes, and refocus around a topic. Make sure to use it frequently within your company or organisation.

What can a review workshop do?

- **Eliminating resistance to change**—You identify the barriers to change and the issues that are getting in the way. Once these obstacles are removed, change will follow. Simple and efficient!

- **Strategy Review**—People often request a strategy workshop, but the are usually wrong. They do not want to create a brand new strategy, but just update a part of their current strategy, which a review workshop is perfect for. We read the old strategy together and answer questions; what is good and should be kept and what are the challenging parts that need to be reviewed.

- **Process Development**—When developing existing processes, you often do not want to create a totally new process but you want to find the pain points that need to be developed.

- **Team Health**—When developing teams you do not want to just discover problems—that creates a feeling that our team is in serious trouble. It is good to show the team what they are already doing well along with identifying areas for improvement.

- **Developing Services**—You can dig into the customer experience by asking for pleasure and pain points. However, in this case we often do not only work with pain points, we also try to increase and further leverage what is already good about the customer experience.

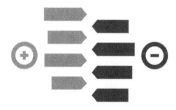

CHAPTER 5:

Problem-Solving Workshop

5.1: Problem-Solving Workshop: Clarifying Challenges with Dynamic Facilitation

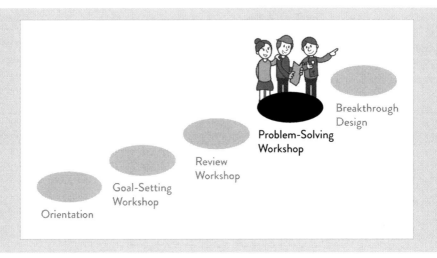

What's here

- **Case Study:** Clarifying challenges using Dynamic Facilitation and Me/We/Us variations
- **Tools:** Hello, Dynamic Facilitation, Me/We/Us, Me, We/We/We/Us, Signature

How it helps

Dynamic Facilitation is a tool created for dealing with social conflicts in situations that can be complex or emotionally tense. Me/We/Us is a tool that provides a sound structure for the workshop by giving time for work individually, in small groups, and then together as one large group.

Success and conflict

Facilitators and group leaders are frequently asked to mediate a disagreement or help a group work through a conflict. Some companies will wait until the atmosphere turns toxic before calling in outside help.

Even though workshops often take place to reconcile differences, I sometimes see participants try to diminish any hostilities and appear as if everyone was getting along just fine. When this happens, we facilitators get people talking about the issues in an environment that feels safe for them. This helps bring the conflict to the surface so that it can be understood and resolved. When I began working with Brilliancy Electronics, a manufacturer of computer graphics cards, I did not need to invest any energy in helping the group reveal the conflicts and disagreements they were struggling with—these things were already at the surface and impossible to ignore.

My work with Brilliancy Electronics began when I received an email requesting to facilitate a session that could help the company deal with some growing pains that they were experiencing. Brilliancy Electronics (B.E. for short) develops and manufactures graphic cards for specialised gaming computers. The Dublin-based company has done a steady level of business for decades until last year, when their product became immensely popular due to its ability to function well in cryptocurrency mining setups. During my initial contact with B.E., I learned that in less than 12 months the company had gained almost 20 new employees to their sales team and were in the process of expanding their services to new key markets worldwide. The company had even hired a press team to help market B.E. to potential investors as they prepared to transition from a private to a public company by launching an initial public offering of stock and being listed on the London Stock Exchange. Once I became familiar with these details, I felt that I could help B.E. find solutions to some of these changes, so it was agreed that I would travel to Dublin to facilitate a workshop for two dozen of their managers and high-level employees. All normal and cordial so far, and no evidence of any drama—at least not yet. That came later, about a week before I was set to travel to Dublin. The drama emerged from an email that was sent out by B.E. to the employees that were set to attend the workshop. The email simply listed the date and time, and a general outline of the topic, which was *dealing with growth*.

Once again, this was business as usual and nothing seemed amiss. But it kicked off when Angie, one of the B.E. employees invited to the workshop, replied to the email:

Thank you for the invitation. It sounds like an interesting workshop, but I am unfortunately unable to attend due to other work-related responsibilities. I hope that I get to hear all about it!

Not twenty minutes later was a reply from Jackie, the Manager of B.E.'s Marketing Team:

Thank you, Pepe. I confirm that I will be attending, no matter how busy I am. Angie, do you see what I did there? I decided to make time for this workshop, no matter how busy I may be. I suggest you reconsider and do the same.

This sounded a bit harsh to me, but I thought to myself that at least there is a culture of accountability and open communication there. This made me optimistic; *People holding each other accountable and communicating directly—this might be an easy session for me,* I thought.

I realised that this would not be the case as the email replies continued:

Angie: *Enough Jackie. I know how to delegate and do not need you breathing down my neck. Stick to your role and I will stick to mine. I used to have your job, remember? But I still give you space to do as you see fit. Can't you let me have the same chance?*

Jackie: *I am not reviewing your work and cleaning up your messes for fun. Do you want to compare our performance as manager? I sincerely hope that you are not STILL upset that I took over as manager. That was ages ago.*

Angie: *No hurt feelings here, and there is nothing to even get upset about. What I was asked to do as Manager and what you are doing now are as different as day and night, so the only similarity I see is basically just the job title.*

Things were beginning to get out of hand, and this was simply an emailed invitation to a meeting! The company's Vice President Simon tried to put a stop to the bickering with a brief email asking Jackie and Angie to *put their differences aside and the company first,* but I noticed that this did not have much of an affect as the two ladies continued to antagonise each other. I had seen enough. I did not need to keep reading further to know that I was going to have my work cut out for me.

A dispute in Dublin

Standing in front of the two dozen workshop attendees for the first time, I did not need any help identifying Jackie and Angie, the two feuding B.E. employees. On the left side of the room was one woman who wore a scowl on her face, and on the other side of the room was another woman who was staring daggers at the first. *These two must be Jackie and Angie*, I thought. In the centre of the room was Simon, Brilliancy Electronics' Vice President. He stood to briefly shake my hand and introduce himself.

"Nice to have you here, Pepe. We can use the help. We are growing like crazy and signs of stress and fatigue are beginning to show. Old friends are even fighting like cats and dogs—you saw the emails!"

I shook Simon's hand and told him I was happy to be there, and even confident that some progress could be made. "I think that today will be a big step in the right direction, but there is a lot to do, so I best get started."

Simon sat down and I turned to the entire group to begin.

"Good morning, everyone! My name is Pepe, and I am a facilitator from Finland. I am here today to help all of you from Brilliancy Electronics to find some solutions to some of the rapid growth challenges you are facing. Our objective this morning is to identify the current challenges that B.E. is facing during this new period of growth, and in the afternoon, to find solutions and to make a concrete action plan. To fulfil this objective, I will have all of you do a lot of talking with one another. We will investigate all the details of the current challenges and I will record everything that you all have to say. By the end of the day we hopefully will have a clear picture of the challenges and you all will know what to do next. But first, we need to collect some more information from all of you. Please divide into six groups of four."

Everyone began separating off into groups, and I noticed that Angie and Jackie were keeping their distance from each other. When everyone was ready, I continued my instructions.

"Now I am going to assign each group a question. Your job is to try to interview every single person in this room and to record their answer to the question. You only will have about three minutes for the interviews, so you will need to be super quick. Also, be sure to write down their replies. You will need them later. But before we get to the interviews, you have a few minutes to prepare. Grab a pen and paper and make sure you have everything you need for the interviews. You may even start interviewing each other in the small groups."

The questions given to the groups were:

- Why are we here?
- Who are the people here?
- What is the purpose of life?
- What is our common goal?
- What are our strengths?
- How does everyone feel today?

After the planning stage, I told everyone that they had three minutes for the interviewing. When I said go, everyone began rushing around and launched into chaotic conversations—the method was going exactly as it should be. Out of curiosity, I wanted to see if Angie and Jackie crossed paths, but I did not see them talking to each other.

"OK everyone, your time is up. Please get back into your original groups. Now you have five minutes to record the results. I have given each group a flipchart which you can use to write on, and please write large enough so everyone can see. You will present the results to the rest of us. If there are no questions, you can get down to it and begin now."

Now the chaos was in the small groups as everyone frantically transcribed the interview results to the flipcharts and then discussed how best to present the results. Once the preparation was finished, it was time for the presentations.

"OK, we have six different questions to discuss here. For the sake of time, each group must give their presentation in thirty seconds or less. Who wants to go first?"

The first group to present was assigned the question: *What is the purpose of life?* Their representative Mary shared the results; "Over half of the interviewees said the purpose of life was friends and family, about a third said that it was knowledge, a few people said that it was service to community and one person said the purpose of life was work. I am not sure if that person was only kidding or trying to kiss up to the boss."

Why are we here?
Replies:
10 people: To make a plan
5 people: To develop teamwork
4 people: To solve growing pains
2 people: To improve professional relationships
1 person: To drink good coffee
1 person: To collect a day's pay
1 person: To make sure Angie does her job

We continued through the rest of the presentations. I noticed that a few of the answers referenced Angie and Jackie, the only two people to be mentioned by name in the replies. I assumed that their conflict was still not resolved, and that they were now bad mouthing each other in their answers during the Hello warm-up activity. We will get this sorted, I thought.

A dynamic day

"As you determined during your interviews, most of us know why we are here—to discuss the challenges that Brilliancy Electronics is facing during this rapid period of growth and to find solutions to these challenges. That is the topic of the day. The goal of our work is to create a better understanding of the situation and to find the key issues to deal with for the afternoon session. Your task is to talk, one person at a time, and to give all your ideas related to this topic. My task is to record as much as I can by writing on these flipcharts that are posted on the wall. I will try to do my best to record your thoughts under one of the four columns listed on the wall: *Facts, Concerns, Problem*

Statement, and *Solutions.* When we have all your thoughts on the wall, we will summarise the key issues. Are there any questions about how we will work today?"

"One question here. Are we supposed to tell you which column our comments go under?", asked a voice from the back of the room.

"No," I replied. "That is my job. You only need to share your ideas and listen to what everyone else has to say. But if you are not happy with my writing, you may take a marker and write your thoughts exactly where they belong before returning to your seat."

"I'll begin," said Jackie. "I think that a lot of our current issues are a result of unclear working processes. As we have grown, so has the team and our own responsibilities. We are growing faster than we can update our ways of working."

I summarised Jackie's comment by writing *unclear processes* under the *Concerns* column. Jackie's comment launched a stream of comments and I had my work cut out for me to try and keep up. I did not need to talk or ask questions to the group—as is often the case when using Dynamic Facilitation, I simply was there to document what people had to say.

Angie and Jackie were both contributing to the conversation, but they still had not addressed each other directly until Angie raised her hand to reply to a seemingly innocent comment about how B.E.'s company culture was in a rapid cycle of change.

"From week to week projects and even jobs themselves change and become unrecognizable. I remember what I had to do as Director of Marketing when I occupied that role a year ago, and now the job and what it aims to accomplish is something that I do not recognise."

Upon hearing Angie mention the role of Director of Marketing, Jackie had a reply at the ready; "Of course it has changed and of course I am doing things much differently to you. A year ago, we all may have been working for a different company! We were small and had the time to be deliberate if needed. We could talk things over and get an idea of how a certain campaign fit in with the overall package that is Brilliancy Electronics. Now look at us. I don't even know everyone's name here anymore and everything is *grow grow grow* and *go go go.*"

Dealing with rapid growth

Facts	Concerns	Problem statements	Solutions
1. Lots of new orders	1. Pricing not optimised in some regions	1. How should company culture adapt to new reality?	1. New workflow to eliminate time-wasting and micro-managed ways of working
2. 20+ new members to sales staff	2. Press coverage does not reflect reality	2. How much agency should employee have vs. bureaucratic and micromanaged processes?	2. Product demonstration and orientation for sales team
3. Regular press coverage for the first time	3. Lack of empowerment compared to pre-growth stage—more bureaucratic	3. How can press releases be revised to accurately to reflect current situation?	3. Establish opportunity for Press/IPO/Investor Relations Team to meet with employees, and map out examples of damaging or untrue press coverage
4. Miscommu-nication, lack of empower-ment	4. Sales team does not know product well	4. How can we improve feedback channels to become more agile?	4. Research key markets instead of generalising price approximations when entering new region
5. Rapid expansion	5. Company culture lost or changing	5. What is our common goal?	5. Prior to launching in new region, compile research report regarding pricing, competitors, etc.
6. More capital coming into company	6. Outdated ways of working		
	7. New management team not acting on feedback		

I did my best to take notes as Angie and Jackie began talking to one another, and as the conversation flowed, it became apparent that the perceived issue between them was not the role of the Director of Marketing, but a lack of understanding of the rapidly changing company goals in the turbulent times. This problem was not only Angie's and Jackie's. It was a challenge for many others in the team too.

"You all have a lot to say, obviously. Now take a few moments to individually think about everything that is written on the board up there. Is anything missing that needs to be added? If so, write it down. You have two minutes to do this."

After everyone had the time to review the flipcharts, it was time to move on.

"Now find a partner and share your ideas with them. Decide together what we still need to talk about!"

Once the pairs had the chance to determine what was still missing, I drew everyone back together and I continued to write down their ideas and fill out the four columns as the discussion continued. People had a lot more to say after having the chance to think about it individually and talk it over with a partner.

Bringing everything together

"Now that you have all shared so many issues, I want you to take a few minutes to think individually about which are the most important issues that we should discuss today. Write them down on a piece of paper as you think of them," I instructed.

Once I gave everyone about five minutes, I asked that they work in pairs to continue the discussion. "With a partner, share your ideas and choose the best ones together."

I watched as about a dozen pairs formed and began conversing. After another few minutes had passed, I asked each pair to join another pair and continue sharing and writing down their key ideas.

"Great job," I said. "As I look at these groups of four, I see that a lot is happening. Let's see what happens if we continue down this road. Each group of four needs to find another group to join. Share the most important issues that need to be discussed today in your new groups. Once you agree what the top issues are, write them down and post them on the wall by taping them to the wall."

I was happy to see that when the groups of eight formed, Angie and Jackie were in the same group, and even better, communicating civilly! People began taping their papers with the top issues to the wall as agreement was reached in each group. Once finished, there were about a dozen key issues taped to the wall.

"Everyone, please pick up something to write with. Read the issues that you all agreed upon and sign your name next to each issue that you want to solve today. Pick any issue you like, pick as many as you like, even if someone else has already signed their name by it."

Key issues that need to be solved today

- Training and integrating Sales Team
- Aligning Press Coverage and P.R. Team with rest of company
- Pricing in new markets
- Empowering employees
- Developing new ways of working
- Keeping company culture during growth
- Clarifying the common goal
- Allocation of time and budget going forward

A diplomatic end

Everyone stood back and admired the results which were a list of key issues that the group decided were most important—an impressive result considering the chaotic situation that B.E. employees found themselves in.

"Now find a partner to chat with. Discuss how we did this morning and if we reached our objective of the first stage and found the key issues or the true pain points."

People paired up and had a brief chat, after which I called for the groups attention and asked for three comments to close the day.

"I would like to hear from three of you before we leave today. How did it go today, and did we reach our objective?"

"The objective was reached, we have the key issues, and I feel like we have a better handle on things now," a voice from the back said.

The second comment also was positive and echoed the first.

As I was considering who to choose among the raised hands for the third comment, I noticed Angie putting her hand up, so I called on her.

"I finally feel that we have shifted towards positivity now after so many months of negativity and arguments. I hope that today has opened up some communication channels which have not existed here for a long time."

She was looking at Jackie as she was saying this, and I saw Jackie return the friendly look back. It was a satisfying ending to a session that had a rocky beginning.

Brilliancy Electronics workshop schedule

• One and a half day session

CLARIFYING	SOLUTIONS	SOLUTIONS CONTINUE
• Three hours long including a 15-minute break • Give an hour lunch break before next stage	• Four hours long including a 15-minute break • End of day 1	• One and a half hours long

		ACTION
		• Two hours long including a 15-minute break

Analysis

This session was the beginning of a day-long workshop to help the company Brilliancy Electronics cope with change related to their rapid growth. The aim of this part of the workshop was to get the group to identify and agree on the most important issues that need to be discussed and solved, which will happen later in the workshop.

Check-in

Hello is a tool that was created by Sivasailam Thiagarajan, who commonly goes by the name Thiagi. He has created dozens, if not hundreds of warm-up tools and games that make meetings and work more fun and playful.*

---

* Thiagi is a true authority on meeting tools and has made great contributions, which I admire. You can find out more by visiting his website: http://www.thiagi.com

Hello (interviews)

Hello is a tool for collecting information quickly, e.g., about the topic to be discussed during the meeting. The method also helps people to get to know each other.

1. Division into small groups with assigned questions
Divide the group and give each small group a question. The task of the small groups is to make a mini-survey about the topic assigned to them by interviewing all participants. Prepare the topics beforehand. Try using both easy / funny questions as well as questions about the day's topic. For instance:

- Expectations?
- Experience with the topic?
- How do the participants feel today?
- Vacation plans?

2. Quick preparation for the interviews
Assign roughly 3 min for the groups to prepare themselves for conducting the interviews (for the groups to think how they are going to interview all participants).

3. Quick interviews
Depending on the size of the group, assign between 3–7 min for conducting the interviews. The aim is that all participants are interviewed for all topics (including the members of one's own group).

4. Analysing and documenting information
Participants meet with their small group members and document the gathered info on a flipchart to be presented to the others (around 3–4 min time).

5. Presentations
Each small group presents their findings (around 30 seconds per presentation).

I like using Hello for a few different reasons. First, it gathers a lot of information related to the workshop. You can begin a session with serious topics, and it is still engaging because it is so fast paced and chaotic in nature. People are forced to work in teams to decide how to even pull off the task of interviewing the entire room. It also gets people to connect with each other right off the bat. It is not a tool for deep discussion, but it opens people up and gets them focused on the topics and themes of the day.

The questions can be adjusted to the situation, and some fun questions like *What is the meaning of life?* can be mixed in to keep things light.

There are some questions that I like to keep in the mix:

- Why are we here?
- Who are the people here?
- How do the participants feel today?

The remaining questions are a mixture of light-hearted and workshop-related questions. For example, if the topic of the workshop is developing values, I would ask about personal values, company values, when values are important, and so on.

There are people who do not like the Hello activity, and if you run enough workshops, you will come across them sooner or later. Hello is challenging for those who don't like chaos. The allotted amount of time given during Hello is always going to be less time than what is needed to interview and talk with everyone. This is by design, but can cause participants to become frustrated, or think that the activity is poorly designed or that you do not know what you are doing as a group leader. Nevertheless, it is a great tool for connecting and focusing participants. If someone does not like a certain part of a meeting then they will not have to wait long for a new stage to begin, complete with new tools and ways of working.

Emergence with Dynamic Facilitation

The emergence tool we used is called Dynamic Facilitation. It was developed by Jim Rough in the 1980s as he attempted to improve communication and working life at the Simpson Timber Company. The website www.dynamicfacilitation.com, an authority on the tool and its history, goes on to explain that Jim did not even think he was doing anything special. In his mind he was simply facilitating. But his approach, which helped people get together to thoroughly discuss a topic, was exciting to the Simpson Timber Company employees, and they even began using Dynamic Facilitation in their home lives. Jim continued to refine the tool, and he has been teaching it professionally in seminars and conferences since the early 1990s.

Dynamic Facilitation is a tool for emergence in that helps people deeply understand new ideas and perspectives and lets them discuss and collaborate to create even better ideas. People naturally tend to shoot down ideas that are not their own. This is why early brainstorming methods did not allow criticism of any kind. However, Dynamic Facilitation works in a totally different way. When someone comes up with an idea, the method encourages people to discuss and examine it from all angles: facts, concerns, problem statement and solutions. The magic of the tool comes from its non-linear structure; someone can comment on the solutions first, instead of saving that for last and only after the facts have been explored, which is often the normal progression. This way, someone's framework and logic are understood and the problem changes as more comments are recorded on the board; the issues, topics discussed, and the conversation is fluid and dynamic. This dynamic nature of the tool is what gives Dynamic Facilitation its name.

Dynamic Facilitation requires the group leader to disappear for a while and simply write comments under one of the four columns which are displayed on the wall: *facts, concerns, problem statement, solutions*. Hours can pass as the group explores the issue while the leader simply records the comments. Recording has two important functions. First, people feel that they have been heard, information is not repeated, and this helps keep focus. Second, people are more objective when they see the problem on the wall. This process is similar to how problems are framed in psychotherapy. The therapist often wants the patient to try and view problems outside of the body, sometimes through writing exercises. This allows for old fears and issues to be seen in a new light, and when this happens everything can suddenly seem so simple and clear for the patient. This is how Dynamic Facilitation works; you can look at your challenges and emotions in front of you and gain a degree of objectivity that is impossible to reach otherwise.

This space for conversation—a dynamic and free-flowing conversation at that—allows breakthroughs to occur. Once I was using Dynamic Facilitation to facilitate a session involving a complex IT change and why it was not advancing. This group was talking for well over two hours, and they fell silent (which is completely normal at times during Dynamic Facilitation). Suddenly, someone stood up and exclaimed, "I've got it!" One she explained, I asked the others if they understood, and everyone nodded. The solution arrived to everyone in the same moment. Proving this, one of the participants stood up and began drawing some arrows around three key elements on a flip-chart. As he drew, a few others smiled and confirmed that they were thinking the same thing. Sure enough, the issue was solved directly by this breakthrough which happened using Dynamic Facilitation. This was actually my first experience using the method, and I came away impressed with its problem-solving power. Jim Rough is so confident in his method that he says he can solve any social conflict, no matter how big or small, in three sessions of Dynamic Facilitation. I believe him, and this is a method that I love. Unlike Jim, I do not give a group three separate sessions of Dynamic Facilitation. Instead, I use the tool more than any other tool during the first *clarifying stage* of a workshop to get the participants on the same page. After, I continue with other tools.

I love using Dynamic Facilitation because it helps people resolve conflicts that people could not solve on their own, like the issue between Angie and Jackie, for example. In our case, there were many layers that needed addressing. First, there was a personal issue be-tween Jackie and Angie. Next, there were questions that existed across departments about unclear working processes. Next, there was a lack of common goals. All of these issues came to the surface during the long, open-ended discussion. Dynamic Facilitation gave the group a platform to discuss all of these things, and through the discussion an understanding was reached.

The power of Dynamic Facilitation lies also in dealing with emo-tions. In a normal problem-solving process, there is no place for emotions. You are supposed to be deliberate and logical. However, we are emotional beings, and it is not always possible to think with a cool and calculating mind. Just think back to the confrontational emails that Angie and Jackie were sending each other. Dynamic Facilitation offers a place for emotions and concerns. I often begin a session with participants complaining. When they see that they have been heard—it is all written down in front of them—people begin working more efficiently and start solving the issue together.

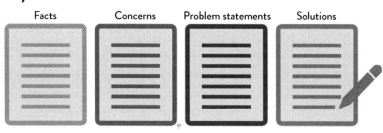

Dynamic Facilitation

Facts Concerns Problem statements Solutions

Facilitating:
- Fill the wall with blank flipchart papers and write down the categories; facts, concerns, problem statements and solutions.
- Agree on a topic to be discussed and post it for everyone to see.
- Communicate your role as a neutral recorder.
- Invite conversations.
- Let the conversations flow freely.
- Write down as much as you can.
- Choose a relevant category for the ideas / thoughts discussed.
- If someone is criticising somebody else's idea, write the critique down in the concerns category.
- In the end, take a new flipchart and ask the group to summarise the discussion.

One shortcoming of Dynamic Facilitation is that it favours vocal and outgoing people. Some people have no issues commenting and taking charge of a discussion, while others naturally want to sit quietly and listen. The extroverts will always talk more during Dynamic Facilitation. In order to keep the most talkative people from running the whole show, I like to change the process a bit. Instead of having one long discussion as the tool traditionally is used, I divided it into two separate parts. In the middle, I had people individually write down what information and issues were missing from the board, then discuss in pairs, and then again in larger groups; the Me/We/Us structure. This way, the introverts would have more of a chance to contribute and share their thoughts in a way that they are comfortable with. However, you can't begin Dynamic Facilitation with individual thinking. Unfortunately, I learned this the hard way. When I tried to begin Dynamic Facilitation with some time for individual thinking, people wrote down their ideas, but instead of discussing them, they expected the facilitator to write the ideas down one at a time while everyone was waiting.

Having a little Me/We section in the middle is not how the tool was originally intended to be used, but I am not writing an instruction manual about how to use these tools as they were originally designed—I just want you to be the best group leader possible, so that means that I am teaching the tools and structures that have helped me get the best results. In my years of experimenting with different formats of Dynamic Facilitation, I strongly believe that adding Me/We/Us in the middle of Dynamic Facilitation has significant benefits, and few, if any, drawbacks.

Convergence

Jim Rough would end a session of Dynamic Facilitation by taking out a new flipchart and summarising the discussion and its key points on it together with the entire group. This works well if there are a few shared key breakthroughs, but it is a challenge to catch many small breakthroughs and all the key points if there are a variety of issues, which was the case with B.E.'s session. This is why I used a variation of Me/We/Us for the convergent phase.

I used Me/We/We/We/Us, also called, 1-2-4-8 (due to the number of people chatting at a time). As I always do, I set aside a significant amount of time for convergence, as convergence may take as long as emergence.

After the convergent period, I asked the groups of eight to write and post their key issues on the wall. Then I used a tool called Signature to check for commitment and to help everyone prioritise the issues. People sign their names next to the issue that is most important to them. This way I can see who is committed to what issues, and in later stages of the workshop I can split the group or spend time on the issues with the most signatures next to them, instead of wasting the group's time talking about something of little importance.

Since Dynamic Facilitation is one of my favourite tools, I also want to highlight its versatility. You can use Dynamic Facilitation in many scenarios, especially the ones involving emotions and complexity.

Check-out

I like circling back to revisit the objective during the check-out stage. This is a good practice, and the comments let you know if you achieved the goal, or if you need to backtrack and dedicate more time to convergence.

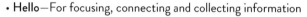

What tools were used and why

- **Hello**—For focusing, connecting and collecting information
- **Dynamic Facilitation**—A tool for creating shared understanding of a topic when there is complexity and emotions involved
- **Me/We/Us**—A tool for inviting group participation
- **Me/We/We/We/Us**—A tool for increasing the participation level
- **Signature**—For prioritising, for forming small groups

Workshop process: Clarifying

Objective: To clarify current challenges
Time: 180 minutes

Check-in (25 minutes):

1. Presenting the objective of the stage and the workshop process.
2. Using Hello method for Interviewing all participants to answer following questions:
   - Why are we here?
   - Who are the people here?
   - What is the purpose of life?
   - What is our common goal?
   - What is our common purpose?
   - How does everyone feel today?

Emergence with Dynamic Facilitation and Me/We/Us
(120 minutes with a 15-minute break)

1. "Our topic today is _____, the goal of our work is to create a better understanding of the situation and to find the key issues to deal with for the afternoon session. Your task is to talk—one person at the time—and to give all your ideas related to this topic. My task is to record as much as I can under the titles Data, Concerns, Problem Statements and Solutions. When we have all your thoughts on the wall, we will summarise the key issues. Is the way of working clear?"
2. "Does anyone have a solution already on mind?"
3. Write what you can and where you can. It is not always clear in which category the ideas belong, just do your best. Try not to interrupt the discussion by clarifying every word and asking in which category the ideas belong, but if participants indicate a category, do as you are told.
4. "Look at everything that has been recorded so far, think individually what is missing" (Me)
5. "Discuss in pairs—what do we still need to talk about?" (We)
6. "Now let's continue the discussion. Who has a thought to share?" (Us)

Convergence tool; Me/We/We/We/Us (30 minutes) and signatures

1. "On your own, write down issues we should discuss here today!"
2. "Share and choose the most important wants with a pair."
3. "Join with an other pair, share and choose the most important issues for today."
4. "Join with an other group of four and choose the most important issues."
5. "Post your issues. Everything clear?"
6. "Now sign the issues you want to discuss today."

Check-out: Pair discussion (5 minutes)

1. "Find a cool person next to you and discuss weather we reached the objective."
2. "Now I would like three of you to comment."
3. "Thank you, we did a great job!"

5.2: Problem-Solving Workshop: Finding Solutions with Open Space Technology and Consent Decision Making

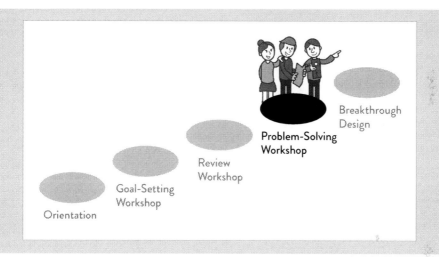

Orientation

Goal-Setting Workshop

Review Workshop

Problem-Solving Workshop

Breakthrough Design

What's here

- **Case Study**: Finding solutions using Open Space Technology and Consent Decision Making
- **Tools**: Six-Zero, Open Space Technology, Consent Decision Making, Five Fingers

How it helps

Open Space Technology is an extremely efficient group method that allows participants to self-organise to connect knowledge and direct their energy as they see fit to get optimal results. Consent Decision Making is a structured framework that guides the group towards agreement.

A physical challenge

After lunch, tired faces returned my gaze as I looked at the group of around twenty B.E. employees that filled the conference room. The day had got off to a great start with a successful beginning to the workshop. We already managed to outline the key challenges that they were facing as a company, squashed a conflict between Jackie and Angie, and had people show their commitment to fixing key issues by signing their names next to them. Not a bad day's work—and all before lunch! But instead of basking in their success and eagerly wanting more, the group was lethargic. A few people were resting their heads in their hands and I suspected someone in the back of the room was catching up on the latest news that crowded their social media news feeds, or perhaps even doing some online dating! *Time to change the energy in here*, I thought.

"Everyone on your feet, please! We are going to begin the afternoon with a test. Spread out from others so that you have a bit of space to yourself. The first part of this test is to stick your right foot out and rotate it clockwise in circles."

So far, everyone could keep up easily enough. "Now I want you to extend your right hand out in front of you."

Someone called out that the test seemed a bit below their level, so I gave the final piece of instructions; "I am a powerful wizard and I have just cast a spell on your leg! This spell gives me control on how your leg moves, and I say that now whenever you draw the number 6 with your right hand, your leg will change the direction that it is rotating! Give it a try and draw the number 6 in the air with your right hand."

I knew what was coming next; laughter and failure at following the instructions. One by one, as people tried to draw the number 6 while keeping their legs rotating, their legs would stop rotating clockwise, or change direction.

"Nice effort, everyone. I am ashamed to say that I may have set all of you up for failure. You can't draw a 6 with your hand while rotating you leg clockwise. Does anyone know why? It is because the nerves that control your hand and feet are connected, and if you switch the rotational direction of your hand, your foot will follow. Pretty cool, right? Anyway, now that we all have woken up and have enough energy, let's begin."

A multitude of meetings

"Our objective today is to solve the key challenges you outlined this morning. Now it is time to create solutions with each other and to come up with the best possible ideas. One more thing, I think this may work better if I put all of you in charge." I saw a few people exchange looks of confusion before I continued, "You are going to run your own meetings today. You decide what challenge you want to talk about, and for how long. In fact, I will take things even further. If you don't think you have anything to contribute, you are not obligated to attend any of the meetings at all."

"Are we going to have the meetings in this room?" someone asked.

Immediately following this question was another; "How do I organise a meeting, and what happens if no one shows up?"

I replied, "You all are very clever. I can tell by the great questions that you are asking. Let me first introduce the meeting roles. There will be meeting leaders who are responsible for holding and recording the meetings. The meeting leader's most important job is to come up with a concrete proposal about what to do at the conclusion of the meeting. But it is OK if you want to delegate the role of leader to someone else so that you can attend a different meeting. The most important rule here is called *the law of two feet*."

A laughing voice from the back of the room said, "Does this law involve rotating our feet clockwise and drawing numbers like before?"

"Hmm, I have never considered that before, but I like the idea! But no, the law of two feet is much simpler. It means that you must go to where you think you can contribute the most. This means you can spend the entire time in one meeting or attend all of them. And if there is anyone here that feels like they don't belong in any of the meetings, I have organised a table with some cookies and coffee available, so feel free to relax and enjoy some caffeine and sugar. Just make sure you are in the right place where you can give the most, OK?"

Everyone seemed to be following along well and there were no questions. I pointed to the wall and said, "You can see all eight challenges you wanted to solve today in front of you."

Key issues that need to be solved today

- Training and integrating Sales Team
- Aligning press coverage and P.R. Team with rest of company
- Pricing in new markets
- Empowering employees
- Developing new ways of working
- Keeping company culture during growth
- Clarifying the common goal
- Allocation of time and budget going forward

I continued, "There will be two rounds of meetings each set lasting 60 minutes. On the time and space matrix you may see Post-it notes with a starting time and place. This tells you if the meeting begins right away or in the second round which begins in 60 minutes. I know you only see a time marked on different colour Post-its and you are wondering what I mean with the place. The colour is your indicator where the meeting takes place. For example, here is a pink Post-it note. Look around the room. Can anyone guess where this meeting will take place?"

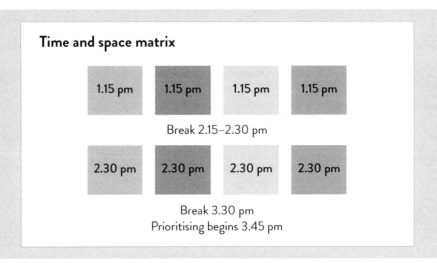

Time and space matrix

| 1.15 pm | 1.15 pm | 1.15 pm | 1.15 pm |

Break 2.15–2.30 pm

| 2.30 pm | 2.30 pm | 2.30 pm | 2.30 pm |

Break 3.30 pm
Prioritising begins 3.45 pm

Pointing to the back-right corner of the room, Marcus said, "Back over there, where the pink Post-it notes are stuck to those tables and chairs.

"Marcus is exactly right. Each topic is assigned a colour which indicates where the meeting is. Look around. There are coloured Post-its placed around the room that show each meeting's location."

Before I could continue, a hand shot up accompanied by a voice; "One question here please!" It was Todd. He asked, "Are you preparing all of the meetings or is there anyone in charge at each meeting?"

"Great question, Todd. Each meeting does have a leader, and we are going to decide who that will be now. We will decide who the meeting leaders are based on motivation—if you want to be a meeting leader and are ready to take responsibility for solving one of the challenges, please take a Post-it note from the time and space matrix, write your name on it, and place it next to the challenge. Once all the challenges have a leader assigned to it, we will be ready to go!"

Marcus started things off by committing to lead the meeting dedicated to the challenge pricing in new markets. Others followed his lead until there was only one challenge left that needed a leader: *clarifying common goals.* No one seemed interested in taking responsibility for this one. Perhaps it was too broad, or maybe it seemed too difficult. Simon finally stood up and claimed it for himself, which meant that each challenge had a designated time, place, and leader. The meetings were now ready to begin.

Key issues, time, space and meeting leaders

- Training and integrating Sales Team | 3.10 pm Hans
- Aligning press coverage and P.R. Team with rest of company | 1.30 pm Jackie
- Pricing in new markets | 3.10 pm Marcus
- Empowering employees | 1.30 pm Bruce
- Developing new ways of working | 1.30 pm Mary
- Keeping company culture during growth | 3.10 pm Todd
- Clarifying the common goals | 1.30 pm Simon
- Allocation of time and budget going forward | 3.10 pm Angie

"One last thing before you all begin. I have one golden rule and some principles which may help you run your own meetings," I said as I pointed to a flipchart on the wall. "The meetings have four important principles. The first principle is *those who come to the meeting are the perfect people to be there*. This means that you should not worry about the amount of people that show up. If you are the only person attending the meeting, great! This means that you have the chance to define the topic and explore it on your own! The second principle is *whatever happens is the only thing that could have happened*. In other words, be flexible. There is no specific path that needs to be followed to get the results that we want. Start new meetings, divide meetings, or do anything else that you feel will help you contribute the most effectively, and don't worry about what process you use or how you do it."

Heads nodded as I explained further, "Speaking of not caring, this brings me to my last two principles; *It starts when it starts* and *it's over when it's over*. Each meeting lasts as long as it needs to, and you can manage the timing of the meetings as you best see fit. My final words of wisdom are to simply follow the golden rule of two feet: trust your feet to take you to the place where you can contribute the most. You may start the meetings!"

After my long set of instructions, B.E.'s employees were ready to go. Everyone began by looking at the time and space matrix to see where the meetings were happening. The meeting leaders were the first to take their places around the large conference room, and the meeting attendees soon followed. Some took a seat and did not move for an hour, deciding to stay in one meeting the entire time. Others adopted the opposite approach of spending five minutes here and another five minutes there, passing from meeting to meeting. Some of the meetings lasted the full hour and started showing signs of slowing down, so I announced to the group that it was time to take a well-deserved coffee break. The second round of meetings were due start 15 minutes later at 2:30 PM, and I was happy to see that everyone was finished with their coffee and ready to go. Hans, Todd, Angie and Marcus took their places as meeting hosts and soon enough each table was filled. At Todd's table, a spirited debate broke out about if company culture should be sacrificed for explosive sales growth. Todd listened and wrote as fast as he could to try and keep up. The other hosts had a lot to record, too, and the second round of meetings seemed like a success. It looked like everyone could keep the conversations up all day, but a small beeping noise from my wristwatch indicated to me that it was time for a short coffee break.

Once everyone returned from the break appropriately caffeinated, I could continue with the workshop. "Look around the room for a moment. You will see all the meeting records and proposals on the walls. Find a person who you have not talked with much today. Walk around the room together and get to know the results. Mark the solutions that you think we should implement by drawing a small heart next to it—this will show that you love the idea! If you don't understand something, someone else nearby probably does, so ask each other for help! I am here too, if needed. Get to it!"

I saw that everyone was eagerly looking at the results posted on the wall, regardless of which meeting they had attended. Even better, people were asking clarifying questions to each other. Small hearts were being drawn next to the solutions, with some being more popular than others. I called for attention so I could give the next set of instructions. "Now it is time for the meeting leaders to finalise the results. Look at all the solutions posted on the walls and take into consideration the amount of hearts each one has drawn next to it. Make a proposal about which solutions should be implemented and be prepared to present your proposal to the rest of the group. Everyone else can help the meeting leaders make the proposals. You have 30 minutes!"

Time flies when you are having fun and before I knew it, it was time to bring things to a close for the day. "Congratulations everyone! You are just about done for today. I want to finish by asking for three of you to comment about how today's work went. Any volunteers?

Marcus was the first person to raise his hand, and said, "I had a lot of fun leading my meeting. I was surprised by how many people had opinions about pricing our services in new markets. I thought I was the only one obsessed with that challenge!"

Mary continued, "I know what Marcus means. It's funny how many ideas and solutions can be created in an hour when we had no ideas for weeks!"

Angie added, "Today was great. Let's keep going! Now that we have answers to our challenges we shouldn't stop here!"

I stepped in and said, "Thank you for your comments, and once again, great work today, everyone. And don't worry Angie, we will get back to work soon enough. But now you all have something else exciting to do! It is my understanding that your kind boss Simon has arranged some dinner plans for all of you, so I hope that you enjoy tonight, and come back ready to go tomorrow. We will spend the first part of tomorrow finishing the solutions stage of the workshop by reviewing the proposals you created today. After that we will enter the final part of the workshop where we make actions for each and every one of you to do that will bring these solutions to life. Have a nice night and see you in the morning!"

Promoting proposals

The next morning, I greeted everyone at the door as they filed into the meeting room to continue the workshop. Angie wore a big smile and strolled in, and Todd gave a thumbs up to me as he walked in. *That must have been one good dinner*, I thought to myself as I watched the happy employees file in. At 9:00 AM on the dot a group of three employees came in and tried their best to give a friendly wave, but their bloodshot eyes and large cups of coffee made me think that the after-dinner drinks must have been pretty good, too. With everyone seated, it was time to begin.

"I hope everyone had a fun night last night, but not too much fun! I need you all at your best today! Our objective for today is to decide together as a group about what the best proposals are. We will do this by watching each proposal be presented, and then talking about it together, as a group. Today's session will take about an hour. But before all that, I need each person to find a partner. Once everyone is ready, discuss together what the key insights from yesterday were, and what should happen today."

Despite the potential headaches that were a lingering result of a fun night out, people got down to it and were soon deep in conversation in their respective pairs. I gave them about ten minutes to talk things through before calling for attention again. "Thank you everyone, you may return back to your seats. Can I have three comments about what you talked about?"

"One key insight from yesterday is that we do not need to rush during this period of growth. We would be getting better results if we took our time to get things right," said Mary.

Hans added, "Mary is completely right. When business is growing like crazy, the natural reaction is to try and speed up to keep pace. But we have unfortunately found out that this is not sustainable or good business."

Simon raised his hand and said, "I think that today we need to figure out just what to do. Yesterday was nice because we created a lot of ideas and that broke us out of a feeling of hopelessness. But if we don't figure out just what to do with these ideas, then I do not see any reason to be too excited."

"Great point Simon, and thank you for the comments," I said. I continued to explain that today's session was about making decisions about the proposals created the night before. "A decision means that no-one objects to the proposal. Is this definition OK for everyone?"

The group nodded in agreement, so I continued explaining what to do. "After presenting the proposals we will have a round of questions and answers. Then we will have a round of opinions, and finally we will vote to see if there are objections. If there are objections, I will take a flipchart paper and we will brainstorm how to solve the issue. If we can't solve it, then no problem. We just decide to save it for another day. Oh, and be sure to celebrate every decision with a round of applause, OK?"

Everyone understood and was up for it, and the group leaders readied themselves to give their presentations.

"Marcus, you can begin please," I said as I pointed to a fellow in the back of the room.

"No problem, Pepe. The topic of my meeting was pricing in new markets..."

Marcus took a couple of minutes to summarise his meeting, and then presented the proposal that his meeting group created:

> Slow down entry into new markets to allow for proper research into pricing to be completed—eliminating uniform pricing policy to ensure best long-term performance.

"Thank you, Marcus. Are there any questions about the proposal?"

At least three hands went up at the same time and Marcus began fielding questions.

"We have been firm in offering uniform pricing for our products, regardless of the market. Isn't this proposal a big pivot away from what made us successful in the first place?"

Marcus replied, "It is a big shift, but one that is a direct response to the new volume we are doing. We have new clients and buyers, and we cannot have one simple MSRP for the end user. Our previous way of pricing was when most of our worldwide sales came from end-users purchasing directly from our website. Things have changed..."

"Marcus, what do you mean by 'proper research' before entering a new market? Who would do this research and what does it entail?"

Marcus continued fielding questions and clarifying doubts and concerns. Once the questions died down, I stepped in once again and asked to hear a few opinions about the proposal. Jackie said, "It is a major change, but it is well-developed, and it's a needed change. I'm just curious about how we will find the time to implement the research. Man-hours are already a bit tight..."

Marcus replied that the research could be done by the Sales Team, or that a new dedicated role could be created. I asked for a few more comments about the proposal before putting it to a vote.

Sampling of proposals from Open Space meetings

Redo onboarding process for sales team (5 hour session in the coming week). After this, make sure sales team is better informed about inventory levels, manufacturing, R&D, etc., by having them present in other meetings or by sharing meeting notes with them.

Establish a liaison between press team and other departments. Allow for feedback from rest of company before a press release is made public to ensure it is accurate and reflects the current reality.

Slow down entry into new markets to allow for proper research into pricing to be done. Eliminate uniform pricing to ensure best long-term fit in a new market.

Reduce managerial interference in inter-team communication (teams can communicate more freely with one another). Less day-to-day micromanaging of KPI's, less pressure on sales team to close deals and more allowance for time to be spent learning product and developing appropriate pricing.

"Now we must make a decision about the proposal. We are going to vote on it, and we are going to vote with our fingers. One finger means you have strong objections, two fingers mean that you have objections, three fingers mean you can live with the proposal, four fingers mean that you like the proposal, and five fingers that you love it. On the count of three, put your fingers in the air. Ready? One...two...three!"

Everyone shot a hand with fingers raised into the air. I looked around the room along with everyone else and saw that everyone was holding at least two fingers in the air, which meant that no one was against the proposal.

"Great! There are no objections which means that this proposal is accepted," I said, as I wrote it down on a new piece of flipchart paper. "Marcus, could you kindly announce the decision?" His announcement was followed by a big applause and some enthusiastic cheers. I called on a new meeting leader to share his proposal with the group, and new rounds of questions, comments, and voting with fingers were conducted.

Group by group, all proposals were clarified and further developed, and finally agreed upon. Some people had objections to a specific proposal, and when this happened, I wrote down the objection on a flipchart paper and asked the person with the objection how to solve the challenge. Sometimes the group helped by sharing their concerns and the proposal was updated so that their objections were met.

A final proposal

To end the solutions part of the workshop, I told the group that I had a proposal of my own. "I propose that we met our objective of solving current challenges...or maybe we didn't. It might be better if you all tell me. Did we succeed in meeting our objective?"

Marcus said, "Our objective was to solve key challenges, and we have not solved anything yet until these proposals are in place and in effect. But we are off to a good start, so I would say the objective was met."

The second comment was also a positive one; "I think that by allowing us to run our own meetings, we made a lot of progress, and the objective was met."

The third comment was the most enthusiastic yet: "Let's get to it! We have a plan, what are we waiting for?"

The comments left no doubt that everyone was happy with the results of the solutions part of the workshop, so I knew that now was the time to move on to the action part of the workshop. I sent everyone off to grab some coffee and enjoy a short break while I prepared the room for the third and final part of the workshop.

Analysis

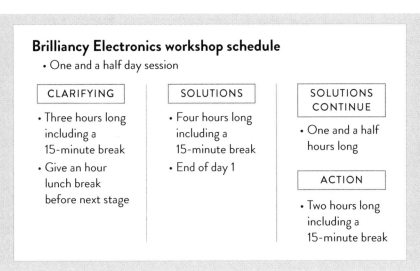

Brilliancy Electronics workshop schedule
• One and a half day session

CLARIFYING
• Three hours long including a 15-minute break
• Give an hour lunch break before next stage

SOLUTIONS
• Four hours long including a 15-minute break
• End of day 1

SOLUTIONS CONTINUE
• One and a half hours long

ACTION
• Two hours long including a 15-minute break

Check-in

To begin this portion of the workshop (which took place only an hour after the morning *clarifying challenges* session), I used an energiser called Six-Zero. Some energisers are structured to get information from a group or take the temperature of a room to see where they stand on an issue or something similar. Unlike those, Six-Zero functions as a fun way to wake a group up and let them have some fun before beginning more serious work.

Six-Zero

A fast-paced exercise which can be used with groups of all sizes.
Give the following instructions to the group:

1. "Stand up and draw the number 6 in the air with your right index finger."
2. "Drop your hand and rotate your right leg clockwise."
3. Explain to the participants that when they do both movements at the same time, the right foot suddenly rotates counter-clockwise by itself.
4. "Now, simultaneously rotate your right leg clockwise and draw number 6 with your right hand."

I have used Six-Zero in groups ranging from just a few people to groups of hundreds of people, so it can be successful with groups of all sizes. The purpose of Six-Zero (and of all energisers) is to get people focused on something completely different than the workshop objective. After taking a break from the workshop topic for a bit, people can come back with renewed energy and focus when it is time to get back to serious work.

Six-Zero is a fun energiser because the results come as a surprise. The instructions, when broken down into individual steps, seem easy. First, rotate your right foot clockwise, then draw the number 6 with your right hand—simple stuff. The reason why most people cannot complete the task is because the same part of the brain controls both hand and foot coordination, and the hand is dominant.

I say "most people" fail at Six-Zero because there are some out there who can complete this task with ease. My colleague once had a group of classically trained ballet dancers in a large group workshop. They all easily passed the task. My son is an avid drummer, and he is extremely coordinated. When I tried to trick him with Six-Zero to show him how cool his father was, he too mastered the movements quickly. Even if some people in the group manage to pull off the instructions of Six-Zero, it is no problem. It is an engaging and fun energiser, nonetheless.

Emergence

Open Space Technology (or simply Open Space or OST for short) served as the tool for emergence during the solutions stage of this workshop. OST is a meeting technology created for large groups of up to five hundred participants. In this workshop I used a variation that works better with smaller groups that have around 25 or fewer participants.

The man most often credited with creating OST is Harrison Owen. Owen lives a rich life and has spent the last 40 or so years being a civil rights activist, an episcopal priest, and a business consultant. As the man himself tells it in his book, *Open Space Technology: A user's guide*, Open Space Technology started out as an attempt to replicate the dynamic conversations that happened during the coffee breaks during a seminar organised. Owen noticed that while the seminar was a success, the most beneficial aspects of it were the coffee breaks where people were communicating candidly and directly. Owen continued to say:

> "So much for a year's preparation...the only thing that everybody liked was the one thing I had nothing to do with: the coffee breaks. My question was a simple one; Was it possible to combine the levels of excitement and synergy of a good coffee break with the substantive activity and results characteristic of a good meeting?"

These questions that Owen was left contemplating were the spark which created the structure of Open Space Technology. Owen is modest about his creation and has stated that was an eight-year collaborative project that involved over 1,000 people worldwide.

I use Open Space primarily for the emergence portion of the solutions stage when there are many different viewpoints and areas of expertise. The unique structure of Open Space makes the tool a powerful one. People have freedom to work together and contribute when and where they see fit. When they choose to come together in the same small group to focus on a clear task, fantastic dialogue is produced, and new ideas emerge. Open Space allows for different opinions and knowledge-systems to come together to deal with complex situations. It also is effectively used in times of conflict like crisis management meetings and conflict resolution sessions. Open

Space Technology works especially well when there are many questions that require solutions and where participants have different sets of skills and expertise. It is used commonly in strategy development meetings since people tend to have many, strong opinions about what strategy is the best course of action. It also is effectively used in crisis management meetings and dealing with complex change.

Open Space Technology

Open Space is based on proactive approach and self-driven interest:

- Any participant can suggest a topic to be discussed (based on the joint theme).
- Meetings will be arranged on the suggested topics. A person suggesting a topic will chair their topic's discussion.
- Participants can freely move from one meeting to another.

Open Space Technology applications:

- Complex problems
- Various kinds of knowhow needed to solve the problem
- Problem includes contradiction, or attempts to solve the problem have led to conflict
- The issue at hand is important

A staple of the traditional Open Space Technology method is introducing the law of two feet, the four principles, and the different types of meeting participants, all in an effort to acquaint people with the way of working and to best prepare them for the open-ended nature of Open Space Technology meetings. The purpose of the law of two feet and the principles are to help participants self-organise.

> ## Open Space Technology — one law and four principles
>
> **The law of two feet**: Trust your feet to take you to the place where you can contribute the most.
>
> **The four principles:**
> 1. *Those who come are just the right people to be there.*
> 2. *Whatever happens is the only thing that could have happened.*
> 3. *It starts when it starts.*
> 4. *It's over when it's over.*
>
> These four principles emphasise that Open Space Technology is built on a free-flowing framework.

After presenting the way of working (the day's theme, the law of two feet, principles of Open Space and meeting roles), Open Space Technology continues with participants coming up and presenting the topics they want to talk about and choosing meeting time and place. This is very simple and works even in very large groups.

I did not follow Open Space Technology completely, though. Instead of letting participants come up with new meeting topics, I let the participants choose from the challenges that the group came up with during the clarifying stage. These were the perfect thing to use because the group had already committed to these topics during the morning session, so all I needed to do was to connect each topic with a meeting leader and assign a place and time for the meeting, and then turn the group loose and give them the freedom to attend the meetings.

The law of two feet needs to be explained and highlighted to the group for Open Space to work. The law of two feet states that people can trust their own intuition to move about the meetings as they please—there is no wrong way to participate. Some group leaders introduce the different roles participants can take during the meetings, ranging from the bumble bee that roams from meeting to meeting, pollinating each meeting with the information that they picked up along the way, to the butterfly who floats out of the room and into an adjoining cafeteria or lounge where they relax while not contributing to the meetings at all. I chose not to mention these roles in this case because they can overcomplicate things or even scare away serious businesspeople from participating to their fullest if they interpret the roles to be a bit silly or off topic. Each group is different (and each group leader too, for that matter!) and you will quickly find out for yourself what works best for you as a leader.

Open Space roles

1. **Convener**: A person who calls together a meeting. They suggest the meeting topic and choose the time and the place. They make sure that meeting is documented.

2. **Contributor**: All other meeting participants besides the convener.

3. **Bumble bee**: A participant who drifts from meeting to meeting. They play an important role in spreading information during Open Space.

4. **Butterfly**: A participant who spends most of their time outside of the meetings. They can be found drinking coffee outside with other butterflies. They often make small talk about sports, the weather, or office politics, but for some reason they usually come up with some key insights related to the workshop topic.

I am a huge believer in the Open Space Technology method, and I think it is one of the most effective methods available. Think about it; people can self-organise based on their own interest, and all the information is recorded for the entire group. Moreover, people can move around during the meetings and come and go as they please depending on their interest and where they feel they can contribute. The result of a good Open Space Technology session is that a lot of work is accomplished, and people feel empowered and listened to.

Open Space Technology is a very efficient communication tool; a large group divides itself into sub-groups to reach alignment and create shared understanding about multiple topics at the same time. This format makes it possible for many breakthroughs to occur simultaneously in the sub-groups, but this format also makes it difficult for these breakthroughs to be understood by the entire group, and it is this shortcoming of Open Space Technology which causes it to be overlooked by some organisations. I can see why—my typical client wants me to help find a common focus and shared solutions, and if I were to only use Open Space Technology, I might not fully reach that goal. Luckily, I found that I can have my cake and eat it too; that is to say, I can still use Open Space Technology and create alignment, simply by adding convergent tools to the workshop.

Convergence

After the meetings, I asked for participants to pair up and review the content that was shared in the meetings. This allowed people to fill each other in about what happened during the meetings. Then I asked everyone to vote in pairs to give their opinions about the proposals. After the voting, I gave meeting leaders additional time to refine their proposals based on the feedback they received from the group. After team leaders refined their proposals, I used Consent Decision Making for group convergence.

In Consent Decision Making, the entire group votes on an idea or proposal. The qualifier here is that it needs to receive a minimum score of at least 'OK' from everyone—meaning that no one is opposed to it. In other words, everyone gives their consent to the idea and its progression, hence the tool's name. There are many advantages to using Consent Decision Making. First, simply talking about making a decision raises the stakes for the group and seems much more serious than other voting or prioritisation activities. If I ask a group to vote on their favourite ideas, then they may feel that they are just giving their opinion, but if I ask them to consider the ideas and then make a decision, then people tend to consider things a bit more carefully.

Secondly, Consent Decision Making differentiates between questions, opinions, and decision making. In other words, the process makes sure that an idea is not shot down simply due to a misunderstanding of the details or a lack of clarity. For example, a close colleague of mine is a wonderful facilitator from France named Jean. However, most of the time I find it nearly impossible to run a new project or idea past him. Whenever I try, I usually receive a confused look from him accompanied by a few comments and critiques all about the small details of my proposal, while all I want is some broad support. Jean is not trying to discourage me or be negative, he is simply a very logical person who needs to get a grasp on the minutiae and details of a project before he can completely commit. Consent Decision Making allows people to understand ideas first, then express their opinions, and finally make a decision when they are ready. It is a very logical process.

Third, Consent Decision Making is equipped to deal with concerns and objections. When people hear an idea or proposal, they rarely have a problem with the entire plan, but only object to a key point or part of it. Or perhaps they are worried about some of the implications of a project. When you write down objections and ask for ideas, most groups find a way to develop the proposal.

There are some shortcomings of Consent Decision Making that come along with the positives I just outlined. For one, some participants find reasons to object simply because they are given the chance to. These people may mean well and are trying to play devil's advocate, but it can create some needless troubleshooting if they are naming potential problems or objecting simply to be contrarian.

Another difficulty with Consent Decision Making is that it is time intensive, and spending a lot of time working with this tool can kill a group's energy. To keep things moving at a good pace, I suggest using this tool with a maximum of four proposals. If you use any more than that, you will need to prepare the group before using Consent Decision Making. In this example with Brilliancy Electronics, we worked with eight proposals. The only reason why this worked was because I had laid the groundwork by preparing the group. The first thing I did was to make sure that everyone had a chance to participate in the creation of the proposals during the Open Space meetings. Then, I gave the group time to walk around in pairs to read all the proposals, and then they were asked to vote to decide what proposals they thought were best. Finally, the leaders of each mini meeting had to rewrite the proposals based on group feedback. All these different steps required participants to be deeply involved in creating and refining the proposals, which meant that they understood them. If I began Consent Decision Making with new proposals that no one was familiar with, then it would have taken hours to get through the activity, perhaps even days! It is possible to use Consent Decision Making with more proposals if you adequately prepare the group, but I encourage you to try and stick with four or so, at least when starting out. This will make it much easier to stay on schedule and avoid having to leave some part of the workshop unfinished.

Consent Decision Making

1. **Present the proposal**
   Ensure that everyone in the room knows what the proposal says.

2. **Clarifying questions**
   Necessary questions to understand the proposal are asked.

3. **Brief response**
   Everyone gives their opinion on the proposal. Keep it short!

4. **Check for consent/objections**
   Consent means that there are no objections. If there are any objections, write them down.

5. **Resolve objections**
   Write down and deal with the objections one at a time.

6. **Announce the decision and celebrate**

When I asked the group to express their objections, I had them to use their fingers to express their sentiments on a scale from one to five. This voting technique is called Five Fingers and it is a quick way to take semi-detailed feedback (more complex than a simple yes or no) from larger groups.

Five Fingers

A voting tool where a value is assigned to each finger, which creates a scale of feedback, that can express anything ranging from strong dislike to strong support.

The following instructions can be used to introduce Five Fingers:

- *Put 1 finger in the air if you really don't like this idea*
- *Put 2 fingers in the air if you don't like this idea*
- *Put 3 fingers in the air if this idea is OK*
- *Put 4 fingers in the air if you like this idea*
- *Put 5 fingers in the air if you really like this idea*

You may take the temperature of a group by using Five Fingers to get feedback about a proposal, plan, idea, etc.

There are many decision-making processes. Some businesses rely more on managerial consent or having a key person decide instead of putting it to a group vote. In cases like this where an idea comes from the top-down, Consent Decision Making as I used in this case study would not be realistic. Fortunately for us, the great Sam Kaner has a solution for us. Kaner, who also created the concept of the Groan Zone (which I introduce and discuss in Chapter 1: History of Group Decision Making), uses a variant of Consent Decision Making that has a key decision maker like a CEO or manager make the final decision after gauging the group's level of support by using a feedback tool like Five Fingers. Kaner calls the intervention by a designated decision-maker the *Meta-Decision*. After a proposal is presented to the group and they have the chance to show their level of support, the decision maker will either make the decision in that moment, or if things are unclear or the group is fragmented, they can decide to discuss things further and create more alignment.

Whenever possible, I try to allow the group to make the decision themselves. If they are in agreement after Five Fingers, then it is a foregone conclusion what they will decide, and if there is still some confusion or strongly diverging opinions, then there is work left to do and we will return back to talking.

Check-out

No matter how good a workshop feels in the moment or how happy the participants seem with the results, I always elicit a few comments about how we did in reaching the objective during the check-out stage. This can be done in small groups or using Me/We/Us, using a polling activity, or by simply asking for comments, which is what I did in this session.

Workshop process: Solutions

Objective: To solve key challenges
Time: Five hours 30 minutes

Check-in (5 minutes):
1. Energiser. Six-Zero.

2. Presenting the objective of the stage.

3. "Is the objective of the next stage clear?"—short discussion.

Emergence tool: Open Space Technology (10 minutes for explaining the way of working and assigning the meeting leaders + two 1 hour sessions + 15-minute break in between = 2 hours 25 minutes)

1. "Let me first introduce the meeting roles. There will be meeting leaders who are responsible for holding and recording the meeting and, most importantly, to come up with a concrete proposal. However, if you do not like this role or you have to attend other meetings, you may always delegate this job to someone else. All participants follow the rule of two feet; they will be where they can contribute the most. That means you can spend all your time with one topic, you can change the meetings whenever you want or you do not have to go anywhere, if you have nothing to contribute—clear?"

2. "You can see all the challenges you wanted to solve today in front of you. There will be two sets of meetings, each set lasting 60 minutes. On the time and space matrix you may see Post-it notes with a time and place. I know you only see a time marked on different colour Post-its and you are wondering what I mean about the place. Look around you and you will see meeting spots around the room with the same colour Post-it notes marking the place the meetings will take place."

3. "If you want to become a meeting leader and take responsibility for solving one of the challenges, you simply take a Post-it from the time and space matrix, write your name on it, and place it next to the challenge. Now everyone knows the meeting topic, the leader, the time and the place. Simple! Who is first?"

4. "You may start the meetings!"

Break (15 minutes)

Convergence tool; Prioritising in pairs (30 minutes), Making new proposals (30 minutes)

1. "Thank you for the great work. You see all meeting records and proposals on the walls. Find yourself a pair, walk around and get to know the results before we make final decisions. If you do not understand something, ask your partner. Mark the solutions that you think we should implement by drawing a small heart next to it."

2. "Now it is time for the meeting leaders to finalise the results. Take the hearts into consideration and make a proposal on which ideas should be implemented and get ready to present your proposal to the rest of the group. Others help the meeting leaders with the proposals."

End of the day (15 minutes)

1. "We are done for the day. Now I would like three of you to comment: How did it go?"

2. "Thank you, we did a great job!"

Beginning the next day (15 minutes)

1. Introducing the program and objective for the day.

2. Discussion in pairs: "Key insights from yesterday and what should happen today?"

3. Three comments.

Convergence continues with Consent Decision Making (55 minutes)

1. "Now, the meeting leaders will briefly present their proposals. Afterwards, we will have a round of comments and questions. Finally, we will check if everyone is ok with the proposals—if not, we will try to deal with the objections. For the actioning stage, we will take only proposals that everyone can live with. Is that ok?"

2. "Marcus, you go first!"

3. "Does anyone have a question?"

4. "Let's hear a few opinions on the proposal!" (in Consent Decision Making everyone shares their opinion, however, in large groups this is rather time consuming.)

5. "Now lets vote with our fingers. One finger means you have strong objections, two fingers mean that you have objections, three fingers means you can live with the proposal, four fingers that you like the proposal and five fingers that you love it. I count to three and we all show our fingers"

6. A. "No objections, the proposal is accepted!"

6. B. "There were objections, let me write them down and lets try to solve them"

7. "Can everyone live with the proposal now?" (If not, in organisations you often have a boss to make the final decision whether to forget, postpone or take the decision).

8. "We made a decision, let's give ourselves a hand!"

Check-out: Three comments (5 minutes)

1. "Now I would like three of you to comment."

2. "Thank you, we did a great job!"

5.3: Problem-Solving Workshop: Creating Actions with Idealogue and Roadmap

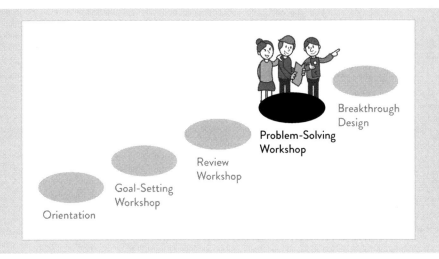

What's here

- **Case Study**: An actioning workshop with B.E. where action points are created to follow and enact recent decisions.
- **Tools**: Idealogue, Roadmap, Floorball, Talking Stick

How it helps

Idealogue is a great emergence tool to help people create, prioritise, and understand ideas. Roadmap helps people visualise the ideas in the weeks and months following the workshop.

Let's play ball!

It was already the second day with the group from Brilliancy Electronics, and they began to know what to expect from me. The group was back after a break, I had just taken my place at the front of the room and right away the participants began to expect that I was going to continue the workshop by asking people to pair up and have a chat...and they were right—this is standard opening procedure for me. I saw that some participants were preparing to stand up from their desks and began making eye contact with each other, the preliminary dance steps of pairing up. I noticed this and saw that I was becoming a bit too predictable, so I decided that it was time to switch things up.

"We are nearing the home stretch for today. Our objective for the final stage of the workshop is to develop concrete actions in response to the proposals you just created. But first, I want to share a little bit of culture from my native country, Finland!"

"Oh, are we going to try some polar bear meat?", guessed Jackie.

"I'm from Finland, not Svalbard, Norway," I replied. "We are going to play a sport that is popular in Finland, and before you get too excited, I am not talking about hockey. This is a sport that people play inside during work breaks, and there are teams in offices all around the country. I am talking of course, about floorball!"

No one gave any indication that they had the slightest idea about what I was talking about, so I just moved right to the instructions.

"In order to play, we first need teams. Each team should have 6 players, so all of you split into four teams now!"

Once divided, I asked each team to think of a team name while I explained how to play.

"Each team stands in a line facing the other team. Keep about ten feet between the two lines. Stand with your feet firmly planted, about shoulder-width apart. Spread your feet so that they are touching your neighbour's feet. Once your feet are set, you can't move them for the rest of the game. The object of the game is to throw this ball into the other team's goal which is the space between their feet. You can use your hands to defend and to pass the ball or throw it through the goal, but remember, no moving your feet and the ball should stay on the ground!"

I lined the four teams up and passed a tennis ball to each group while I asked for their team names.

"On this side of the room we have the Sassy Shamrocks versus Brilliancy Floorball Squad! And on the other side of the room we have the Hungry Hippos taking on the Supreme Sales Team. The first team to score 3 goals wins, and you can begin now!"

As usual with an active game that breaks up long workshop stretches, the group really seemed to enjoy playing floorball. All four teams were laughing and even taking it somewhat seriously. *Everyone loves to win, no matter what the game* I thought.

"You can all take your seats, and congratulations to our winning teams, the Shamrocks and the Hungry Hippos. We will have a championship game at the end of the day, and I have some chocolate from Finland for the winning team. But first, back to business. Our objective as I mentioned earlier is to create actions that will help us realise the decisions you made earlier today. To help us think of the best actions and make sure that they are all understood, I have a method which requires time for thinking of your own ideas individually, and then more time for stealing the best ideas from others around the room. Are there any questions about the objective or how we are going to work to achieve it?" There were no questions at this point, or perhaps people were tired and still recovering from their intense floorball matches. Regardless, it was time to proceed to Idealogue method.

A great idea

"Before we go any further, I want you to think about the proposals that you made earlier today. Take a moment to review them and I have them posted on the wall over there if you need to refresh your memory."

Decisions from Open Space meetings

Redo onboarding process for sales team (5 hour session in the coming week). After this, make sure sales team is better informed of the status of inventory, manufacturing, R&D, ect by having them present in other meetings or by sharing meeting notes with them.

Establish a liaison between press team and other departments. Allow for feedback from rest of company before a press release is made public to ensure it is accurate and reflects the current reality.

Slow down entry into new markets to allow for proper research into pricing to be done. Eliminate uniform pricing to ensure best long-term fit in a new market.

Reduce managerial interference in inter-team communication (teams can communicate more freely with one another). Less day-to-day micromanaging of KPI's, less pressure on sales team to close deals and more allowance for time to be spent learning product and developing appropriate pricing.

As people reviewed their notes or the proposals that I posted on the wall, I said, "You have five minutes to write down the actions that need be taken to achieve these proposals. These should be individual actions for yourself. Please write your actions down on a personal piece of paper."

Pen hit paper, and it did not look like anyone had much trouble coming up with actions to be taken to achieve the proposals.

"Fantastic job, everyone. You are a nice group to work with, and I am sure you all are kind people. Which is why the next part of the activity may be a bit uncomfortable for you; I am going to ask you to ruthlessly steal from one another. That's right, you job now is to find only the best actions that exist in this room—it does not matter who they come from, and it does not matter if you give proper credit to the person whose it is...if you hear an action that you like, steal it and write it down on your own piece of paper. You can also combine different actions to make new ones, so if you hear an idea that inspires a new and wonderful idea of your own, write it down. Any questions at this point?"

"You are having us steal from each other?" asked Jackie. "Why don't we just talk about it in groups like before? Is there a point to this?"

"Great question and thank you for challenging me, Jackie. There is a point to it—sometimes I think competition brings out the best in us, like when you all were playing floorball like a bunch of happy maniacs earlier. The game now is to get the best actions on your piece of paper, and please feel free to be as competitive as you like. My hope is that the results will be as good as the entertaining floorball games I was just watching."

Jackie agreed to suspend judgement and give it a try, so I asked for people to get into groups of three and begin stealing. "You will have about fifteen minutes in these groups of three to share your own ideas and listen to and steal from the others, so you may begin!"

"OK, tell me the good actions," someone demanded as they formed a group of three. I watched while this demand played out in different ways across the large room. I looked at the group in front of me as someone explained their action point of *beginning the search internally to fill the role of liaison to the Press Team*. Apparently, this was a good idea, because the other two group members were writing it down.

On the other side of the room I watched Jackie as she outlined several actions to help B.E. expand into new markets. "The first step is to reconsider the timeline for expansion and map out more detailed stages," she said. "We want to land and expand well, but to do so we will need to create an outline of the market conditions, our competitors, and unique challenges to that area."

"Good thinking, Jackie," said Todd. "Those ideas are definitely worth taking."

After fifteen minutes I called for attention. "Well done, all! Now we are going to do the exact same thing, except in new groups. Look around the room and find two people with whom you normally do not work with. These people are going to be your new group members. Another fifteen minutes for sharing your action points and, most importantly, stealing the best ones for yourself! Go ahead!"

As people began sharing their ideas during this second round, I noticed that the actions they shared were more developed and detailed in comparison to how they were during the first round of idea-stealing.

Todd had already added on some new details to the ideas he had taken from Jackie just a few moments earlier, and I watched as he explained it.

"When we enter a new market we will need to first do our due diligence in 4 key areas: competitors and pricing, alternative solutions, legislative issues, and additional factors, like any cultural or geopolitical issues that would call for a different approach to entry than what we normally do."

"Wow Todd, where were these ideas and details four months ago?", exclaimed an obviously impressed Robin.

After another round of group discussion, I told people to find two colleagues for a final round of discussion and stealing with pride. During these fifteen minutes I noticed the continued development of the actions—they were more focused and sharper still. Five more minutes passed, and it was time to proceed.

"Thank you, everyone. Fantastic job. I think that you are ready for the next step, based on the great actions that I heard during your stealing session. Stay in your current groups. I am going to pass out some jumbo Post-it notes to each group. Your job is to decide within your groups what the best actions are, and then write them on to the Post-it notes. One action per note and make sure to include the important details: *who, what,* and *when*. If you write someone else's name, make sure they agree first. Once your Post-it notes are ready, put them on this roadmap with a timeline behind me," I said, as I pointed to the flipchart on the wall behind me.

What can we make better?

Once the roadmap was covered in Post-its, it was time to restart individual thinking with some stealing in small groups. "Take a moment to look at the roadmap and appreciate your own work. You have some great actions there, thanks to some expert stealing. Just think for a moment; are these actions the best that they can possibly be? Could they be improved in any way? Do we have the right people responsible for the actions? Is the timing, right? Reflect on those questions individually for a few moments and write down your new and improved actions, if you can think of any."

Who: Simon **What:** Organise cross team collaboration sessions to brief sales team **When:** next week	**Who:** Jackie **What:** Use new onboarding process (longer) **When:** Beginning Q2	**Who:** Jackie **What:** Fill PR Team liaison position **When:** 3–6 months	**Who:** Simon/ Everyone **What:** Plan and attend review workshop **When:** Beginning Q4
Who: Jackie **What:** Outline P.R. Team liaison position **When:** 2 weeks	**Who:** Marcus, Hans **What:** Refine and begin using flex pricing **When:** Q2		**Who:** Hans, Simon **What:** Review flex pricing performance **When:** End financial year
Who: Todd **What:** Design and demonstrate new market research process **When:** 1 month	**Who:** Bruce, Mary, Angie, Hans **What:** Transition to new performance review system **When:** Q2		**Who:** Simon/ Jackie, Hans **What:** Review new performance review system **When:** End Q4
Q1	Q2	Q3	Q4

It took some time for people to make improvements on the already-solid actions, but after a few moments some began writing. "Now that you have written down some changes to the actions, we are going to steal again. I am not trying to corrupt you or get you to abandon any moral code—it's just that it was so successful the first time that we need to try it again. So once again, your mission is to get into groups of three and share your ideas, listen to others, and steal the best of the bunch. I will pass out the Post-it notes again so that you can make any changes and post the new ideas on to the roadmap. Once you are done, you can sit back and read the roadmap and all of the new actions silently to yourself."

Ending with a nice talk...thanks to a stick?

"Great work. As you can see, we have a full roadmap in front of us. It looks to me that you all have managed to map out a busy and productive future, congratulations!"

"Thanks, Pepe," said Omar, one of B.E.'s managers. "We appreciate your help here and guiding us in the workshop, thanks again."

People began to thank me and begin to gather their things, thinking that now that the roadmap was done, so were they.

"Woah, woah, woah! Thank you for the kind words, but I am not done just yet. I have one final tool that I need to show all of you, perhaps the most valuable tool that I use."

This dramatic introduction got their attention, so I seized the moment, reached down into my briefcase, and pulled out the tool that I was referring to: a large, ugly stick.

"As you all can see, I have a stick here in my hand. But this is not just any ordinary stick, this stick talks...with your help of course. This is called a talking stick, and it is a Native American tradition. I have heard that during their tribal meetings, anyone could talk, no matter what their age or rank. The catch was that they had to be holding the talking stick to have permission to talk. Once they had the stick, they could talk for as long as they wanted, and when they were finished, someone else reached for the stick and the discussion continued that way. This was a highly successful method that they used, and we also are going to use it. Now this stick is coming to you and you will have a chance to give us feedback."

Jackie was the first to take the stick. "I really like the roadmap and it will be helpful. But are we supposed to keep it set up in this room for the months ahead?"

Taking the stick from Jackie, I replied that I would be taking a photo of the roadmap and emailing to everyone after the workshop.

Hans, a member of the Sales Team, took the stick and mentioned that the workshop was great, and that he also had some unfinished business to take care of. I was not sure what he meant until I saw him stand up with a group of five others and form a line. It was time for them to finish the floorball games that they started at the beginning of the workshop, and who was I to argue with them?

Analysis

Brilliancy Electronics workshop schedule
- One and a half day session

CLARIFYING	SOLUTIONS	SOLUTIONS CONTINUE
• Three hours long including a 15-minute break • Give an hour lunch break before next stage	• Four hours long including a 15-minute break • End of day 1	• One and a half hours long

ACTION
• Two hours long including a 15-minute break

Check-in

I used an active energiser called Floorball to warm the group up. The point in using this activity is to get everyone moving and engaged. This session was towards the end of a one-day and a half long workshop. After hours of different activities that are much different than a normal day's work, I find that people sometimes slow down or lose focus towards the end of a session. Floorball is a fun way to get everyone energised and focused. Depending on time and group size, you can run the activity a number of different ways; a single match between two teams if the group is small and time is short, or you can create a tournament with this game. For example, ask different tables of people to form teams and give themselves a team name. The games start in the morning. Then after lunch there is another round of games, and at the end of the day you can run the championship game and award funny prizes to all the teams.

Floorball

Materials needed: clear space, a soft ball (foam or rubber ball works well)

- Have everyone stand up.
- Divide the group into two equal lines that are facing each other. Everyone must stand with their feet shoulder-width apart.
- The space between each person's feet serves as the goal area. Teams can pass the ball to each other and try and throw the ball into the goal (between the other team's feet).
- People can defend by moving their hands, but the feet are planted and cannot be moved.

Emergence

This portion of the workshop was based around a tool that is close to my heart—Idealogue*. With the help of some colleagues of mine, I created Idealogue as an alternative to traditional brainstorming methods, which I found were limited in creating group understanding and alignment.

The history of how Idealogue came to pass is a simple one; when I was facilitating creativity sessions, I was having a difficult time creating group alignment. More specifically, I saw again and again that people loved to share their own ideas, but really had a hard time listening to other people's ideas. Idealogue's simple core rule of *steal with pride* solves this. First off, when people are tasked with collecting the best ideas from around the room, they are forced to listen to other ideas and understand the reasoning behind them. This keeps them in the important and sometimes elusive emergent zone.

---

*   www.idealoguemethod.com

Idealogue is made up of five steps: *Individual, Steal with Pride, Repeated Stealing, Idea Selection,* and *Idea Evaluation.* The order of the steps always stays the same, but the amount of time spent on each step can change, depending on the size of the group and the complexity of the topics being discussed.

Step 1: Individual

The amount of time given for this step depends on the complexity and number of potential ideas. If I am leading an actioning session where people are expected to think of specific tasks related to a simple process, then one or two minutes of time for the individual step is enough. If I am conducting a creativity session where ideas are more abstract and complex, around 5-10 minutes is fine. And sometimes even more time is needed for this step, like when people are asked to try to explain and map out their own logic.

Step 2: Steal with Pride

In this step the leader introduces the ground rule, *steal with pride,* and places people into small groups. The ground rule *steal with pride* gives permission to take other people's ideas. I typically explain that this would involve participants explaining their ideas, inquiring about the ideas of others, and then developing ideas together. In the small group discussions, the ideas lose ownership and become common property of the group. This begins to create group consensus. I've been asked more than once if this ground rule could be worded more softly because participants might resist the notion of stealing. For some, the world steal has strong, negative connotations. People are taught from a young age not to steal, and some of us may have heard a story about a person who lost their job or ruined their career due to theft-related reasons. In the ground rule of Idealogue, the word steal can be replaced with something softer like *take* or *exchange* if need be, but I have to say that "exchange ideas with pride" does not have the same ring to it.

A key instruction I give to the group during this step is to *collect the best ideas on your own piece of paper.* This is the very core of the method and relates directly to the ground rule *steal with pride.* If I asked the participants to share, that would be a group task without an individual objective. If at this step I asked the participants to agree on the best ideas, I would have a group arguing about what the best ideas are before they have had a chance to understand them.

Asking the group to collect the best ideas for themselves and on their own piece of paper makes it an individual task, and it makes each participant personally responsible to fulfil it. It has a clear goal and is motivating. Also, there is no need to argue about the best solutions. If you find something that you consider to be a good idea you write it on your own paper, then you simply move on to the next idea.

The method shines because it is impossible to write down other people's ideas without first understanding them. When people ask the important question "why?", they are forced to think about the ideas in broader contexts and on a deeper level.

The etymology of Idealogue

Dialogue = dia + logos (Greek) = through meaning

Idealogue = idea + dialogue = conversation to discover through meaning of ideas

When I divide people into small groups, I instruct them simply to form groups of three. Why groups of three? Sometimes pair discussion just does not work. Based on my long experience working with groups around the world, I have seen people working in pairs struggle to maintain conversation. On the other hand, when you have more than three participants, the silent ones tend to drop out of conversation and just fly under the radar. In groups of three you typically have enough diversity of ideas and shy or quiet people feel comfortable enough to participate without feeling overwhelmed. In most cases you can't have only groups of three because the number of participants cannot be divided by three. In that case you may have some groups of two or four.

The amount of time spent on this step depends on the complexity of the session's context. A typical round of stealing takes about ten to fifteen minutes. However, I have held creativity sessions where technical experts were sharing and discussing ideas for almost two hours in groups of three until we formed new groups to repeat the stealing process.

Step 3: Repeated Stealing

New groups of three are formed and the ideas are further developed.

The simplest way of forming new groups is just to tell the participants to stand up and quickly find two new people to form a group with.

Why do we repeat the stealing step again in different small groups? It is repeated to further promote the exchange and comprehension of ideas. The first group of three now has a good understanding of each other's ideas and probably even a common understanding of the best ideas. But they don't understand what else is happening in the room, so you must connect the first group with the other two groups, too.

Idealogue is a strong consensus-creating method. The more times people form new groups to share, the better understanding you create within the whole group. I sometimes joke that you need to keep changing groups and having people share again and again until the point of exhaustion, so that they are tired and will agree with just about anything! In practice I don't try to tire the group out quite that much, and I typically have three to four rounds of sharing in small groups. Anything past this and we reach a point of diminishing returns; the energy starts going down as people get a little tired of talking, thinking, and developing each other's ideas.

If the first round of sharing takes ten minutes, you should give a bit more time for the subsequent rounds. This is because after each round of sharing, people have more to talk about due to the ideas that they have stolen from others. On average about ten to fifteen minutes per round should be fine.

Often I place an individual round of idea development between each round of stealing. In between stealing sessions, I tell the group something like this: "Now take a careful look at your precious list of ideas, develop them and create new ones. You have four minutes."

I am just a strong believer in giving people an opportunity to think. We do not think enough! Well, at least I don't.

Convergence

Step 4: Ideas Selection

People remain in small groups and select the best ideas. Once a group has agreed on what they are, they post them at the front of the room so everyone can see what they came up with. The previous steps had an individual focus; to collect best ideas on your own piece of paper. Now the participants should seek agreement and consensus, which should come relatively easy after rounds of stealing and creating understanding of the logic behind ideas.

The number of chosen ideas is not limited. You can't ask participants to post a specific number of ideas; it is crucial that they are not limited at all during this step by such requirements. What if the group has five excellent ideas, or just one? Instead of forcing the group to agree on a certain number, I ask them to simply post the best ones. However, not every idea can be considered the best, so groups will need to choose their favourites.

Step 5: Ideas Evaluation

This is where the group leader makes sure that the entire group understands the posted ideas by giving time for questions as needed. Once the ideas are understood, the group can evaluate them together.

Interestingly, the participants do not need to present the ideas they posted with their small groups because a shared understanding of these ideas already exists on a group level. The repetition of group formation in the previous steps has guaranteed increased and inquisitive dialogue, which contributes towards everyone understanding the content they talked about. The person most likely wanting further clarification would be the one person who did not participate in these conversations, the group leader. At this point it is enough to ask the group to read all ideas in silence and if some of the ideas are not understood to ask other participants to elaborate and reply to any questions.

Many facilitators and experienced leaders like to group ideas while the group evaluates them. Grouping or organising the ideas beyond this point is not needed. I am an enemy of grouping ideas, and I will explain why by using the topic of what to have for dinner as an example.

Pretend that you are trying to decide what to have for dinner. Your friends have suggested salmon, beef, perch, lamb, pork, and cod. Now you group the different suggestions as meat and fish. This will not help decision making at all. When you group ideas, you lose the real content, and it makes decision making more difficult. When defining a problem, grouping can even be dangerous. You group the problem, and it becomes something else and you cannot see the real problem anymore. Grouping ideas also can be difficult due to people trying to group things that do not really belong together, which can lead to unnecessary arguing.

Now it is crucial to evaluate the results. For instance, if you are clarifying the problem, you ask the group: "do we have the problem here?" If you are creating a common vision, you inquire whether the group feels that the vision is common. If you have created new ideas, you ask whether the ideas meet the goals of the creativity session. And if you have created an action plan, you want to make sure the actions cover all the solutions you have agreed on before actioning. But what if the group is not happy with all ideas? Then you ask for new ones. For instance, you may have one more round of small group work in groups of three, with the discussion topic being how to improve the results of the session.

In the session with B.E., once ideas had been created and posted to the roadmap, another round of developing in groups of three was given. First, people were asked to individually review the actions that were posted on to the roadmap. Next came idea development in groups of three, and finally all of the new actions were reviewed by the group as a whole. Groups of three worked the same during convergence as it did during emergence, with the difference being that during emergence people were focused on stealing ideas to develop new ones, and during convergence, ideas were discussed in groups with a focus on improving the actions.

A typical Idealogue session takes about an hour and a half and consists of an introduction and focusing for 15 minutes; the individual ideas phase for 5 minutes; stealing with pride in changing small groups for 45 minutes; choosing and posting the best ideas for 15 minutes, discussion for 10 minutes, one or two minutes to evaluate the results and get group feedback, and finally another minute or so to thank the group and end the session. The length of the session can vary depending on the number of participants and the topic. The longest

Idealogue session I have been a part of was a creativity session which lasted almost 6 hours!

Idealogue is perfect for groups ranging from 6 to 24 participants, although it can be used effectively with larger groups too. In very small groups you may have to use pairs instead of groups of three. Ideologue has been successfully used in groups of hundreds of participants. Even in a large group setting it will help people develop their ideas. However, in large groups building consensus becomes harder simply due to the number of connections that exist between participants. In a workshop, Idealogue can be used to clarify a problem or a goal, to share best practices, to create new ideas, and for action planning.

Steps of Idealogue

Step 1: Individual stage
Participants are asked to write down their ideas in silence.

Step 2: Steal with pride
- At this stage, the facilitator introduces the ground rules and groups of three participants are formed.
- Steal with Pride!
- Collect the best ideas on your own piece of paper.
- Share, listen, and develop ideas.

Step 3: Repeated stealing
New groups of three are formed and the second stage is repeated several times.

Step 4: Idea selection
At this stage, the participants remain in groups of three and select the best ideas.
- Choose the best ideas.
- Try to reach consensus.
- Write down best ideas on a piece of paper with a marker.
  (The number is not limited but just the best ideas can't be many)
- Just one idea per paper.
- When your group is ready post your ideas on the wall.

Step 5: Idea evaluation
The facilitator makes sure the group understands the posted ideas and the participants evaluate the results.

Why Idealogue in actioning sessions?

As people repeatedly share their action points in small groups, they gain confidence and new allies as sources of support are discovered. Furthermore, the actions are made real. By repeatedly sharing what you are going to do, you are internalising the action point, and are becoming more accountable for it. The same principle applies here. The action points are refined and further developed during the group sharing sessions as well. People may offer support or knowledge from an unexpected source, and it is common for people to realise that their action points overlap with those of another person, creating an ally.

This is a strong advantage of Idealogue; it works great as an idea creation tool, and also for idea selection. It may seem counter-intuitive at first—after all, the instructions to the method remain the same, to steal other ideas with pride. But you will find that when people share ideas (in this case their action points) with others in multiple rounds, the action points are stolen again and again and this process of repeated stealing works as a sort of prioritisation tool; the most effective and best ideas are stolen and then posted to the roadmap at the end of the activity.

Roadmap

I used Roadmap with Idealogue. The two tools are a great fit together. Idealogue requires a lot of talking and sharing in groups. Roadmap displays visually the actions in a logical way on a timeline for everyone to see. This appeals to those who like clarity and perhaps want some time to consider and develop actions and the complete action plan.

The road mapping activity makes the individual actions of everyone more concrete, and more likely to happen. If you have a personal goal, you can keep it to yourself and work very hard to achieve it. Maybe you will. But if you write your goal down, then you have a better chance of making it come true. And if you really want to make your goal come true, then write it down, share it with others, and display it in a public place. This is what the Roadmap activity effectively does.

Roadmap

It also contextualises the personal action points by placing them onto a timeline. Do they happen now, or will they happen in the future? The roadmap lets people decide.

Finally, the roadmap combines individual action points with those of others, creating a complete picture of what will be done. People can easily see what others will be doing, which separate action points can be combined and collaborated on, and which action points are dependent on others.

Check-out

I brought out my trusty talking stick for the check-out activity. I explained the history of the talking stick first; it is an old Native American custom that was used to grant the power to speak during tribal meetings. The backstory is not important though, and you can use a talking ball, talking cup of coffee, pen, anything you like. An engaging story works to help hold a group's attention, but the main purpose is to have people speak one at a time. After the participants speak, they pass the talking stick to the next person, and feedback is received from around the room. The designated object can be anything—I have used things ranging from markers to a plant with success.

This activity is normally a part of Open Space Technology and used to wrap up an Open Space-based workshop. I find that it works just as well on its own though, and I use it a lot to get feedback from larger groups—those who have something to say simply raise their hand to receive the talking stick.

Talking Stick

- This method borrows from an old Native American tradition and lets everyone share something about their experience or feelings regarding the meeting. Talking Stick isn't meant for giving long speeches or an individual's conclusions, but rather short comments about personal experience.

- Everyone gets to say something. In a smaller group the stick can move clock-wise from person to person. In a bigger group, the eager ones can start the discussion by saying something. You can use a small object like a microphone as the talking stick.

- The amount of time needed for implementing this tool depends on the number of participants, but you shouldn't use more than 30 minutes. It is good to plan your check-out to ensure that the energy level rises instead of drops. Try doing Talking Stick by standing in a circle.

What tools were used and why

- **Floorball**—Active energiser
- **Idealogue**—A tool for creating shared understanding and breakthroughs
- **Roadmap**—For visualising action points
- **Talking stick**—A tool to get group feedback at the end of the workshop

Workshop process: Action

Objective: To agree on concrete actions for the decisions/solutions
Time: 120 minutes

Check-in (15 minutes)
1. **Energiser:** Floor Ball
2. Presenting the objective of the stage and the workshop process.
3. "Is the objective of the next stage and way of working clear?" (Short discussion).

Emergence tools: Idealogue and Roadmap (70 minutes)

1. "I have posted the decisions on the wall. Look at the decisions you want to implement and individually write down actions for yourself on your piece of paper."
2. "Steal with pride! Try to get the best actions on your own piece of paper by stealing ideas from your colleagues in groups of three. Share, listen and develop."
3. "Steal with Pride!—but this time try to form groups of three with people you usually do not work with."
4. "Steal with Pride!—this time form a group of three with your closest colleagues."
5. "In the same group of three, choose best actions—the ones that need to be implemented—and write on jumbo Post-it notes and post on the roadmap on the appropriate place on the timeline."
6. "Read the action points in silence. Do you have questions about the actions?"

Convergence tool: Idealogue (20 minutes)

1. "Individually take a critical look on the actions. Is something missing or duplicated or overlapping? Do we have all right people responsible for the actions?"
2. "Steal with pride! In groups of three explain, listen, and develop."
3. "Now make your changes!"
4. "Read the action points in silence. Is everything clear?"

Check-out (15 minutes):

1. "I have a stick in my hand, but not just any stick! This stick talks... with your help of course. Talking Stick is an activity where a stick is passed around the room. Only the person holding the stick has the right to talk, and everyone else has to listen. Once they have said their piece, they pass the stick to whoever wants it next."
2. "Thank you!"

5.4: Problem-Solving Workshop Review

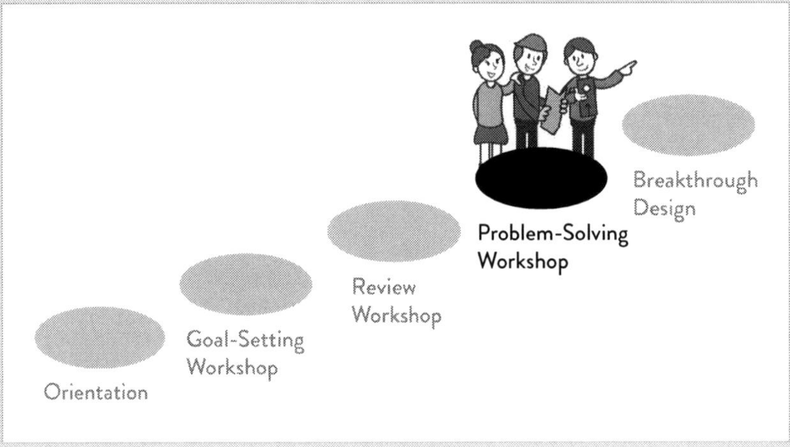

Problem-solving workshop

Brilliancy Electronics workshop schedule

- One and a half day session

CLARIFYING

- Three hours long including a 15-minute break
- Give an hour lunch break before next stage

SOLUTIONS

- Four hours long including a 15-minute break
- End of day 1

SOLUTIONS CONTINUE

- One and a half hours long

ACTION

- Two hours long including a 15-minute break

Chapter 5 covered the problem-solving workshop I had with Brilliancy Electronics (B.E.). B.E. was experiencing a period of rapid growth and change, and the theme of the workshop was *dealing with growth*. The entire workshop lasted around 10 hours and took place over two days. The aim of this workshop was to identify the real problems that B.E. was experiencing, find solutions to these problems, and then create specific actions that could be followed to enact the solutions. The environment was complex; the company was rapidly changing after years of stability and facing challenges that were completely new to them. To make things even more difficult, there were interpersonal conflicts between individual employees. The cause of the conflicts needed to be identified and then solved.

To deal with these multiple issues, I used a combination of workshop tools that I was most confident in. In fact, the combination of tools that I used in this workshop is my most common choice when I deal with complexity and there are strong emotions involved, like those we saw with Angie and Jackie and their disagreement. This workshop followed the 3-stage CSA workshop structure just like the other workshops we reviewed in previous chapters. The workshop began with clarifying challenges, then came identifying solutions, and finished with creating actions.

Brilliancy Electronics workshop tools

CLARIFYING	SOLUTIONS	ACTION
Tools	Tools	Tools
• Hello	• Six-Zero	• Idealogue
• Dynamic Facilitation	• Open Space Technology	• Roadmap
• Me/We/Us	• Consent Decision Making	• Floorball
• Me/We/We/Us	• Five Fingers	• Talking Stick
• Signature		

Clarifying

Time: Three hours
Objective: Discover current challenges

This workshop was my first experience with B.E. I was called in to help identify the important problems that the business was facing due to rapid growth. The issues identified in this stage of the workshop would carry over to be discussed in the later stages of the workshop. The issues were not clear cut; they were ambiguous and there were a lot of them. Therefore, I needed to use Dynamic Facilitation, which is a good for dealing with both emotions and complexity.

Solutions

Time: 5 hours
Objective: Find solutions to current challenges

This was the second stage of my workshop with B.E. We continued working with the problems identified during the *clarifying* stage and began to create solutions to these problems. People had lots of different ideas about what issues they wanted to solve and how to solve them, so I gave the group as much freedom as I could by using Open Space Technology, which lets people self-organise. By the end of this stage we had proposals outlining what needed to be addressed to solve the current challenges the organisation was facing.

Action

Time: Two hours
Objective: Make and commit to actions to achieve the identified solutions

The final stage of the problem-solving workshop has the objective of agreeing on the concrete actions that need to be taken in order to realise the solutions that were created previously. The final product of the workshop is a roadmap with the actions placed, eliminating any doubt or uncertainty about what is going to be done. With this map to success, all that is left is to execute the actions and regularly check in on progress by referring back to the roadmap, which should be kept and displayed in the office or distributed digitally within the group.

Leading the workshop

Before we can come up with great solutions, we need to deal with emotions and clarify the daunting problems. The workshop with Brilliancy Electronics dealt with two different types of problems: a personal disagreement between two members of the team, and the growing pains experienced throughout the company as Brilliancy Electronics rapidly expanded. First off, there was an emotionally charged disagreement between people. These types of interpersonal issues rarely just affect the two parties directly involved because the energy between the two arguing people usually spills over to negatively impact the rest of the team. In order to get the team ready to perform at its best, this issue needed to be fixed right away. Then there were the larger problems that the whole company was facing. The rapid growth was causing challenges that Brilliancy Electronics had never had to deal with previously. It was new territory for everyone, and there was more uncertainty than enthusiasm.

In this workshop I chose from the best group tools in the world, and selected those tools that I was most confident in using. By the end of the workshop, the interpersonal issue was resolved and there were solutions and actions in place for everyone. As you use the tools demonstrated in this book, you will find that you like some better than others. Perhaps a specific tool fits your leadership style well, or maybe you understand the purpose behind a certain tool better than the others, making it your favourite. I could have created a different workshop structure with other tools that would have worked too, but I would not have been as confident or comfortable, so I chose my favourites. You should too. If you need to lead a workshop to deal with something particularly difficult, or if you are just starting your journey helping groups with decision making, then use the tools that you know and have confidence in using.

When to use a problem-solving workshop

- Creating a project plan or defining project goals
- Creating a strategic goal or project goals (in this case your title is "Our goal" and you summarise the discussion with listing the goals)
- Creating values (again your title is "Our values" and you summarise by listing the values)
- Clarifying mission or purpose
- Developing customer experience
- Developing co-operation
- Dealing with interpersonal or group conflict (we use this method in my company to deal with interpersonal conflict)
- Process development (for finding the pain points)
- After presentations for discussing practical implications
- Change implementation
- Team Development
- Problem solving

CHAPTER 6:
CSA Method for Workshop Design

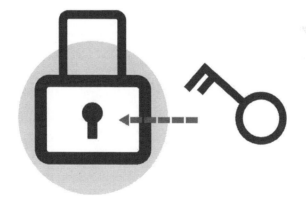

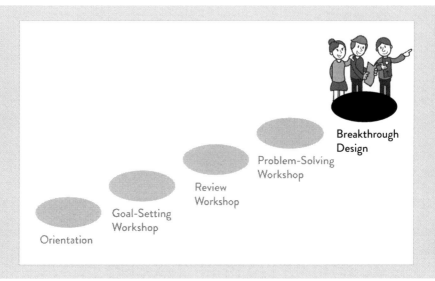

What's here

- CSA workshop structure defined
- Identifying which workshop stages to use
- Matching the right tools within a workshop for emergence and convergence
- Adding supplementary tools to begin, energise and end a workshop

How it helps

Building effective workshops is a necessary skill for group leaders. Workshop design goes beyond tool selection. In this chapter I lay out how to create practical and engaging workshops.

Workshop design for breakthrough decision making

Breakthrough decision making and the associated tools are versatile, and they have served me well in situations ranging from boardroom meetings in billion-dollar companies to small church committees.

As a group leader, you are tasked with tailoring your methods to fit whichever situation you find yourself in. Different topics and attendees will create unique environments for you to navigate, but almost every situation will have at least one thing in common; you will be leading a group through a workshop you designed.

Put simply, a workshop is an intensive meeting that is dedicated to a specific topic. Workshops are normally a bit longer than standard meetings and can range from a single session of a few hours to an extensive multi-day event. When I meet with new clients, I need to first identify the deliverables—what do they want me to provide? Conflict resolution? Change deployment? Group consensus? Once I understand what they want, I must figure out if I am helping clarify a problem or a goal.

Once this is established, I need to determine how to structure the workshop and decide which tools to use to best meet the client's needs. I also need to come prepared with tools to begin sessions and be equipped to energise the group throughout the workshop and to its end.

Designing a workshop

1. Understand the desired outcome
2. Choose the stages and understand whether you are clarifying a problem or a goal

CLARIFYING	SOLUTIONS	ACTION

3. Choose the core tools for each stage
4. Add additional beginning, energising and ending tools
5. Check the schedule

Does this sound bit confusing? Well, to be honest, it can be. Designing a workshop from scratch is much more advanced than using tools individually, and it is a constant learning process that is never finished.

I have been facilitating well over twenty years, and I still have a-ha! moments where I realise how tools can be tweaked and combined for better results. The arrival of new online technologies has also opened the door for change, and the possibility of virtual workshops have brought in new tools, benefits, and challenges that are developing and unfolding right behind the technology that drives it. To make it easier, thankfully there are core elements that always must be considered when designing workshops:

1. **Identify the key deliverables**
2. **Identify the appropriate workshop stages to use**
3. **Choose the core tools for emergence and convergence**
4. **Add tools for beginning, energising, and ending**
5. **Check the timing**

When you are familiar with these concepts and can apply them yourself, you will be well on your way to creating world class workshops.

Identify the key deliverables

The essential first step towards designing a successful workshop is figuring out the answer to the following question: *What is the point of this workshop?* When I began leading groups, I realised early on that the answer to this question is not always straightforward. In fact, discovering what the client really wants is the most challenging part of designing workshops. Your client may think they know what they want, and they will tell you confidently that they want you to solve some conflicts, perhaps implement a few solutions and give their employees the chance to air feelings and doubts, but this list of wants does not help. If you were to listen to every surface-level wish of the client and incorporate them into your workshops, the structure would be confusing and unfocused. Instead, your aim as the group leader is to focus on one primary goal for the workshop and then give space and opportunity for workshop participants to decide for themselves how to reach that goal. This is what identifying the key deliverables means, and it is the indispensable beginning to every workshop.

Of course, you will encounter clients that want more control. Maybe they already have firmly in mind what they want their employees to do and they crave control and a predictable outcome above all else. If this is the case, a participatory workshop is not needed. Instead, your job could be to help participants understand and agree to this course of action that management has decided on taking.

Questions to define the key deliverables

- What is the desired outcome of this workshop?
- What do you hope to achieve?
- What problem or issue does this workshop address?
- Do you have a decision that you want to implement or do you want the group to decide?
- What are your existing concerns that require a workshop?

Once I have discussed with the client what they hope to achieve with the workshop and what high-level problems or challenges it addresses, I have a much better idea about the situation and how to best approach it.[*]

What it looks like: My friend Mike complains about millions of small details that are wrong with his production facility. After hearing him out, we come up with the objective of a workshop: improve production efficiency.

---

[*] In my experience, the client soliciting the workshop is usually a person with decision-making power. They can answer questions about their goals or what they hope to achieve with the workshop. However, sometimes an assistant or lower-level employee will be tasked with setting up the workshop, and you will need to find a way to prepare and ask the questions to the right person.

Identify the appropriate workshop stages to use

When I plan a workshop, I use the 3-stage structure of CSA, which stands for Clarifying, Solutions, Action.[*] The clarifying stage is where a group determines where their focus should be and what questions need to be answered. The solutions stage is finding alternatives and answers to these questions, and the action stage is where concrete actions are outlined and committed to.

People tend to think in solutions. I remember a session I facilitated with a publishing company in Finland that illustrates how different solutions lead into conflicts. It was a small workshop for only a handful of managerial types. About a week or two before the session was set to begin, an invitation was sent to all the participants inviting them to a workshop to create a new strategy. When it began, half of the room had already made up their minds that the right solution would be domestic expansion, while the other half of the room was sold on the idea of entering the largely untapped Chinese market. It was obvious to me that these eager participants had already reflected on the goal themselves and decided what the best solution was. They argued in circles about what the best course of action would be. The *domestic expansion* proponents insisted that it would be a quicker timeline for the expansion, and the *Chinese Market* believers were saying that they should "go big or go home" and that the real money was in the Asian markets. To resolve this, I brought everyone back to the beginning by asking, "What is it that you all really want?" Once everyone had the chance to answer, the room realised that there was a shared goal: sustainable business growth. We were able to use this as a point of departure to think of solutions and actions, and a third option was eventually decided on—expansion into other EU countries where the existing contacts and distribution channels could be used for maximum effectiveness.

---

[*] CSA is summarised in more detail in Chapter 2: Cornerstones of Breakthrough Decision Making.

The 3 parts to a workshop: CSA structure

CLARIFYING	SOLUTIONS	ACTION

The flow is always the same—as a group leader you need to decide whether to clarify the problem or the goal.

People don't just think in terms of solutions, they also have the tendency to argue about solutions, too. Therefore, it is necessary to take one step back and clarify the goal or the problem. This is the key question; are you clarifying a goal or a problem? The answer is situational. You will need to assess each case as it comes and have some candid discussions with the client before the workshop even begins. But there are some guidelines which you can follow to make the determination a bit easier:

- If long-term development is the topic, you should be clarifying a goal.
- If an obstacle stands in the way of your goals or if there is any urgent issue that needs immediate resolution, then you should clarify a problem.

For instance, if we need to plan a new project, we first clarify the goals of the project. If the project runs into trouble or needs to be reviewed, we clarify the problems that stand in the way of achieving the project goals.

There is a third option that is relatively common. Some sessions come with a goal being handed down from the board or management to the rest of the company. In this case, the goal is already defined. The session can begin with the group leader making sure everyone is on the same page with the same understanding and definition of the goal. Once the goal is understood, the solutions and the subsequent actions would be created. These workshops are called implementation workshops and they are often related to implementing new strategies, projects, technologies, or ways of working.

> **Implementation Workshop Structure**
> 1. Communicating the Goals
> 2. Solutions
> 3. Action

Some people decide that they want to try and clarify both a goal and a problem in the same workshop. They attempt this by having two clarifying stages, a solutions stage, and then an action stage: a CCSA structure for the workshop. Their thoroughness is admirable, but I find that this is challenging to do in practice. Let's use a personal goal of mine as an example: to be happy. If I participate in a session designed to clarify goals, I will arrive at this goal of happiness. If I spend time clarifying my problems later on, one reoccurring problem of mine that could come up is lack of time. These two topics, seeking happiness and lack of time, share some solutions in common. For example, I could reduce my workload, which would both give me more time and make me happier. In this sense, the results of clarifying goals and problems are often related. If you clarify both the problem and a goal you will often get many overlapping topics; the same issues and discussion points appearing again and again on different levels.

> **What it looks like:** Mike is excited about the workshop to improve production efficiency, and I agree to lead it. I will use the 3-stage structure of Clarifying, Solutions, and Action. I will begin by clarifying a problem because Mike wants to fix the existing production process, not create a new one. If Mike wanted a new production process, then I would start by clarifying a goal.

Choosing questions for CSA stages

Questions for clarifying the goal

Asking for the goal
- "What is our project goal? List ideas!"

Expanding the list of goals created
- "Look at the list of goals you created. Ask yourself why these goals are important, and write more goals!"

Wishing
- "Thinking about the future of our department, list wishes. I wish..."
- "Thinking about our company, finish the sentence: It would be great if..."

Negative Brainstorming
- "List the worst things that could happen to our team. Now, think about what our team goal is and list ideas!"

Question for choosing the goal should have both *who* and *when*
- "Choose the goals you want to achieve in the next 6 months."

First, I choose the questions for the clarifying stage. The choice of my question depends on whether I am clarifying a problem or a goal.

To clarify goals, I sometimes just ask, "What is the goal?" Creative goal-setting activities like Negative Brainstorming are also useful. Negative Brainstorming requires participants to list undesired outcomes first. Interestingly, listing what you do not want helps people understand what they really want. Another opportunity to help a group further clarify their goals is to ask them to expand on their reasoning. After everyone has listed goals, I sometimes ask why these goals are important. This question brings out deeper motivations related to the goal. This creates new goals which are often more important than the original goals. For example, a goal of mine is to make lots of money. Why is this important to me? Because I want to feel more secure about my family's future. Feeling secure about my family's future is the new goal which is far more important than simply making money.

My favourite goal-setting activity is Wishing. When people wish for something, they connect their wants with their emotional desires. In other words, they put aside logical thinking for a while and think with their heart.

The instructions for choosing the goals matter, too. Asking someone to think of the "best goal" can feel a bit broad. Be more specific and include a timeframe and who the goal is for. For example, instead of saying, "Please choose the best goals.", you can ask, "Choose which goals your team should accomplish within the next 6 months."

Questions for clarifying the problem

Asking for the problem
- "What are our production problems? List ideas!"

Expanding the list of problems created
- "Look at the problems you listed. Ask yourself why we have these problems and write more. You may ask why many times to see how deep into the issue you can get."

Force Field Analysis
- "List successes and challenges."
- "List benefits and challenges" (if there is no practical experience).

Question for choosing the problem should have both *who* and *when*
- "choose the challenge you want to solve today."

To identify what specific problem a group is facing, I sometimes just use the simple question, "What is the problem you are facing currently?" At the very least, this can open conversations about what the issue is, and get people thinking about the problems they are struggling with. Problems tend to be multi-layered and complex. A way to help individuals find the problem is to first guide them into a deep analysis of what their true challenges are. An example: I am always traveling, and I would say that I take close to 50 flights a year. This means that I am always fighting jet lag, and always missing my family. On top of that, I am also living out of hotels most of the time, and not eating and exercising like I want to. Why? Because my home is in Europe but most of my work is in Asia. Why? Because I live with my old father and he does not want to move to Asia. Why is my father holding me in Europe? Because I feel responsible. Why? I am not sure... my dad is just a great guy who has taken good care of me.

We can already see a few different problems that are caused by my constant traveling. But which ones to solve, and how? Root cause analysis helps us focus on the right problems instead of the superficial symptoms of a problem. Some of the most common tools I use for exploring problems deeper are 5 Whys and the Current Reality Tree. Sometimes I will use a simpler tool like Force Field Analysis to identify the problems. Force Field Analysis asks the group what is going well, and what is not working. It gives a balanced picture of the situation by calling attention to the accomplishments and achievements that have been reached so far. I think that this is very important because if you spend most of the time working with what needs to be changed, it makes it easy to forget all of the hard work and positive results of the past.

To help the group make a choice about which problems need solving, I might ask, "Which problem do you need to solve today?" I make sure to ask the group to be specific and include *who* and *when* along with the problem. Most people, even very responsible people, tend to externalise problems and fall into the trap of choosing problems for other people to solve. You can force people to resist this tendency by asking them to choose challenges they need to solve themselves.

Instructions for each part of CSA

CLARIFYING	SOLUTIONS	ACTION
Clarifying a goal: • What are our goals? • Which goals should we reach in next three years? **Clarifying a problem:** • What is our problem? • Which problem should we solve today?	• What are the solutions? • Which solutions do we want to implement?	• What do I do? Which actions do we need to develop and how?

To find solutions, I first ask the group what they think the solutions are. Creative tools can be used to dig deeper, just like other parts of the workshop. For example, asking the group to list obstacles first frees up thinking and helps people create stronger solutions. *Benchmarking* is thinking what industry leaders would do and is an effective tool for creating better solutions. When it comes time to choose solutions, I ask the group to choose the solutions that they want to implement. When you ask people directly what they want to implement, they cannot externalise the solutions to others or think of them in a broad way.

During the action stage, the solutions are split into concrete personal steps. The action stage scales back to one key question, like the clarifying stage. The key question here is, "What am I going to do?" If you have asked for personal actions in the beginning, you normally do not need to prioritise actions. Participants have committed to actions that they deem important and you will most likely have the correct amount, but even with commitment and the correct quantity of actions taken care of, the work is not done. The actions need to be fine-tuned even further, which is what convergence is for. Perhaps the correct people are not entirely committed, or the timing is a bit off. Instead of prioritising, I ask the group what can be developed and refined.

Actioning is hard work, and there are some challenges that routinely come up. People leading groups often do not ask for personal actions, instead they brainstorm actions for others. As a result, you have dozens of great actions, but when it comes time for people to volunteer to see specific actions through, no one says a word. After hours of creating this content, no one wants to commit to it!

Another common challenge is the group leader asking for participants to nominate other people to take ownership over a specific action, which can possibly create action points that no one is committed to. This can be a natural occurrence that comes from the tendency to deflect blame and look for the problem (and solutions) outside of one's self. I have seen too many action plans where human resources, the boss, or the administration are outlined as being responsible for this or that, but when I follow up with the people or departments identified and check to see if they are committed, I do not get a positive answer.

To fight the tendency of creating actions outside your zone of effectiveness, I ask for people to think of individual actions first. By forcing people to think of individual actions first, you lean into the hardest part of actioning: commitment. If it is necessary to involve another person who is not in the room into the action too, you can create another individual action point that evolves around speaking to the other person and convincing them to help.

> **What it looks like**: Since Mike's workshop is about **clarifying** a problem, I will begin by asking the group what is stopping them from being efficient. After hearing their responses, I will ask which challenge they want to solve today. To discover **solutions**, I will simply ask them directly what solutions they can think of to solve this challenge, and which ones they want to implement. For the **action** stage, I will ask each participant what they are going to do. After visualising the action points and identifying the who, what, and when, I ask everyone to review the actions and improve them.

Choosing tools for emergence and convergence

After determining if you are clarifying a problem or a goal and setting the workshop stages, you continue to build the workshop by selecting your primary tools. There are many tools to choose from, so where do you begin? We can make things a bit simpler by categorising workshop tools into three different types; **basic tools**, **communication tools**, and **tools that deal with complexity**.

Basic tools are used when the situation is straightforward—one key question or topic, and a group of participants that are neutral to change and to each other. These tools are most often used during the clarifying stage of a workshop where there is one question/goal to clarify.

Communication tools take things a bit further and force participants into the emergent zone, where the logic and framework behind other ideas are analysed. Idealogue and Bus Stop are two examples.

Tools that deal with complexity are those that help understand complicated situations or social conflicts. Think about Dynamic Facilitation, where the entire group shares their thoughts and concerns while the group leader simply records the results. Some of these tools can handle multiple key questions simultaneously, and they are open-ended without many rules. Think about the Open Space method where people can come and go to topical meetings as they see fit.

TOOLS FOR THE CLARIFYING STAGE

Emergence

Emergent tools for dealing with one question

Basic tools
- Listing

Tools for better communication
- Me/We/Us
- Idealogue

Tools for dealing with emotions and conflict
- Dynamic Facilitation

After choosing my questions, I choose my tool for creating ideas. You do not have many questions at the clarifying stage, and the key tool for emergence will be one created for one question*, and you will make your choice based on how much communication is needed for

---

* An attentive reader might say that Force Field Analysis always has two questions: supporting and restraining forces. If this is the case, then how can I use a tool for one question for doing the analysis? It seems to work because there is only one theme that is analysed and both positives and negatives are related to that theme. If the questions were not interrelated, a tool made for dealing with several questions would work better.

that specific topic. Sometimes, not much communication needs to be created—it can be a challenge that everyone is already aware of or something that is straightforward and easily understood. In this case, it is enough to take a piece of flipchart paper and write down the challenges. If the topic needs explaining and reflection for the true picture to emerge, you may use Me/We/Us or Idealogue for even deeper communication. However, as a professional facilitator, I am most likely to be invited to conduct a workshop when there is a conflict, complexity and emotions are involved. When this is the case, I choose Dynamic Facilitation, which happens to be my favourite tool.

Methods for visualising priorities

- Stickers/markers
- Participants sign their name next to ideas they find interesting/ want to commit to
- Traffic lights (include=green, maybe=yellow, exclude=red): Keep the green and yellow ideas
- Investment Activity: Each participant is given $15 that they can invest into the ideas they like
- Voting with legs: Move towards the preferred option, line, coordinates
- Raise your hands to show support
- Drawing dragons (or any symbol) next to ideas that are supported

Each stage of a workshop will need to balance emergence and convergence. This means that tools for aligning priorities and visualising priorities are also needed. Most would choose a voting tool that visualises results, like Dot Voting. This is a sound choice for visualization, and you do need to decide how to visualise priorities, but voting alone does not create group alignment. It will only show the opinions of participants at a specific time. If no tools for aligning priorities are used, then the logic behind ideas is not understood, which means that the job is not done. When a workshop ends, everyone should understand the logic behind the ideas that were selected, even if they do not agree with ideas themselves.

It may sound strange, but the key tools used for convergence and group alignment are mostly the same as the tools that I use to help groups create ideas. I even choose them the same way, by determining how much time I need to spend nurturing communication within the group. First, I let everyone determine what their own priorities are after they review all the options created by the group. Then, I let them discuss and prioritise further in small groups. If I want more alignment, I mix the groups into new small groups for further refinement of ideas until all the priorities are clear. Remember, discussion in small groups will bring consensus, especially after repeated discussion.

Finally, I evaluate the results with the entire group to make sure that the decision-making process was a success.

What it looks like: For the first clarifying stage of Mike's workshop I used Idealogue for the emergence part of the workshop. Mike said his employees have a history of blaming each other, so I wanted everyone to have a good talk and figure out what the real problems were. I chose Me/We/Us for convergence; it is a good communication tool for choosing key problems. For visualising group priorities, I asked people to sign their names next to the key problems that they are committed to solving.

TOOLS FOR THE SOLUTIONS STAGE

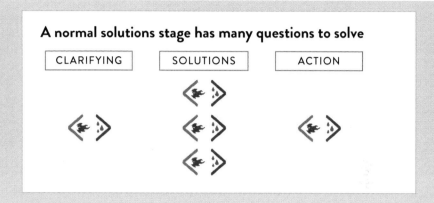

A normal solutions stage has many questions to solve

| CLARIFYING | SOLUTIONS | ACTION |

Emergence

The second part of a workshop is the *solutions* stage. This is where ideas and alternatives are thought of, and then the best ones are selected to be solved in the action stage of the workshop. The solutions stage is structured similarly to the clarifying stage; emergent and convergent tools are used to first elicit ideas from the group and then get people to agree on the best ones.

In my decades of experience leading workshops and helping people make decisions, I have noticed that it is extremely difficult for people to think of just one problem or goal. Perhaps we humans are blessed with entirely too much creativity. This tendency to produce many problems or goals means that the solutions stage is a bit different in that there are many questions in play simultaneously, and a few rounds of ideating, discussing, polling, group voting, or other prioritisation are required. Most likely participants will identify 3 to 5 key common questions. With this many questions you will need to select a tool that can deal with multiple questions simultaneously; World Café, Bus Stop, and Open Space are natural choices to use. On the other hand, Idealogue (a great tool to explore one topic in-depth) would not work during this stage of the workshop.

Emergent tools for multiple simultaneous questions

Tools for discovering participant knowledge
- Gallery walk

Tools for better communication
- Bus Stop
- Café

Tools for dealing with expert questions and complexity
- Open Space Technology

Again, you will make your choice based on how much communication is needed for the specific topic being discussed. The fastest way to collect information is a tool called gallery walk—the participants walk around in silence and list ideas on flipcharts. Gallery walk is a fantastic tool for collecting information, but it falls short in creating a deeper understanding of ideas and the supporting logic.

If I want to have more communication, I form small groups that discuss ideas while recording them onto flipcharts and then I rotate the flipcharts along the small groups. This gives everyone the chance to contribute. One downfall or risk of tools that rotate content among groups, to have comments build off other comments left by other groups, is the telephone effect. In other words, the original message can get a bit off topic and distorted along the way. Did you ever play a game of telephone with your friends when you were a child? For those who are not familiar, telephone is a game where one person starts by whispering a phrase into the ear of the person next to them. This continues until the secret has been shared about 10 times. Then the person at the end of the line shares the secret with everyone, and the entire group laughs and laughs because the ending phrase is always much different than how it originated. This is the telephone effect, and it can also happen when flipcharts are rotated around the room for comments.

If I want to safeguard against the telephone effect and make sure it does not happen, I choose Café; a tool where groups rotate, but someone always stays behind with the flipchart to explain it to new groups as they are exposed to the material for the first time. This way, the message remains true to its original form as new groups add their comments and contributions.

Last but certainly not least is Open Space. It gives total freedom for everyone to work with whatever topic that they like. Open Space is the perfect tool for dealing with complexity—situations where there are multiple topics that require the correct people to contribute, but that also do not apply to everyone.

Convergent tools for aligning priorities with multiple simultaneous questions

Basic tools
- Prioritising individually
- Silent Moving

Tools for better communication
- Me/We/Us
- Me/We/We...Us
- Bus Stop (rotating sets of solutions between small groups and prioritising)
- Group Ranking (rotating sets of solutions between small groups and ranking)

Convergence

The solutions stage needs sound tools for creating alignment about decisions. For this stage, which deals with many questions, each with their own set of solutions, there are a few options that you can follow, depending on the amount of time and focus you want to spend on creating alignment within the group. The first option is to ask everyone to prioritise individually (me stage). Then you can poll the group to get the results and discuss them in one large group (us stage). This format will not create a lot of alignment. It is time effective, but I would rather add a short we stage and have the group divide into pairs for more discussion on priorities. If you want to create even more alignment, you can add in a round (or several rounds) of discussion in groups of three where people are tasked with listing the very best ideas, and then transition into visualising these priorities as one large group.

I also love to split everyone into small groups and have them discuss the solutions in short rotating conversations, instead of just having one large conversation together. This requires everyone to explain their decisions to others and consider alternate viewpoints.

As facilitators and leaders, it is our job to create alignment, so don't be afraid to spend ample time with convergence during this stage-it is a crucial part of the workshop.

> **What it looks like:** For the second part of Mike's workshop I chose Open Space for emergence because there are many questions to consider, and everyone has their own areas of expertise. I wanted people contributing where they are most useful, not discussing questions that do not need their attention. I chose Bus Stop for convergence. Mike wanted the group to come to a collective decision about what needed to be done to improve production efficiency, and Bus Stop forced everyone to understand all the options before they actively took part in decision making. Finally, I used the fun polling activity Dragons to get the group to prioritise the results.

Tools for action stage

When planning the action stage, you must decide between simply listing action points, having small groups discuss the ideas, or using Idealogue (which means having changing small groups of three to discuss and develop the action points). The more time you spend having the actions discussed in small groups, the better people will understand them and become aligned together around the actions. Once everyone agrees on the actions, it is time to visualise them with the names of the people who are assigned to carry the actions out, along with the timeframe of when they will be completed. Now you should help the group visualise and organise the actions—Blossom, Roadmap and Kanban are your go-to methods here.

Emergent tools for dealing with one question in the action stage of the workshop.

Basic Tools
- Listing

Tools for better communication
- Me/We/Us
- Idealogue

When choosing tools for convergence, I have a choice of working individually or using tools that give participants the chance to talk in small groups. I once worked with a group of twenty people, and two managers began arguing about who should be the right person to implement an action. Neither wanted to give an inch, and the argument dragged on and on. When the dust finally settled, they continued their disagreement by focusing on a new action to bicker about. Meanwhile, the rest of the group was growing restless as more and more time was spent focusing on two people arguing.

Convergent tools for dealing with one question in the action part of the workshop.

Basic Tools
- Prioritising individually

Tools for better communication
- Me/We/Us
- Idealogue

Going through each action individually can be tedious, and people generally take sides in big group discussions. I think it is more effective to first look at the actions and give time to think individually about what can be developed and refined. Then I form small groups and give the following prompt: "Find the people you need to talk to and form groups of three or smaller to discuss possible changes. Once identified, change the actions accordingly." People are productive in small groups and deal with conflicts efficiently.

Finally, we look at the actions together again as one large group and evaluate the results. Is everyone happy? If so, great! But if not, they can be placed back into small groups to continue to tweak the actions by making small change until everyone is content with the results.

> **What it looks like**: I used Idealogue and Blossom for the third part of Mike's workshop. Executing the solutions requires cooperation from everyone. Idealogue allows participants to align actions with other people. Blossom is a practical tool that connects actions with solutions. I used Me/We/Us for convergence because it is a good communication tool for developing actions and ironing out the small, but crucial, details.

A complete tool set: beginning, ending, and energising tools

Every workshop begins the same; participants are advised that they will need to be attending. This can happen via email, a calendar invitation, an announcement from the boss during a meeting, or via phone. The common thread here is that the people attending a workshop have an idea of what it is for. They are often more aware of the changes or challenges a company faces than the external consultant or facilitator is, so the aims of the workshop are clear to them. If the participants understand the key themes and aims of the workshop, you may think that you can leap right in and begin clarifying with your main tools and the CSA structure, but this would be a mistake.

Each successful facilitated workshop needs something before this; a beginning (often called check-in) stage. The purpose of this stage is to help people focus on the objective and to connect with other participants.

I begin by stating the objective for the sessions and explain how they will be working to achieve it. One tip; do not name the tools you are using. Instead just describe *how* people will be working. Tool names are often not understood and sometimes scare people. Once you have presented the objective and the way the group will work towards it, ask for participants to discuss in small groups and to give feedback. "Does this sound OK?", or "Are there any questions or concerns?" are two quick and effective questions I ask at this point. If anyone has any doubts, then you will need to address those and use your skills to make a deal with the group and get everyone onboard before continuing to the CSA stages of the workshop.

It is also important to build a connection between participants so that they feel comfortable and psychologically safe. Psychological safety helps people open up and discuss the real issues facing a team. I connect participants by giving the group an icebreaker activity. This can be a fun game, a survey or key question that people need to reply to and discuss related to the workshop theme, a round of trivia—there are hundreds to choose from. The icebreaker gets people working in a way that is different from their normal routines, and establishes new ways of working early on in the workshop so that people will be able to try the new tools and tasks that they will experience in later workshop stages. By beginning with an activity that requires talking in pairs or groups, you are also helping people loosen up and get accustomed to sharing their thoughts and talking with others—something that quite a few people get nervous about. People feel psychologically safe as they talk in pairs and connect with each other. Interestingly, you cannot create psychological safety by introducing yourself in front of a large group, which is a common practice. My job is to talk to large groups of people but when I wait for my turn to introduce myself I blush and only think about what to say to make a good impression, consequently, I do not pay any attention to what others are saying.

What if the participants do not like icebreakers? I still connect and focus the group by asking to have a discussion in pairs about a question related to the workshop like, "Why am I here?" The question is serious enough to be discussed even between high level participants and with this simple activity I accomplished two objectives: I got the people focused on the topic and had them talk to at least one person in private—which is the minimum for creating psychological safety.

What if I don't do anything in the beginning? I am most likely to have a workshop where it is difficult to activate people, people do not talk about the right topic and the participants do not connect well with each other.

Energisers are yours to choose and use as you see fit. Energisers are often not related to the topic at all; their purpose is simply to get the people to focus or refocus. The times I most often need them are after breaks or lunch—when people are re-joining the workshop after a brief respite. I find that it is best to ask the group if they want an energiser, and if they do not, then there is no need to give them one. On the other hand, if they are open to the idea, then you'll know it is beneficial and can proceed.

How do you choose which energisers to use? You need to use tools that feel comfortable for you, which also fit the group you are working with. If I am working with an outgoing group of energetic school-teachers, then I can count on them being up for all sorts of creative games and activities, and I will build these parts of the workshop accordingly. But if I find myself in front of a room full of overly serious businesspeople, then I will keep things more solemn and professional instead of having them draw pictures or run around on imaginary lines. However, you cannot completely tell at first glance what a group will want—some groups will surprise you! When in doubt, go with your instincts and everything will be fine.

Success does not hinge on your choice of the perfect energiser or warm-up method; there are multiple effective paths. Your main responsibility is to set the mood, help the group become comfortable, and re-energise and focus participants as needed.

Purpose of ending (check-out)

1. To check if the goal was achieved
2. To check how the people are feeling about the process and results. This also gives a sense of closure

The ending (check-out) stage of the workshop focuses on two areas: one related to content and the other related to people. Has the goal of the workshop been achieved and how do participants feel about the process and results. You can have people discuss in pairs and ask for results, or you can just call on volunteers to share their thoughts. Concerns and shortcomings, if any, usually come to light before this during the CSA stages, but it is important to check with the group one final time to see how things went and if you need to circle back to improve the workshop results. This can be done in a fun way, too. For instance, having everyone stand up and creating a line with "amazing" on one end and "horrible" on the other. Then ask everyone to line up accordingly and watch as people scramble...hopefully towards the positive side of things.

What it looks like: I began Mike's workshop by dividing the group into pairs and asking them to respond to the question, "Why am I here?" Mike told me that the production workers are a no-nonsense group, so I wanted to begin the workshop in a straightforward way. After the lunch break, I energised the group with the Floorball activity (covered in section 5.3). I ended the workshop by giving everyone the chance to give feedback using the One Step tool (covered in section 4.3).

Check the timing

Good workshops take time. My workshops using the CSA structure take between half a day to two days for groups of 6-20 people. With most of the tools in this book you can finish a workshop in 3.5–4 hours. If you do not have time in one day, then split the workshop. You can begin with clarifying, continue the following week with solutions, and finish with action planning. I have learned the hard way that it is better to negotiate more time for the workshop with the client than it is to rush things[*].

When people get into having real conversations about topics that are important to them, it is difficult to stop them. Quality workshops share little in common with the average meeting, so different time allocations are required. One way to look at it is that giving ample time for a quality workshop now will save many hours down the road. In other words, the client is investing their time now into a workshop that will improve efficiency and result in fewer meetings down the line.

Mike's workshop
9.00 Welcome, objective, program and getting focused
9.20 Clarifying
10.45 Break
11.00 Solutions: first round of meetings
12.00 Lunch
13.00 Energiser
13.15 Solutions: second round of meetings and choosing key solutions
15.00 Break
15.15 Action
16.45 Check-out
17.00 End of workshop

---

[*] The outline I used for each workshop is presented at the end of each chapter. Refer to it for any doubts about the timing or sequence of tools and activities.

Who should attend the workshop?

How can you increase the ROI of a meeting or a workshop?
Don't invite everyone just for the sake of inclusion.
Consider the role of each participant:

R responsible   Invite all the people who should be doing the work.

A accountable   Invite the person who will approve the work. This person will make sure that the right people do the right tasks at the right time.

C consulted   Interview people whose opinions are needed before the meeting. You can also organize a separate data gathering workshop beforehand.

I informed   Inform afterward those people who need to be kept up-to-date on the progress. This is one-way communication and no actions are expected from those that are being informed.

Additional considerations—Who is invited?

When I am asked to provide services to a company or organisation, usually there is already a list of participants that the bosses or company has in mind. If it is an initiative that affects three departments, then those teams will be in attendance, usually along with some members of management.

But what if you are responsible for organising the participant list for your own workshop? Just how do you go about it? Basically, think about some of the potential actions or results of the workshop. What new tasks may be created? What team would the responsibility of completing these tasks fall to? It is these people that you want to invite. Invite those who will be doing the work or affected by the topic of the workshop. Invite their bosses too. It is important that the people who have to approve the workload and time allocation attend the workshop.

A workshop does not have to be for the entire company. In fact, this can become counterproductive after a certain point—you only want to invite those who are going to be directly affected.

Additional considerations—Combining workshops

Workshops are not isolated events that are independent of one another. They are all inter-related, and great leaders know how to chain them together over time to achieve larger goals or improve an organisation. This process typically begins with a goal-setting workshop. Then you review the results and check in regularly to deal with any obstacles that have sprung up, as well as to keep people motivated. In Volume II of this book we introduce the concept of the breakthrough organisation— a nimble and aligned system that is connected by dialogue across all levels. Volume 2 presents numerous examples of how to combine workshops to create organisational development processes.

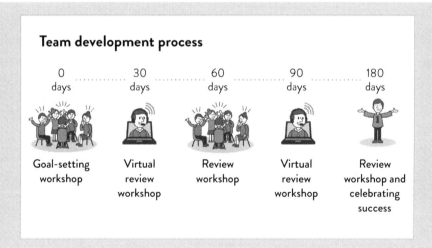

Team development process

0 days	30 days	60 days	90 days	180 days
Goal-setting workshop	Virtual review workshop	Review workshop	Virtual review workshop	Review workshop and celebrating success

A final word on workshop planning

Are you feeling a bit overwhelmed? Perhaps you are looking back over this chapter and asking yourself just how the heck you are expected to keep track of all these important principles of workshop design. Stop, and take a breath. If you have made it this far, then you now realise that there are a lot of things you need to keep in mind to plan great workshops, but it is not that complicated. You know that you will be using the CSA structure, which means that there are going to be three stages: clarifying, solutions, and action. If you find yourself trying to add more stages, then you are making things too complex for both yourself and the workshop participants.

Next, when choosing tools, consider the situation at hand; is there one key question or topic? Are there many? Are the participants generally aligned with each other, or do you need to use a tool that takes more time but fosters communication? Once you have an idea about the situation, choose your tools accordingly, and add some group activities for the beginning and end of the workshop, and have a few energisers ready to use. I have included an appendix of all the tools I used in this book and you can refer to it to see where in the book they are discussed, and what purpose they serve you, the group leader.

As a parting word of advice, I recommend you take it slow. A well-designed workshop is the key to effective group leadership. I have trained thousands of people to become facilitators, and the ones who invest enough time in planning their workshops always succeed. At first, workshop planning will be time consuming and feel complicated, but as you gain experience it will become second nature. You know that the CSA structure is the foundation of your workshops, and you have the tools needed for any type of workshop, so you have every reason to be confident!

What's next?

Congratulations! You just completed quite the journey! You have travelled back in time to learn about the history of group decision making and how the most influential tools came to be. You have learned about the cornerstones that make up breakthrough decision making. You have seen what effective group leadership looks like by analysing multiple case studies, and you have taken a step back and looked at the bigger picture of workshop design and how to use the CSA structure. I am confident that you are now much better equipped to leading groups to make decisions than you were before.

Our journey together does not end here, however. Just turn the page to continue with the *Handbook of Professional Facilitation: Theory, Tools, and Design Volume 2*. It will build off the material covered here and demonstrate how to deal with complex situations that group leaders encounter, like defusing conflict and identifying what clients really need.

Other free resources to improve your leadership are available.

I publish a free newsletter that you can sign up for by visiting www.grapepeople.com. By signing up, you will receive free essays, eBooks, and invitations to webinars and live events.

One last piece of advice...remember to have fun! You are armed with the tools needed to help groups solve problems, dream bigger, and reach their goals. I hope you find that as rewarding and enjoyable as I have.

Handbook of

Professional Facilitation

Theory, Tools, and Design

VOLUME 2

The Professional Path

It's not always clear what separates the best from everyone else. For athletes, it seems to be a mix of good genetics and years of training. In chess, some people are blessed with a gifted mind that can visualise seventeen moves in advance. What about group leadership? What's the difference between a competent leader and a true master? In *Handbook of Professional Facilitation: Theory, Tools, and Design Volume 1*, I said group leadership is easy. I claimed that anyone could be an effective leader if they know how to design workshops and use a few different group tools. If these are the only requirements for outstanding leadership, why do some leaders stand out among the rest? I remember when I had been facilitating for about two or three years. I knew how to design a workshop, and I had mastered about a dozen group tools. I thought I was ready. Yet, I could not understand what separated me from my teachers and group leaders that I admired. I didn't know what skills I lacked, so I attributed it merely to a lack of experience.

Tool selection and workshop design are the foundation of effective leadership. They are fundamental keys that all leaders need to learn before working with groups. However, there are advanced competencies that can bring your leadership abilities to the next level. These are the things that separate the best group leaders from the rest of the pack, and I will teach you all about them in *Handbook of Professional Facilitation: Theory, Tools, and Design Volume 2*.

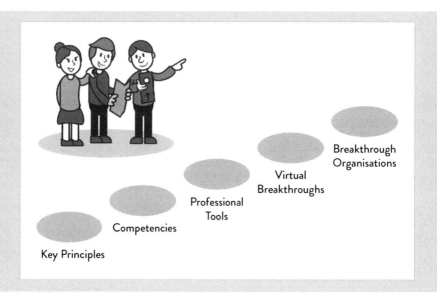

You will understand how to design workshops that help people solve problems, create new ideas, and more. You also will learn about emergent and convergent thinking. These are different thought processes that help people's creativity and understanding. If you read Volume 1 of this book, you are already familiar with these key principles. Now I will take things a bit further and show how you can play with these concepts to lengthen or shorten different parts of your workshop to provide optimal results, no matter the situation. Knowing how to organise and lead a workshop is one thing, but top-notch leaders understand how to shift the group's focus to unlock better results.

Once you've mastered the key principles, we can move on to study the competencies that I believe most great leaders possess. Over the decades that my colleagues and I have spent studying leadership and leading groups, we have identified eight core competencies of successful leaders. These are things that a leader does while conducting a meeting or workshop, such as remaining content-neutral or making sure to use group memory. When you combine these competencies with the leadership fundamentals you already are familiar with, you will be on your way to world-class leadership.

The third part of this book is devoted to professional tools. Anyone can use professional tools, but I call them that because these are the tools that professional leaders rely on to achieve crucial things. Do you find yourself guiding a group through an emotionally charged session? I will show you the tools to make it manageable. Need to help a group solve a complex problem? Try using Challenge Mapping. Is there a nasty argument between two opposing sides? The 3-Step Intervention Model is just the tool for the job. Do you have a client who is oblivious to reality and unaware of what they need? You can help them discover their actual needs by using STP Analysis. Not every great leader needs to act like a rock star, but they must be able to tell a good story, and they know how to get others to share their stories, too. I will finish the professional tools section by teaching you how to incorporate storytelling into your meetings and workshops.

Next, we will move on to the timely subject of virtual break-throughs. It feels like most of the world has transitioned from office life to working from home. The commute has changed from driving to a physical workspace to logging into a virtual one! Expert leaders know how to provide the support and guidance a group needs in any environment, including virtual ones. To lead effectively in a virtual setting, you will need to make adjustments. Some might be obvious, like taking the time to get familiar with the meeting software you will be using. Other adjustments might catch you off guard. For example, if someone is disruptive in a face-to-face meeting, you can address the situation head-on. What about virtually? You can put guidelines and rules in place to get a group performing at its best in remote sessions, and I will show you just how to do that.

Finally, we look at the big picture to see how you can create organisational change. Great leaders don't run average meetings, and they are not part of ordinary organisations, either. I've met all sorts of leaders, coaches, consultants, and even a guru or two throughout my career. Out of all these brilliant people, I've had two or three mentors that deeply impacted me. They all had their unique views on leadership, but they shared one thing in common; a set of skills that transcended an individual meeting to change a whole organisation. I will show you how to regularly schedule meetings and workshops to develop positive working habits and create habits that promote collaboration and communication.

Each chapter of this book includes a case study or several short stories from my career that illustrate common group leadership challenges. Each chapter ends with an analysis section where we look back at what happened and review the methodology of the tools used and how you can apply them.

Whether you want to brush up on modern group leadership techniques or if you're going to be leading a workshop for 500 people next week, you are in the right place. I will equip you with everything you need to be a world-class leader.

CHAPTER 1:

Key Principles of Breakthrough Decision Making

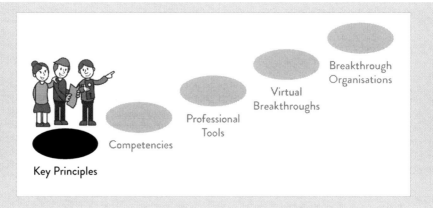

Key Principles · Competencies · Professional Tools · Virtual Breakthroughs · Breakthrough Organisations

Chapter Preview

What's here
- Emergent and convergent thinking
- The CSA structure of workshop design
- Managing group dynamics

How it helps
Mastering the key principles of breakthrough decision making allows you to understand the methodology behind leadership tools and why they work.

Missing money and breakthrough decision making

It was a Friday afternoon, and I was thinking about robots. Not the kind of robots that build cars or sort packages in a massive warehouse. I was thinking about the type of robots sent from some distant planet to destroy humanity. And before you ask, no, I'm not crazy. Why was I dreaming of destructive robots? Because on Fridays, my wife and I have a tradition of going to the movies together and eating too much popcorn and candy while enjoying the latest blockbuster. And if the robots did not clue you in, it was my turn to pick this week. Unfortunately, as I was getting ready to leave to watch the movie, disaster struck. No robot came down to attack us, but I saw something almost as disturbing; my wallet was empty. That very morning, I counted seventeen euros in bills and coins, but now it had vanished! It was no mystery who committed this crime either. My teenage daughter Hannah was just in my room an hour ago before she went out to spend the afternoon with her school friends. Instinctively, I snatched up my phone and began angrily typing a message to her, but I stopped myself. I took a minute to think. *Pepe, instead of shouting at her for being greedy and shattering the sacred father-daughter bond, try something different this time. If you can't get through to her, you can always shout later.* So, with a somewhat clear head, I decided to enjoy an evening with my wife watching killer robots. I would talk with Hannah later that night.

"Hi, Dad!" Hanna smiled and gave a small wave as my wife and I returned home after our evening at the movies. I took one look at my happy daughter and thought I could see right through her act. I decided to cut right to the chase. "Hannah, I was counting my money to see if I had enough to buy a sufficient amount of candy at the theatre, and I quickly saw that there was no money to count! We were almost late and missed out on reserving our favourite seats!"

"Oh, sorry about that. I was in trouble, though. Today was the student council meeting at school. I needed a few euros for the bus, and the meeting lasted a few hours, so we decided to get something to eat after."

"I see. You had things to do that you needed money for, and you knew where I keep my wallet."

I was beginning to see where Hannah was coming from and the thought process that led her to take my money, but she did not understand my thinking yet, so I continued talking. "When you take my money without asking me, I feel betrayed. It hurts my feelings and makes me feel like I can't trust you."

My daughter is a sensational young lady, but she takes after her mother and has a bit of a temper. As my words sunk in, I noticed that her cheeks were turning a dark shade of red, and her eyebrows were pointed sharply downwards in a dramatic V-shape that I had not seen before.

"Dad. Are you calling me a thief? Are you SERIOUS?"

"I'm not calling you a thief at all, Hannah! I just feel like it is an invasion of my privacy to put money away in my wallet, only for it to disappear later. I want to be able to trust you one hundred per cent."

"I took the money because we trust each other, Dad! You always say I can count on you, and you push me to do activities like the student council meeting. But I needed money to get to the meeting! Whenever I ask you for money to buy a new album or clothes, you ramble on how you prefer to support my constructive activities! I figured you wouldn't mind if I took the money since I was spending it on something you want me to be a part of."

At this point, I understood my daughter's motivations much better. "That's fine, Hannah. Next time just text me when you need to take money from my wallet."

Hannah nodded. We understood one another and reached an agreement. We enjoyed a great evening together as a family where Hannah and my wife made fun of my taste in movies while I tried to defend my love for giant robots.

We were able to move past the money issue by talking things out. Instead of getting angry and taking away Hannah's car for a year or dishing out some other harsh punishment, we had a conversation and began to understand our actions and why we did the things we did. Once we understood each other's logic, we agreed on an action plan. This is breakthrough decision making.

Breakthrough decision making =

A participatory dialectic process focused on creating understanding and making a choice.

The benefits of breakthrough decision making are:
• New insights
• Better decisions by combining group knowledge
• Acceptance and commitment to ideas

Breakthrough decision making requires an attitude of exploration and curiosity. You must want to understand another person's thoughts and feelings to engage in breakthrough decision making and ultimately collaborate with someone else. Breakthrough decision making helps groups make better choices and can be used in many different situations.

A breakthrough idea is an idea that:

1. Overcomes any resistance that others have towards it
2. Gains acceptance
3. Is agreed to on a group level

Many people share a common tendency to resist a new idea. This makes breakthrough decision making crucial. Have you ever shared a bold new idea in a team meeting? Perhaps you proposed a strategy that was different from how your organisation typically does things. When you shared your new idea, what happened? Most likely, people were reacting with reasons why your idea would not work. This hesitant reaction is not because your idea was bad, but rather because it's hard for people to get their heads around things that challenge their current view. Hearing new ideas challenges the listener's framework of thought. When this happens, the first reaction is usually resistance and criticism. This negative reaction does not come from a place of jealously or close-mindedness but rather from a lack of understanding. People often just want to know more about your thinking when you share a new idea, but unfortunately, the typical reaction is to criticise new ideas before they have the chance to flourish.

Two heads are better than one

Now Hannah and I understood each other and why we acted the way we did. This mutual understanding stopped us from arguing further and turning an argument into a serious problem. But our work was not done yet. We were still in the middle of a collaborative phase called emergence.

> Emergence is when people share their ideas, logic, and beliefs. Ideas gain acceptance (or die), and ideas are combined to create breakthroughs.

Although Hannah and I weren't arguing anymore, I wanted to make sure we agreed to a plan moving forward. So, I caught her attention and asked, "Do you think the plan for you to send me a text when you need some money is OK? I thought I saw a negative reaction on your side when I suggested it."

"I guess it's fine, Dad. I don't think I will be taking much money from you anyway from now on."

The idea of my daughter getting a job and funding her activities was music to my ears. But I knew my moody teenage daughter well, and somehow, I was sure that this was not what she meant.

She continued, "All this talk about trust makes me feel weird about taking your money. I can take a cheaper bus, but it goes on a longer route and takes an hour longer. I also can stop buying lunch every other day or just say no to my friends when they suggest that we eat out at places I can't afford, like McDonald's."

Hannah's vision for her future sounded bleak. "Is there anything your mother and I could do to help?"

"Yes, there is, Dad! You could make some money available to me, so I don't have to look for it myself when something comes up. I'm not talking about a huge amount, but something that I can use for transportation or food when I need to."

"Right. I could leave my spare change in a bowl in the kitchen. You can help yourself to it when you need to. Or I could give you a monthly allowance at the start of each month. Another option is that I buy you a transit card. Which one of these sounds best to you?"

Hannah and I reached the end of the emergence phase. We were creating new ideas together and understanding each other. Our original ideas, like texting when needing money, had died and were being replaced with better ones. Now we were entering a new phase called convergence. In convergence, people compare and sort ideas and then make a choice.

> Convergence is the phase where people compare ideas and make a choice.

"An allowance sounds awesome, but what would I do if I spent it all in the first week? I'd be raiding your wallet again in no time. The coin bowl makes sense, but what do I do if I need money when I'm away from home? I don't like the idea of carrying around a bag of coins."

I thought back to my school days and remembered how mean kids could be. I agreed that carrying a bag of coins around high school was a bad idea.

"I guess that leaves the transit card as the best option. It'd be great if you can get me one, Dad."

"But you can't buy food with a transit card, can you? What will you do if you get hungry?"

"I guess you could also leave some coins around that I can take if I have plans or if I'm going to be away from home all day."

"Perfect, I'll give you some money so you can buy yourself a transit card, and I'll start to leave my extra change in a bowl in the kitchen. I think that is a plan that works for both of us."

"Thanks, Dad! You're the best! I need to remember that beneath your cold and angry exterior is a reasonable person," said Hannah. With that final insult (or was it a compliment?), my daughter gave me a quick hug and ran off to find more important things to do.

I didn't share this story to show off my parenting skills or showcase how challenging teenagers can be. I shared this story to illustrate the two phases of breakthrough decision making: emergence and convergence. Understanding how these phases work and knowing how to lead groups through them will help you make better group decisions in your personal and professional life. Emergence and convergence are essential concepts, but they fit within a broader system called CSA when you lead a meeting or a workshop.

The Clarifying → Solutions → Action (CSA) workshop structure

Breakthrough decision making is combining people's knowledge and ideas to make better decisions. When people understand each other and collaborate, they create something more valuable than they could alone. In other words, breakthrough decision making can be represented by the following formula: $1 + 1 = 3$. Aligning people and resisting our natural tendency to shoot down new ideas is not easy, but anyone can do it with the right tools. Great leaders build their workshops around a tool called CSA. CSA is a 3-stage structure for designing workshops. Each stage helps people understand the content they are working with, leads them towards finding solutions, and requires that they develop actions to complete.

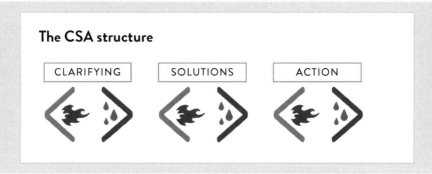

The CSA structure

CLARIFYING   SOLUTIONS   ACTION

CSA reflects how people naturally think about problems. People tend to approach a problem by immediately thinking of solutions. To put it another way, when someone walks into a meeting about increasing sales, they usually have an idea or two about what to do before the meeting even starts. Their predetermined solutions can clash with what other people already have in mind. Each person has their unique perspective and way of understanding things—their framework. It is hard to get someone to stop thinking about their framework to take the time to understand your framework. You can help people understand each other by defining the shared context. What is the common problem that everyone is at the meeting to discuss? What goals do people have in common? People begin to understand each other once they have a shared point of reference. The clarifying stage of CSA creates this shared point of reference. The solutions stage comes next, and it is where people develop solutions together. Finally comes the action stage, which is about splitting your solutions into concrete actions by assigning each aspect of the solution: who, what, when.

Questions for each part of CSA

CLARIFYING	SOLUTIONS	ACTION
Clarifying a goal: • What are our goals? • Which goals should we reach in next three years? Clarifying a problem: • What is our problem? • Which problem should we solve today?	• What are the solutions? • Which solutions do we want to implement?	• What do I do? • Which actions do we need to develop and how can we develop them?

Each stage of CSA has one primary question for both the emergent and convergent phases. The leader presents this question to the group, and it serves as a topic for that part of the workshop. So, for example, in the Clarifying stage of CSA, you can ask, *What are our goals?* Then there is a clarifying emergent phase followed by a clarifying convergent phase. Then the same structure repeats for the Solutions and Action stages of CSA. In practice, this means that you take the group through a decision-making process consisting of six questions.

Managing group dynamics

Taking a group through the right set of questions helps, but it is not enough. You do not always get everyone to participate. Some people dominate the conversation, and people frequently argue about ideas when working in big groups. You have probably seen this yourself and been a part of a conversation that goes in endless circles as each side defends its position. These types of circular conversations waste time and energy. A great leader avoids these wasteful interactions by using Me/We/Us. Each part of Me/We/Us has participants working differently. During Me, people work individually, We is for work in small groups, and Us brings everyone back together as one large group.

Managing group dynamics

Me/We/Us:

1. **Me/individual thinking**
   - Connects people with their own thinking and logic
   - Creative!

2. **We/small groups**
   - Ideas are refined in pairs or small groups
   - Helps new concepts and understanding to emerge
   - Alignment!

3. **Us/everyone together**
   - Sharing the ideas with the whole group
   - Informing and checking for group understanding and acceptance
   - Inform and decide!

Me

The Me thinking mode is about giving people time to gather their thoughts at their own pace. Sometimes we need time to think on our own. It helps us connect with our logic and create new ideas. I'm from Finland, the land of shy and introverted people, at least according to the stereotypes. It just so happens that many stereotypes are based on truth, and when I go to a local factory and ask the engineers about their current production challenges, I don't get any answers. If I give them a piece of paper and ask them to write down their current production challenges, I will get dozens of ideas or challenges. Giving people time to think independently helps them organise their views and beliefs without feeling rushed or pressured.

We

The We thinking mode is about sharing ideas in a small group of around two to five participants. When I get an idea, talking about it helps me understand it better. It brings clarity and makes me more confident. Some of my ideas simply fade away as I talk about them and realise that they are not very good. Other ideas grow and become stronger as I talk through them. When my colleagues tell me their ideas, I gain new perspectives, and I become invested in their views, too. As people talk in small groups, some ideas are discarded while others become clear options for decision-making. I find that the We stage is crucial when I work in China. Many organisations in China have a very formal way of working and adhere to strict hierarchies. You simply do not present your ideas in front of your boss without first making sure they are acceptable. The we stage allows people to share their ideas in small groups first. This creates a sense of psychological safety.

Us

The Us thinking mode is for sharing the best ideas with everyone in the room. It effectively creates a shared understanding of ideas and the logic behind them. Then, when everyone is back together as one large group, it is easy for the group to check whether people understand the ideas and want to commit to them.

Managing group dynamics during emergence and convergence

Experienced group leaders combine emergence and convergence with Me/We/Us to help groups make decisions effectively. This is how great leaders form a solid foundation of key concepts that support their meetings and workshops. When I lead a group through decision making, I am thinking about how I will use each part of Me/We/Us during emergence and convergence. Let me present a leadership situation that I was in where I brought these concepts together.

I was working with a famous Chinese brewery in Shanghai, China. The brewery used state of the art machines which automated the production and bottling process. Most of the workers were highly educated and experienced. Even though the facilities and the workers were top-notch, I was hired to lead a workshop to increase production efficiency. The big boss, a friendly man called Tony, with grey hair and a belly that showed a fondness for food and drink, warned me that working with this group would not be easy.

"Everyone is competent, and they know what they are doing. A lack of experience and knowledge is not the problem. The issue is everyone seems to be shy and introverted. Cultivating teamwork is a problem."

I told Tony that I understood his concerns, but I was confident. I came armed with a powerful tool called Me/We/Us, and I planned on using Me/We/Us for the emergent and convergent portions of the workshop, and I was sure that this was just the thing that Tony and his Team needed.

Emergence

Me: After warming the group up a bit with a short icebreaker activity, I said, "Everybody, please take a piece of paper and a pen and write down the challenges that get in the way of production efficiency. This is an individual task, and you have five minutes to complete it, OK? If anything is unclear or you have any questions, please let me know. You can begin!" Pens and pencils began scratching paper as the group started writing down their challenges. So far, so good!

We: Once the time for individual writing was over, it was time to move to the We part of Me/We/Us. "Thank you! You have done a great job! Now it's time to share your important thoughts with your colleagues. Please form groups of four. Now your job is to share the challenges you wrote down. If you don't understand something that someone has written down, ask for clarification. Keep sharing until everything's understood. Once all the challenges have been shared and understood, your job as a group is to agree on three or four challenges that we should solve today. If there are any questions, ask me! You can begin now."

Us: "Now we will come back together as one large group. It's time to present the challenges you have agreed to solve! Who would like to go first?"

I went around the room and called on each group of four to share the challenges they agreed on. Suddenly, a hand shot up in the air. Someone had a question. Jane Wu, the Assistant Controller, asked, "A lot of these challenges are the same, or at least very similar. Should we combine them if they are close to the same thing?"

"Great question, thank you, Jane. It's best if we leave them separate. The challenges tend to lose their meaning when they are categorised, so let's keep them as they are. However, if two challenges are identical, we can remove one. Would you like to help me remove the duplicates? That would be a big help!"

Convergence

Me: "Now we have all of the challenges written on the wall with the duplicates removed. Please take a few moments to review them by yourself. Think about which ones should be solved today. Is that clear?"

"Not really, no," said Mike Zhang, a production manager. "Are you saying I should pick just one challenge?"

"Pick as many as you like, Mike. The only restriction is a time limit of three minutes to do this. Please begin. And remember, it's a good idea to write down the challenges you choose."

We: "Now, form groups of three. Once you are in these groups, try to convince your group members why your chosen challenges are the best ones to solve. I will give each group $12. Use this money to invest in the challenges you want to solve. For example, if there are three equally brilliant challenges, you might invest $4 into each of them. If one challenge is clearly the best one, you might want to put all $12 into that challenge. It's up to you, and you have twelve minutes with your group to share your challenges and invest together!"

Us: "Now it's time to put your money where your mouth is. Please have someone from each group come to the wall where the challenges are written and write down the amount of money that you have invested in each challenge."

I watched as group representatives came to the wall and began investing. I was interested to see what the group priorities were. After a few minutes had passed, everyone was seated again, and I took a look at the final result. "I see that there are five challenges that have a lot more money invested in them than the rest. I think that these are the ones that we should focus on today. But it's not what I think that matters. I want to hear from you, so please let's go around the room for a quick round of feedback."

After everyone had the chance to comment on the result, it was clear that the group agreed on what needed to be done. "It seems like you all agree on what needs to be solved today. That means that our work is done for now, and the first stage of our workshop is officially over! Relax and enjoy some coffee. We'll meet back together in fifteen minutes to continue."

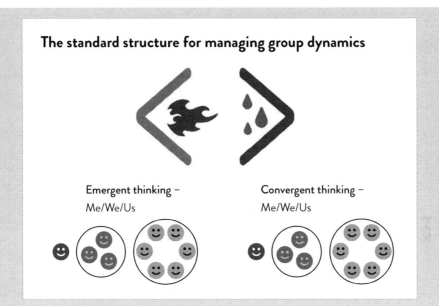

The standard structure for managing group dynamics

Emergent thinking –
Me/We/Us

Convergent thinking –
Me/We/Us

A double dose of Me/We/Us

I used Me/We/Us two twice in this workshop. First, I used it to help the group think of challenges that blocked production efficiency, and then I used it again in the second part of the workshop to help them choose. I used Me/We/Us twice to make sure that the decision-making process was balanced. Group leaders tend to spend a lot of time leading groups through emergent thinking, the phase where ideas are created. Unfortunately, they tend to rush through convergent thinking, where ideas are understood and prioritised. If a leader neglects convergent thinking, it is tough for participants to understand the logic behind the choice.

When the logic behind the choice is not clear to participants, your workshop will end with people feeling confused. The results will be weak and short-lived. As a rule of thumb, you should balance the two stages. I used Me/We/Us for emergence and convergence to ensure that the structure of my workshop was symmetrical.

In addition to clarifying a problem or challenge, you may use the same structure to clarify a goal or agree on solutions. Just change the question. For clarifying a project or strategic goal, you simply ask, "What is our goal?" For creating solutions, you first present the problem or the goal. Next, you ask, "What is the solution?" The key to success is remembering to use Me/We/Us twice to balance your workshop in both emergence and convergence.

Balancing emergent and convergent thinking

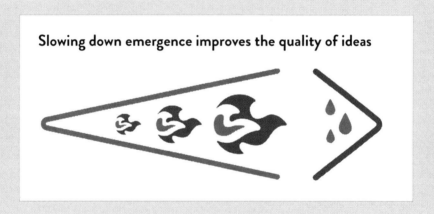

Slowing down emergence improves the quality of ideas

You just learned why it is essential to plan a decision-making process with equal parts for emergent and convergent thinking. If you followed this simple structure in all your workshops, you would do just fine. But you have more power, knowledge, and ability than to aim for *just fine*. You can slow down convergence and emergence to create a more focused workshop. If you slow down emergence and allocate more time to it, you will improve the quality of the group's ideas. If the most crucial workshop objective is to create breakthrough ideas that combine everyone's knowledge, I do this. In practice, I would give everyone an extended amount of time for individual thinking, which is the most effective thinking mode for creating new ideas. Then I repeatedly alternate individual work and small group discussion, which is the most effective thinking mode for combining ideas to create breakthrough ideas.

People often ask me to lead workshops for groups that understand the available options but need to make a choice. If the workshop's most important outcome is a clear decision, I will slow down convergent thinking by devoting more time to it. More time for convergence means more time for creating a shared understanding of each option and its practical implications. Understanding the consequences of a decision empowers people to make better decisions. And it is no secret that people find it easy to commit to good decisions that they under-stand rather than shaky, ambiguous choices. I slow down convergence by giving plenty of time for discussion in small alternating groups. Multiple rounds of discussion in small groups create alignment and understanding. I also use numerous rounds of polling or voting to expand convergence.

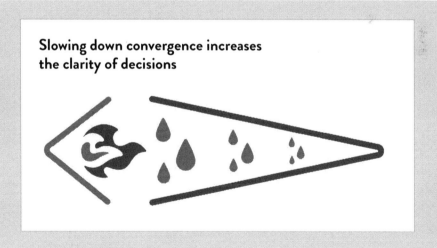

Slowing down convergence increases the clarity of decisions

To summarise...

Leading groups through the decision-making process is not so much about the individual tools you decide to use. Instead, it is about being aware of these significant concepts; CSA structure for workshop design, emergence and convergence, and managing group dynamics with Me/We/Us. These three things are different from one another, but they all fit together to create an environment where groups can work together and solve complex problems. CSA is a structure for designing workshops that contains three stages: clarifying, solutions, and action. Each stage focuses on a different part of the decision-making process. Emergence and convergence are two distinct modes of thought. Emergence is about sharing ideas and their logic. Convergence is about choosing the best ideas. And finally, Me/We/Us is your tool for managing group dynamics that forces people to work individually, then in small groups, and eventually all together. These concepts form the foundation of a successful group session, and really, they are the guiding forces that world-class leaders use to help group decision making.

CHAPTER 2:

Competencies of a Group Leader

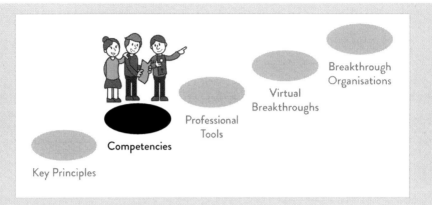

What's here
- The eight core competencies of professional leadership

How it helps
Avoid the most common leadership mistakes by mastering these competencies and keeping them in mind as you run your meetings and workshops.

Superior group decision making

I love to share my knowledge with inexperienced group leaders and watching folks progress from being complete novices to expert leaders. Sometimes this can happen in a matter of weeks, if not less! I have identified eight core competencies that form the foundation of successful leadership. I use these eight competencies as my evaluation criterion for the facilitation certification exam. The exam requires candidates to demonstrate their skills by leading a sample workshop. To pass the exam, a candidate will need to demonstrate competence in these eight areas successfully.

1. Neutral role

Group decision making is complex and requires a person entirely focused on the decision-making process. An experienced group leader remains 100 % content neutral.

Be neutral

- The leader is content neutral and does not favor some ideas over others. They do not group, censor, or edit the ideas created during the workshop.

It means that the leader does not show any preference for the group's ideas. A content-neutral leader also does not feed solutions or give answers to the group. Instead, the group leader focuses on leading the group process and ensuring that the workshop transitions smoothly from one part to the next.

Remaining neutral implies you are not pushing for any specific outcome, even if you hope for one particular result. The content-neutral group leader hopes that everything goes well, but it is a harmful shortcut to try and ensure success by giving hints or suggesting ideas to the group. Your suggestions are probably going to complicate the group decision-making process.

The International Association of Facilitators considers neutrality the most important competence for professional facilitators. I remember way back when I was becoming certified as a facilitator. I was in the beautiful town of Portoroz, Slovenia, at the European Conference of Facilitation. There were nine of us attempting to pass the certification test. We were a mix of trainers, coaches, managers, and consultants. Five of us passed the test, and four did not. Coincidentally enough, the four that did not pass were all consultants. What was it about the consultants that caused them to fail while the rest of us succeeded? They were just as capable as everyone else, but the nature of their role as consultants made it very difficult to remain neutral. It makes sense that neutrality would be a challenge for a consultant; after all, they are brought in to share their expertise and experience to guarantee that a project succeeds. During the test, the consultants began their workshops well enough; they knew how to lead a group in creating ideas. But in the end, they all involved themselves in idea selection, grouping and prioritising the ideas, as they would in their everyday work.

The leader as a neutral party

Groups will ask you for your thoughts and opinions when they are stuck. It is important in these moments to deflect their questions back to the group quickly. Acknowledge that the situation is difficult and ask a question to get them thinking:

- Damn, this is quite the challenge. What do you think should happen next?
- Wow, I can see why this is a struggle. Can you think of any solutions?
- This is a tricky topic. Do you have any other ideas or can you try thinking about this in a new way?
- Hmm, what a situation. What do you think you should do?

The phrases above are just examples. The key is to show you understand the issue (empathise) while at the same time deflecting the issue/topic/question back to the group so that you remain neutral.

Remain neutral, even if people directly ask you what they should do. If someone asks me for my opinion about a challenging situation, I acknowledge that it is difficult, but I do not suggest what to do. Let people know you understand that it is difficult, but at the same time, give the group complete decision-making control.

2. Choosing the correct stages for the workshop

Clear and logical stages to a meeting or workshop are the backbone of group decision making. If you link the workshop stages in a logical progression, then the tools and methods will flourish. On the other hand, nothing will work well if the group leader doesn't organise the stages of their meetings or workshops correctly. I use the three-stage CSA process for workshop design. This process was presented in Chapter 6 of the *Handbook of Professional Facilitation: Theory, Tools, and Design Volume 1*. However, I want to mention it again because it is a core competency great leaders have.

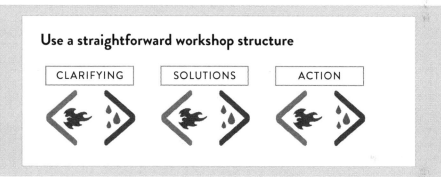

It is common for people to use too many stages in their workshops or neglect stages entirely. I have seen novice group leaders build workshops with two solutions stages and no action stage.

Another mistake inexperienced leaders make is not distinctly separating the stages of their workshops. When the division between the stages is blurred, participants have a hard time focusing on the correct objectives of the workshop.

Each workshop stage contains time for emergent and convergent thinking. The decision—making process is promoted by questions that invite participants to develop or choose ideas. I often see candidates using the wrong questions to clarify the goal or problem in facilitator certification events. I remember one specific certification test where I observed the clarifying stage of a workshop led by an experienced trainer called Dani. Dani had constructed a great workshop intending to increase employee wellbeing and happiness. I could tell from the workshop outline she submitted that she designed it well. Her workshop got off to a good start, but everything fell apart when she asked a group to clarify the problem with the question, "What do stability and satisfaction mean in our context?" Dani used this question as the starting point to lead the group to create answers, solutions, and actions. This question, however, was not the correct starting point, and it set everything off course. The results were not in line with the objectives of the workshop. Be sure to give clear prompts to the group and be careful when giving a topic to clarify. Dani's mistake was that she had an overly specific question that did not clarify the goal or the problem. Dani did not distinguish between the different CSA stages, which caused her to mislead the group with ineffective questions.

3. Choosing the right emergent and convergent tools

To be a great leader, you need to know how to use quite a few different group tools, and you also will need to know when to apply them. By having a wide selection in your toolbox, you can design workshops that fit varying time constraints and objectives.

Choose the right tools

- The group leader knows how to use both emergent and convergent tools. They can pick the right tool to match the group's needs and they can select tools that fit the available amount of time.

To prevent you from making the same mistakes, I want to highlight a few common errors I see people repeatedly make during their facilitation certification test.

I remember evaluating a new facilitator by observing a practice workshop. She was in command, and everything was going well until she arrived at the solutions stage. The group had defined five key challenges, and she began using a tool called Idealogue*. The solution stage of a workshop has multiple questions to deal with, and Idealogue only works with one question at a time. This mismatch of tool and situation is a common error, so be sure to know the tools and what they do and adjust accordingly. Like the tools a mechanic would use, facilitation tools have their specific purpose; they fit certain situations perfectly while being completely wrong for other cases. Just like you would not use a wrench to clean a car window, you would not (and should not!) use an emergent thinking tool to collect feedback at the end of a workshop.

I frequently see people use too many tools. They try to be overly thorough to guarantee that they meet the workshop objectives. This results in leading a group through repeated activities that do the same thing. Using too many tools can make things cluttered, making the later stages of the workshop less effective. I was once sitting in on a goal creation workshop, and the facilitator began by leading the group in a needs analysis activity. This activity created answers to the prompts *I need...* and *Our company needs...* Then, the facilitator led the group in a wishing activity that used the prompt, *I wish we...* Unfortunately, the Wishing activity and the needs analysis activity produced almost the same results. The leader should have only used one of these two activities.

Think carefully about what each tool provides and where to use it. By reviewing these things beforehand, you can avoid misusing tools or using redundant tools.

---

* Idealogue is a method I developed as an alternative to traditional brainstorming. You can read more about Idealogue in my book, *Beyond Brainstorming-Idealogue* (2016).

4. Creating a sense of psychological safety

One of the most notable things about attending a meeting or workshop with a competent leader is the sense of psychological safety during the session. People feel relaxed and engaged. The group leader helps people open up and participate in remarkable ways, which gives excellent results. It all starts with you, the group leader. Your job is to create psychological safety by connecting participants, being transparent, and having a friendly and attentive presence.

Create psychological safety

- The group leader is transparent and clearly explains the workshop goals, the agenda, the instructions, and participant roles

- The group leader is friendly and approachable

- The leader connects individuals together by giving time for conversations in pairs and small groups

---

First, let's talk about connecting participants. You want to do this early on, so it is best to work towards this at the very beginning of the workshop during the check-in stage. The way to do this is to have people talk in pairs. Pair discussion is less intimidating than talking in larger groups, and no one can hide to avoid talking when in pairs. This one-on-one discussion links the individual with another person and eliminates nerves. As people respond to your questions (which can be light-hearted), they build confidence talking with their partners. The pair discussions connect individuals with someone else, which makes everyone feel good.

You also need to remain transparent to inspire trust in the group and make participants feel comfortable. The primary way to be transparent is to clearly explain the aim of each stage and the way of working. Tell everyone what they will do, why, their expected roles, your role, and the duration of the activity. This makes tasks seem manageable and helps people understand the purpose of each activity and why they should participate. Group activities that do not have a clear objective can feel like a waste of time.

Be Transparent

- Clearly share the objectives for the workshop or session

- Explain how you will guide the group towards these objectives (ways of working, not tool name or method)

- Share expectations (time allotted for work, active participation, etc.)

- If the workshop is not going well, address it and ask for feedback from the group to find out why

- Frequently ask the group if there are questions or feedback

Let me tell you about my recent visit to the dentist to illustrate the importance of being transparent. It was my appointment with a new dentist, and I was a bit nervous. I hate going to the dentist. To be honest, I was looking for an excuse to jump out of that chair and leave. I almost did exactly that when I saw that the dentist had picked up an oversized angry-looking drill in her hand. But before I could make a break for it, she said, "OK, I am going to use this drill to clean your teeth. The entire cleaning will take about five minutes. I will drill for about thirty seconds and then stop to vacuum excess water from your mouth. If you are in any pain, just raise your hand in the air, and I will stop."

Her explanation of the cleaning process completely erased my fears; I knew what the dentist would do, why she had to do it, and how long it would take. I also had a sense of control; I could raise my hand to give feedback on the process as it was happening, so I was not worried about being stuck in an uncomfortable position. Give your participants the same sense of safety by explaining your processes and the tools you are using.

You do not need to have a specific type of personality to be a group leader. I have seen introverts who do a fantastic job, and many talented group leaders are extroverts who love being around people. There are many ways that you can get the job done. I like to tell silly jokes and even make fun of myself—I want to show people that I don't take myself too seriously and that they should not, either. Setting a relaxed tone works for me and gets everyone in the right mindset for the work ahead. Some of my colleagues would never dream of telling jokes to the groups they are leading. Instead, they opt for a more professional approach. Either way is acceptable. But one needed constant is to be friendly and respectful to people. You lead by example. The tone you set will be mirrored by the groups you lead.

5. Creating alignment on content

You are the leader of the group. You are there to guide the group towards its goals. I see this role as someone who creates alignment. Think about it. When clients request a workshop, they want a people-based solution, an agreement between the participants. They want their employees to work together towards the common good! They hope that a workshop can get people to agree to move forward with a new strategy or policy, solve a conflict, or create new ideas that they would achieve as a team. These different examples are all forms of alignment, and as the group leader, it is your job to create alignment. I would say that creating alignment and shared understanding is the most difficult of the eight competencies.

Create alignment

- Use individual, small-group, and full-group communication

- Invest enough time for both emergence and convergence

Alignment simply means that everyone is pointed in the same direction towards shared goals. There is a unified, understood purpose within the group. A group leader creates alignment by balancing discussion and group activities so that these three categories are present: individual, small group, and full group. But stop me if you have heard all this before, and I think you have. I'm talking about Me/We/US, one of the key principles of breakthrough decision making presented in Chapter 1. Explaining the process and demonstrating early that there will be multiple stages (Me/We/Us) lets everyone know right away that they will have many ways to participate and contribute.

Alignment is needed for emergence and convergence. It is equally important to understand the ideas and why they are chosen. To get the most out of the group, you need to allow time for emergence (idea creation) and then convergence (choosing the best ideas). Let's see how this looks in practice by reviewing an error I noticed during a workshop I was sitting in on.

Tina, the group leader, began by spending eight minutes leading her group using the *wishing* activity to create a common goal. The eight workshop participants created plenty of ideas and wrote them down on Post-its. She made sure that lots of ideas were created by encouraging the group, and finally, there were about fifty Post-its stuck to the wall. She did not have people discuss in small groups nor develop or choose ideas, skipping the most crucial emergence stage altogether. No one understood the ideas, and they had to make a lot of guesses about what they meant and how to complete them. Tina tried to transition to convergence and used Dot Voting for polling the group about the best ideas. She gave five dots to each participant. You can imagine the results; first, the participants never understood the ideas, and now they prioritised without any discussion on what kind of ideas should be prioritised. And what kind of ideas did the participants choose? Their own ideas, of course—those were the only ones they understood!

The common goal Tina wanted to create had become a wall of scattered individual goals. Unfortunately, the results of her activity were incomplete. Tina noticed this and tried to group ideas together. Unfortunately, grouping is not the same as creating understanding and alignment. It is simply an unnecessary practice of putting ideas together.

Avoid grouping

Grouping is the process of combining similar ideas into one idea or placing similar ideas into one group. It is natural to want to do this. Grouping comes from our mind's natural categorization process that we use in our daily lives to remember and process ideas. Grouping ideas helps us in our daily lives, but it is counterproductive and you should avoid it.

Avoid grouping by:
- Giving clear instructions to the group to write down each idea individually
- Write down one idea per Post-it note
- Only combine ideas that are exactly the same (duplicates)
- Monitor group progress regularly and give additional instructions as needed
- Display ideas clearly and separately when using visualisation tools (Roadmap, Kanban, etc.)

What can we learn from her mistakes? The number one takeaway is to use small groups when creating and choosing ideas. The formula is simple; the more you work in small groups, the more alignment you create.

6. Use group memory

Group memory is an ongoing record of the work a group produces during a workshop or meeting. To use group memory, you need to display ideas and other essential pieces of information in the workspace so that everyone can always see it. Group memory is something anyone can master. It does not require any special skills or attributes, yet I see people mess this up again and again. Using group memory to visualise ideas helps people focus on decision making as they can see the subject matter right in front of them, and they are reminded of the task at hand. It also helps the decision-making process because the group can simultaneously keep track of multiple ideas, expanding their brain capacity.

Use group memory

- Use group memory to focus the group and to help decision making.

- Objectives, the agenda (workshop schedule), and instructions are written down and displayed for everyone to see during the workshop.

You also need to visualise the instructions for each group tool you use. Write them down large enough for everyone to see. No matter how well I think I explain my instructions, someone always misunderstands or forgets what I say. So, I usually use bullet points and write down a simplified version of the instructions as I describe them. This helps keep people on task, and they can always refer to the visualised instructions as needed.

Conversely, if there is any uncertainty or confusion about the instructions, people may follow this feeling, and soon, the entire group will be lost. Clear instructions are essential when you are facilitating larger groups. If your instructions are unclear or ambiguous, you can cause disarray and disorder in the group, and if a few people lose focus, this spreads within the larger group, and soon the leader has a real problem on their hands.

Our friend Tina made another mistake; she wrote down the instructions and tried to use group memory, but she used small Post-it notes. The ideas were recorded and displayed, but no one could see them from more than a few feet away! Be sure to come prepared for a workshop and have the right tools to visualise. Some companies will provide a space with a large whiteboard or projector, which makes using group memory easy. But sometimes, you will have to make do with your own materials. Bring a flipchart or jumbo Post-it notes and tape so that you are prepared for anything.

7. Presence

Be present

- The leader actively monitors the group by observing and listening. This lets them know when to step in and help if there are issues that get in the way of the workshop objectives.

All impressive leaders share one thing in common: a strong presence. No, I am not talking about charisma or a bubbly personality. Your presence as a leader is your attentiveness to the group. In other words, you need to be present and monitor how things are coming along. Presence is about observing and listening to the group. If you can do this, you will be able to tell when people run into obstacles and require assistance. If you notice this, you will be able to help clarify a point or explain the instructions differently so that people understand. Maybe you have seen this in practice yourself. Have you ever been in a workshop where the leader seemed to intuitively answer a question you had right before you had the chance to ask it? Or perhaps you had a teacher that always came around your desk at just the right time to help motivate you or clarify a point. This is presence in action.

Leaders who are not entirely present tend to push forward to the next part of an activity, even if the activity's objectives are not met. Pay close attention to the transitional points between different activities and workshop stages. If the group does not agree on the previous stage's results, you cannot continue. If you continue without an agreement, you will simply lead them in the wrong direction and further away from the objectives. Listen closely to feedback and try to understand the feeling in the room to ensure that there are no remaining questions, doubts, or concerns. I use dedicated feedback and polling tools for this, and I also use the simple method of asking people directly for candid feedback.

A present leader also can tell when they need to push people to get back on track and stop counterproductive behaviours. In a dream world, everyone would hang off your every word and give you their complete and undivided attention. Unfortunately, the reality is a bit different, and there are times when I notice people tuning out, pulling out their phones, talking over me, or outright ignoring my instructions. If you spend enough time leading groups, you will see these behaviours from time to time, too. Do not ignore them. Instead, ask people to actively participate by getting back on track and following along with the workshop schedule. If this does not work, be candid and ask why these things are happening. Do not take it personally or get offended. Instead, figure out why these behaviours are happening. Then you can intervene and propose an activity or plan for the rest of the workshop that everyone agrees to follow.

8. Reaching the goal/delivering the objective

The final competency of a great group leader is to make sure that the workshop's objective is achieved. This is your primary job and the reason you spend so much time designing the perfect workshop. But it is not always easy, even for the best leaders. People are unpredictable. You never know who will arrive on time, how focused people will be, the amount of effort they will put forth, or if the right people are even invited to the meeting. You are also working with time constraints; perhaps you are given two hours to tackle a topic, and you suddenly realise that it is so complex that the job would require days.

Reach the goal

- Objectives of the workshop are reached on time

- If targets are not reached, the workshop is paused and the group decides on the next steps

- The outcome is evaluated against the objectives

Most of the time, I come to a workshop prepared with a plan that uses the tools and methods I describe in this book. By planning ahead, I almost always guarantee that I will guide a group to complete the workshop objectives. However, if for some reason you fail to reach the objectives, be transparent. Agree with the group on what the next steps should be and what happens next. This could mean another workshop to deal with a re-framed topic, or it could mean focusing on the delivered content and shifting or abandoning the original objective.

I remember an instance when I was facilitating a strategy workshop. About two hours into the session, it became apparent that the group was not producing enough content to move forward. Some ideas were created initially, but they could not be developed. Why? The participants were not familiar with new markets and other requirements to outline the challenges or develop the ideas in a meaningful way. We stopped the session, talked about it, and decided to put the workshop on hold for two weeks while everyone researched the topic. Once everyone had the chance to prepare adequately, we would have a new strategy workshop and try again.

Talking with the group about failed objectives can turn a bad situation into a productive one. Compare the results against the original workshop goal and evaluate them together. There is always something gained from a workshop, even if it is not the original objective.

Last but not least, assess the results. Show the group the workshop's objective and ask everyone their thoughts about if they reached the objectives. Yes, this can be dangerous—maybe five hands will shoot up into the air, and multiple people will begin telling you that they think your workshop was a waste of time. Wouldn't it be easier just to end things on a high note instead? No! Perhaps someone is unhappy, but it is far better to deal with the fact right there than to have people suffer in silence and talk about it behind your back later.

1. The leader's neutral role
- The leader is content neutral and does not show personal preference, nor group, or edit the ideas created during the workshop

2. Workshop stages
- The leader uses a clear and logical workshop process

3. Tools for creating and choosing ideas
- The leader knows an adequate number of tools and how to choose the right tools to use to meet the needs of the group and complete the workshop objectives

4. Psychological Safety
- The leader is transparent and clearly explains the goal, schedule, instructions, and roles
- The leader is friendly
- The leader connects participants

5. Creating alignment (dealing with the content)
- Balancing individual, small-group, and large-group activities
- Giving importance to both emergence and convergence

6. Visualising
- Visualising the group's ideas to help decision making
- Workshop schedule, workshop goals, and instructions are written down and displayed

7. Presence
- The leader observes and listens to the group and intervenes actively when the group is stuck.

8. Reaching the Goal
- Objectives of the workshop are reached on time
- If targets are not reached, the leader and the group discuss why. A plan on how to proceed and meet the objectives is made
- The outcome is evaluated against the objectives

CHAPTER 3:

Dealing with Emotions

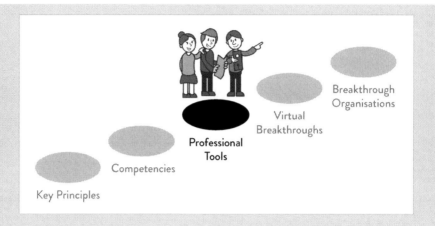

Key Principles
Competencies
Professional Tools
Virtual Breakthroughs
Breakthrough Organisations

What's here

- **Four different case studies that each illustrate an emotionally charged situation and how to approach it:**
  - The therapeutic benefits of addressing emotions
  - Resolving negative emotions within project management
  - Beginning the healing process
  - Dealing with uncertainty, fear, and anger caused by workshop results
- **Tools:** Izard's theory of basic emotions, Archipelago of Emotions, Timeline, Wheel of Emotions, Emotional Goal Setting, Carousel

How it helps

Learn the theories that explain how and why emotions are felt and learn group-level tools facilitators use to work with emotions. This knowledge will enable you to help people use their emotions productively and keep them from being paralysed by what they feel.

There is no crying in baseball

"Are you crying? Are you crying?! There's no crying in baseball!"
The quote above comes from Tom Hanks in the film *A league of their own*. Hanks portrays a demanding coach who manages a women's baseball team competing in the All-American Girls Baseball League. Hanks first tries a hard-nosed approach, complete with a bit of yelling and harsh criticism, which causes one of his players to break down in tears, which causes Hanks to put forth the classic quote that states that there is no place for tears in baseball. Why am I talking about Tom Hanks and baseball, of all things? I do have a point, I promise.

The point is that I have met many people that adopt a similar approach of trying to remove emotions from the business place. "I am a manager, not a therapist," they might say. Or they might question why they need to deal with emotions at all; "That's something for employees to sort out with their families or at the bar in their own time."

Forbes Magazine even put forth an article titled "How to Remove Emotions from the Business Equation", instructing readers to approach situations analytically and take a break and pause a session if things become emotional.

I agree that there is a time and place to minimise emotions; after all, you should not make critical business decisions in a reactionary way. Instead, you should analyse the current wants and key needs and then decide. But with that said, it is simply impossible to lead groups effectively if one does not have the skills and tools to help people address their emotions. As a facilitator, I work with people and enable them to make decisions, unlike business analysts or consultants that operate with a more analytical approach. Because facilitation approaches all situations from a people perspective, a successful group leader must be comfortable in emotionally charged moments and be equipped with the tools necessary to guide groups through them.

There even is a specific branch of facilitation called crisis facilitation that focuses on facilitative techniques for literal life and death situations such as hostage negotiation conflicts that threaten the wellbeing of entire communities. These moments of crisis are always very emotional as people are scared, angry, resentful, panicked, etc. Strong emotions like these cause people to freeze, and their decision-making ability is drastically reduced. As the Forbes article suggests, the answer is not always to take a break and remove the person from the situation. Instead, people need therapy. Yes, therapy. Before you roll your eyes and think that I am asking you to lie down on the couch, let me assure you that I am still talking about group leadership.

Leadership and therapy are more closely related than you might think. Some of the tools and techniques presented in this book have been used in the mental health field for years. For example, Mental Health America, a large non-profit group that has been around for 110 years promoting self-care and wellness for Americans, released a thorough guide explaining how to use facilitation in care groups and self-help groups. Their guide uses group tools to foster understanding and agreement, just like we hope to in the meetings and workshops we lead.[*]

The business meetings and workshops you will find yourself in may not be as emotional as the support groups that Mental Health America refers to, but they are not entirely different. In both contexts, emotions can hold us back and keep us from advancing, or they can guide us and be a powerful tool towards progress.

I saw this first-hand when I went to a large textile factory to help discuss process development. The managing director wanted to reorganise the scheduling to account for new financial constraints. He wanted to increase production levels without increased costs, so he devised new scheduling rules for his employees. He planned to save money by cutting out most overtime pay and enforcing a strict clock-in/clock-out system. The workers were furious and would not let anything progress until they had the chance to voice their feelings and opinions. In the end, they were not upset at all by the proposed changes, but they needed to have the opportunity to give feedback and feel they were heard before things could progress.

---

[*] Mental Health America's guide, *Support Group Facilitation Guide*, was published in 2016, and can be accessed online using the following link: https://www.mentalhealthamerica.net/sites/default/files/MHA%20 Support%20Group%20Facilitation%20Guide%202016.pdf

The fundamental emotions

To properly navigate emotions, we will first need to define our terms better; the word *emotions* is vague and does not tell us much. Thankfully, we can rely on existing work to help us. American psychologist Carroll Izard was a pioneer in developing emotional theory, and he outlined ten basic emotions which everyone experiences.

Izard's ten basic emotions

- Joy
- Excitement
- Surprise
- Sadness
- Anger
- Fear
- Disgust
- Shame
- Guilt
- Contempt

I thought Izard's list was the perfect starting point. I modified it by deleting some emotions and adding *interest*, *love*, *pride*, and *shame* to the list. I wanted to make sure that the list of emotions I was using had terms that participants could relate to. It is worthwhile to use words that are accessible; Izard uses the word *contempt*, but I would replace it with *distaste* or *hatred*. These words are common and well known, so they evoke a stronger response from participants than a less common word like *contempt* does. It is vital to use emotions that trigger a good talk if you lead an activity that uses emotions; you want them to resonate as much as possible, even if they stray from Izard's list.

Emotions that resonate with people and spark conversation

- Joy
- Surprise
- Interest
- Love
- Pride

- Sadness
- Annoyance/Anger
- Fear
- Shame

Now that we have our list of common emotions, let's examine these case studies to learn more about dealing with emotions while leading groups.

Case study #1: The therapeutic benefits of addressing emotions

The scene

Performing at your best is impossible if you are afraid. Imagine trying to drive down the freeway if you are scared of all the other cars on the road. How about trying to cook a delicious pasta sauce while being suspicious of the onions you are chopping up? Fear holds many people back from living their best lives. It can even be so severe that it interrupts daily life.

Fear can be an obstacle for people participating in meetings and workshops, too. As the group leader, it is your job to check if negative emotions like fear are getting in the way of reaching the workshop objectives. If so, you need to address the situation early on to get your workshop back on track.

One example of what this looks like comes from a strategy workshop I led with a group of managers from an athletic apparel company. Ironically, their slogan was *Fear Not!* but I guess this slogan was only for their customers. Early on in the workshop, I noticed that about half of the group seemed tentative and even a bit agitated. The stakes of the workshop were high. Their boss had invited me to lead this strategy workshop to help determine the best strategy to follow moving forward. The company was considering two options; continue to offer a diverse range of athletic apparel and products or scale back down to their core competencies and focus solely on running shoes and clothes. People knew that the decisions made during the workshop could spell doom to their careers.

If the stakes were not so high, I would have laughed at the scene before me; the room was split down the middle. On one side of the room, people seemed serious but also calm. It was evident that these employees worked on the running products—no matter the outcome of this meeting, their jobs were safe. The group on the other side of the room was only a few feet away, but they inhabited a different world; no one was relaxed enough to make small talk, and one lady in the front row was beginning to turn green! When I started the strategy workshop and put them into small groups to participate in a check-in activity, I realised that people were too preoccupied to focus. Many of the conversations I heard also demonstrated that quite a few people were defensive about their jobs being at risk and could not move past that feeling. Observing this, I decided that I needed to intervene. I began to write down emotions on pieces of paper. I knew just what this group needed.

The tool for the job

"It doesn't take a psychologist to see that something is bothering all of you. I understand that the current situation brings out some strong emotions, so I want to pause the workshop for about thirty minutes to explore these emotions. If you look around the room, you will see six different islands."

"All I see are papers," said Martin, the Running Division's Team Lead.

"Excellent, Martin. You've spotted our islands, which happen to be made out of pieces of paper. On each island, you will see a piece of paper with a basic emotion written on it. The rule of each island is to think about that emotion and talk about how you feel regarding your company. For example, this first island has the emotion *Joy* written on it. So, if you come to this island, you will need to think about how the company makes you feel joy."

"So, we are forced to make up things that we like about this situation? I feel quite a few emotions right now, but none of them are close to joy." It was the lady who was turning green, and she had a point.

I continued, "You're absolutely right. There's not much point in talking about the joyful aspects of this situation if you don't see it that way. What you can do is visit a different island if you like. There are six different islands in this room, and you will have time to visit three of them. Each visit will last about six minutes, and I will tell you when to rotate to a new island. If an island is crowded, please consider visiting a less crowded island to balance the discussions. You can begin now by choosing your first island to visit!"

People began distributing themselves among the islands right away. People who seemed stressed out and fearful of the new strategic changes went right towards islands labelled *anger*, *sadness*, and *fear*. The islands marked *pride*, *joy*, and *interest* were filled with the other half of the group that appeared less worried about the impending changes. I circulated the room and passed each island. I walked past the *sadness* island and heard one man who was on the verge of tears say, "Ten years of my life working here, and for what? Only to fail in the end? What was the point of it all?"

On the *anger* island, I saw two red face women agree that the timing of this new strategy workshop was "insulting". I continued walking around the room, listening. I kept my eye on the clock so that I knew when to tell people to rotate to the next island, and after three separate rounds of discussion, I called everyone back together and told them to sit back down in their original seats.

"How did you all like the islands?" I asked.

Paul, one of the managers who was fearful of his job being cut, said, "I found just the islands I needed, so I had the chance to vent a bit with others who feel the same way I do."

"Anyone else?" I asked. More hands went up, and as I called on them, I learned that others echoed Paul's sentiments; they too were able to find the islands that they needed to share their emotions.

"Thanks for your feedback, everyone. It sounds like everyone had an easy enough time to match their feelings with the right island. Was there anything unexpected or surprising that came up during this activity? Did you catch yourself on an island that you didn't expect to visit?"

"I did," said Ronny, the long-time manager of the Men's Running division. "I had a lot to say when I visited the *sadness* island. My job isn't threatened because Men's Running Division is thriving. But even though my job is not at risk, I realised that I am sad and a bit scared of the changes that are coming."

Anna, one of the employees at risk of having her team cut, said, "I had the opposite experience. Unlike Ronny, my team will probably be disbanded, and I will lose my job. I'm obviously sad and angry about this, but I found myself on the pride island with a lot to say. I guess that I saw some silver linings to this situation, too."

Some people still seemed melancholy and nervous, but the overall mood in the room was drastically better than before. I felt that the group was ready to leave the archipelago and return to the scheduled workshop agenda.

Analysing the Archipelago of Emotions

I first heard about the Archipelago activity from an Indian facilitator I knew called Aarav. Aarav was brilliant at leading groups. People loved attending his workshops. Aarav loved to use creative and exciting icebreaker activities that captivated people who attended his workshops. He told me often that he only needed five minutes to transform a room full of dysfunctional people into a happy group of friends. One day I asked him if he had any new icebreakers to show me, and low and behold, he walked me through the Archipelago. He explained that he used topics like movies, books, favourite foods, and other light topics with this tool. I was interested, but Aarav worked a lot with teachers and university students—these funny topics suited a classroom environment well. I could not imagine heads of companies or the serious businesspeople that I worked with making small talk and discussing trivia topics, so I changed the titles of the islands into emotions. The Archipelago of Emotions was born! Interestingly, I have difficulties getting busy high-level executives to talk about movies, but they are happy to discuss their feelings – emotions are fascinating.

Archipelago of Emotions

- This tool creates trust by allowing participants to safely share their emotions and process negative emotions.

- Islands will be established around the room. Each island has an emotion assigned to it. When people visit that island, they can only talk about that specific emotion.

- After about five minutes of conversation ask people to switch islands.

- Repeat about four times.

- You should use Archipelago of Emotions to deal with negative emotions and to create trust.

The reason why Aarav and I love the Archipelago of Emotions is that it creates trust through self-disclosure. Usually, we only explore the surface levels of self-disclosure. For example, my name is Pepe, and I work as a facilitator. I like to travel and go water-skiing. These are the basic facts about me. Somewhere deeper are my emotions, my fears, wants, and feelings. Talking about emotions is self-disclosure on a deeper level than what people usually reach at work. As people share what they feel with others, they become more comfortable and realise that others feel the same way. You feel empathy and relate to what other people are going through, and strong connections are made. Sometimes, a bit of emotional therapy goes a long way!

I use the Archipelago of Emotions when I want to connect participants and create trust. In this case with the apparel company, there was a divide in the room, and people were not emotionally connected.

The new strategy's potential implications did not affect everyone equally; some people were guaranteed to continue as usual with their jobs while others were possibly going to be looking for new work soon. Since the group's emotions related directly to the outcome of this workshop, I used the company's current state as the topic of discussion. Sometimes my topic is change, values or just pure emotions – the participants can share any experience related to the emotion of the island where they stand.

Archipelago of Emotions: process and participant instructions

Check-in (30 minutes):

1. Presenting the objective of the workshop and the workshop process.

2. Introduction to Archipelago of Emotions
   - "Emotions are fascinating, and we are going begin the workshop by exploring some basic emotions related to our current strategy. Are you ready?"
   - "I've placed islands around the room – each one with a basic emotion written on it. That is because each island evokes different emotions and people on that island talk about what makes them feel that emotion. For instance, on the island labeled fear, you might discuss what is it with the current strategy that makes you afraid or worried. When visiting the island with the label *enjoyment*, you could discuss what you like about the strategy."
   - "You are about to visit three islands of your choice. Each visit lasts about six minutes. If the island is crowded, it might be wiser to visit some other island first. If you are alone, you might visit another island first or you can have a good talk with yourself. I'll tell you when to change islands."
   - "Ready? Find your island!"

3. Debrief

   - "How did you like the islands?"
   - "Did you discover anything interesting?"

I don't use the Archipelago of Emotions if the participants have an open conflict. That would be a bit too heavy for this tool, and I would need to use something more thorough, like Dynamic Facilitation.

Using Archipelago of Emotions is quick and straightforward, and the tool can be used with groups of up to hundreds of people. You can set up and run the entire activity within half an hour, regardless of group size. Just be sure to explain the instructions and the process to the group and have a quick debrief after the activity to see if anything unexpected came up and take the room's temperature.

Case study #2: Resolving negative emotions within project management

The scene

The drive from Ballston Spa, New York, to Lewiston, Maine, is beautiful. Trees line the road that winds through the hills and dense forest of the North-eastern United States of America. Perhaps it is fall as you leisurely drive through the picturesque scenery without a care in the world. The drive is so beautiful and well known that several travel books have been written about how to structure and execute drive-cations in this area. Yes, a vacation where the point is to tour around in your car and soak in the scenery. That sounds too much like my morning commute to appeal to me, but hey, to each their own. I have been lucky enough to drive this route a few times myself, but I struggle to find beauty in the surroundings. Why? Not because I am a negative person who lacks imagination. It all begins with a story that is not my own, although I wind up playing an essential part in the end.

You see, Route 56, one of the oldest and most well-known roads in the region, needed a makeover. Potholes filled the highways, and cars congested the road. It was overstrained and quickly becoming outdated. The combination of an influx of tourists and the steady traffic of truckers and locals meant that the road constantly needed repairs of some sort. The State of New York decided that it was important to invest in this valuable infrastructure and redo large portions of the road. One key part of this makeover would be rebuilding the Kristaps Bridge, which crossed a river and an extensive marshland. Residents in the area, truckers, and tourists all needed a new bridge, but it would also be used politically to symbolise rejuvenation and tax dollars at work. The timeframe for this project was eighteen to twenty months, which seemed like plenty of time.

Two firms were the prominent players in this project; Ernesto Engineering to design the bridge and Tella Construction Company to execute the design. Both firms were well-liked and had excellent reputations. They were large and well established, which is most likely why they won the bid for this project in the first place. With the Kristaps Bridge project in such capable hands, what could go wrong? Well, as it turns out, almost everything.

Flash forward sixteen months. Almost a year and a half had passed, and the bridge was nowhere near ready. Tella Construction had only just finished laying the beginning of the foundation for the bridge. What was supposed to be a project lasting a maximum of twenty months was already delayed by another ten months. There was no dramatic explosion or hurricane that derailed this project. Instead, it seems that disaster took shape in a series of minor delays, mistakes and miscalculations that left Ernesto Engineering and Tella Construction pointing fingers at each other and trying to place the blame on the other side. The bridge was a government project, so there were fines to be paid due to the companies not delivering a finished bridge, and the dispute was brought to the State Court of New York for arbitration. The court blamed both sides, and this project was becoming a costly mistake for both companies. The worst part? Enough progress had been made already on the bridge to require both sides to see things through, so in addition to the hefty fines that Ernesto and Tella needed to pay, the court ordered that the two companies devise a plan to be able to continue working together to finish the Kristaps Bridge. Unlike the Sagrada Familia—the famous church in Barcelona under construction for 100 years and built on "gods timetable"—the bridge had a strict deadline.

Where do I come in? I am not a civil engineer, and no, I was not pouring the cement to build the bridge, either. However, I am good friends with Tammy Sanchez, a former New York Councilwoman. She asked me to facilitate a workshop between the management teams of Ernesto Engineering and Tella Construction to help them move past their atrocious start to the project and get to a state of mind where they can continue the project and finally finish the bridge. And so, that is how I found myself in Ballston Spa, New York, in a small conference room in an airport hotel.

The tool for the job

The two sides could barely mask their mutual dislike for each other. The court-ordered arbitration had ended just a few weeks prior, so the disagreement was fresh in their minds. No one was excited by the thought of working together for the next few months, either. The workshop attendees were professionals—men and women who had risen to upper management for their well-respected companies. No one wanted to fight each other, but I could tell that mental acts of violence were being committed as people on both sides of the room sized each other up. I began the workshop by first presenting the workshop's objective, which was to prepare both sides to work together again by moving past negative emotions. I then asked people to find a partner from the other company to discuss why they were here and chat briefly about what they wanted to get from the session. I was happy to see that everyone could speak civilly with someone from the other side, even if they did not seem to enjoy it that much.

With the group adequately warmed up, it was time to begin moving past the negative emotions. "From what I understand, you've been on quite a roller-coaster ride together over the last year and a half. Plenty of ups and downs, I imagine."

"You can say that again," said Ricky, an Ernesto engineer.

"Well, I want every single one of you to tell me all about it," I said.

"Just pick up a newspaper," said Leslie, one of the managers of Tella Construction. She continued, "It's all out there and well documented. Each delay and problem, ranging from the bad weather to the material shortages, and even the protests from PETA when we were following the plans to pave the marshlands and disrupt the nesting habitat of some speckled hens." Leslie was beginning to get angry and spoke faster and louder as she continued, "You can even read about how Tella had to pay over $100,000 in fines for missing deadlines. All the information you need is a matter of public record, and you do not need us to tell you the facts."

"That sounds like quite the experience, Leslie, but I do want to hear from you. I want your perspective on the whole project. After all, every one of you probably has a slightly different experience and point of view." Some laughs came from the group as someone joked that differing points of view are what got them into so many arguments in the first place.

"Here is how I want you to tell your story. Each person is going to draw a line on a piece of paper. On one end of the line, you will write the year that this project began...when was that?"

"2018," offered one of the engineers.

"Great, thank you. On one end of the line, you have that year, 2018, and on the other end of the line, you will write the word *Now*. This line represents the timeline of the entire project. On the line, I want you to label three things: successes, disappointments, and major events. The final thing you need to do to complete your timeline is to draw another line that reflects your feelings during this project. This line will run the length of the timeline and move up or down, depending on if you were feeling a positive or negative emotion at the time. Once you complete it, it will look like a wave that rises and falls as it passes the major events, successes, and disappointments marked on the timeline. This line is called the emotional line. Draw it higher on the page to reflect stronger positive emotions and dip it down to the bottom of the page to represent negative emotions. Is all of that clear?"

No one had any questions, so I gave the group about ten minutes to complete the instructions. Once this was complete, I asked everyone to discuss their timelines and share their emotions. "Please get into groups of four. Each group needs to have two people from Ernesto Engineers and two from Tella Construction, no exceptions! Your job now is to share your timelines. Then as a group, create one shared timeline and emotional line running over it. You should draw these on a piece of flipchart paper when you are ready. Take about 30 minutes to do this, and be ready to present your results when the time is up!"

I walked and watched as people divided into groups and got to it. Depending on the groups, some people laughed as they compared their results, while others took a more serious approach and politely listened to each other. By the end of the allotted time for group work, multiple flipchart papers were on the wall, each with a shared timeline on it. One of the shared timelines marked out the issue that the bridge project faced with the zoning restrictions in the marshland; it was a protected environment, but Ernesto Engineering did not account for this in their plans. At the same time, Tella Construction was also ordering building materials that did not comply with national compliance laws about sustainable building, so both sides made an error around this issue. Yet, each was quick to forgive the other side but still thought that they were being blamed for their own mistake—something that turned out not to be accurate at all. When everyone realised this, they understood that both sides were invested in the same goal and not interested in blaming each other.

"Thank you all for working so hard and so well together. It is now time to look at what you all came up with. Were there any surprises during this activity?"

"I have an answer," said a builder called Joel. "I was shocked at how we were all able to create a common story together. I thought that there would be more disagreement about what happened and why. But after comparing notes, I could see that the engineer's emotions matched my own. When I was assuming that they were angry, they were not! This opened my eyes as to how the other side saw the issue, and it improved communication."

"Thank you, everyone, for sharing. Based on these shared stories, does anyone have any wishes for the coming months as Ernesto and Tella work together to finish the bridge?"

Margery, one of the lead engineers, wished that communication was as open and easy to follow as it was today in the workshop; "Now that I know what the other side is thinking, I'm not afraid of what they could be thinking!"

David, a Tella manager, added, "I wish that we would have been able to communicate this before the courts and lawyers got involved. But, since it's too late for that, the next best thing is to keep this standard up moving forward."

And finally, an engineer seated in the back of the room said, "I wish that we don't jump to blame each other when the next unexpected challenges come up."

I thanked the group for a job well done. I planned on using their wishes later in the workshop to build shared goals for the two teams.

Timeline

1. **Draw three lines on the wall**: Me, Team, and World. Start the line using the year that the first participant entered the team. End the line with now.

   2000 _____ World _____ Now

   2000 _____ Team _____ Now

   2000 _____ Me _____ Now

2. **Ask participants to mark major events, successes, and disappointments** on the whiteboard.

3. **Feelings**: Participants draw a line describing their feelings at that particular time. They should mark positive feelings on top of the timeline and negative feelings under the timeline.

4. **Analysis and storytelling**: Ask participants to create a story based on the timelines; What do the timelines tell about the people involved? About the team? About the world we all live in?

5. **You may ask additional questions** depending on the case. What kind of leadership do we expect? Our strengths and challenges? What kind of ground rules can help us work together? What kind of values would help us to succeed? Where do we want to be in 5 years?

Analysis of Timeline

This workshop was about as emotionally charged as they get, with both sides undergoing arbitration in an attempt to resolve their issues. While the courts settled who has to pay what, an abundance of raw emotion remained. Moreover, these two sides needed to move past these emotions if they were to have any chance at re-joining forces to finish the bridge, as the court demanded. I used the Timeline tool to help each side understand what the other side was feeling. As a result, they could relive the shared history together, but through the other side's perspective, which helped create empathy and understanding and made it possible to start over again.

It's common for strong disagreements to be born out of fear of what the other party thinks. Are they disappointed or angry with you? Are you afraid that they are blaming you for something out of your control? You may think this is the case, but it is not always so. It can be hard to directly ask the other side how they feel about your work. Unless you share your emotions, as was done in this activity, the disagreements and misunderstandings can grow and grow until they reach the State Court of New York! All that Ernesto Engineering and Tella Construction needed was a bit of shared empathy and understanding.

You may explore key events on different levels—what is happening in the world, company, department, team, individual—and you will get an interesting systemic view of what has happened. In this case, we only used one level, their joint project.

Tella Construction and Ernesto Engineering had a history of poor communication, so I needed to use Timeline to create dialogue and bring two opposing viewpoints together. Once I had asked for groups to develop wishes using emotional wishing, I would then use those wishes later in a different session to help clarify the goals of the two companies.

Timeline – Process and participant instructions

Objective: Deal with negative emotions and prepare the project leadership team to work together

Time: 90 minutes

Check-in (10minutes):
1. Presenting the objective and the workshop process.
2. Pair discussion with a partner from the other company:
   – "Why am I here?"
3. Feedback
   – "Would anyone like to share?"

Workshop tool: Timeline (75 minutes)
1. Individual stage:
   – "Draw a timeline starting from the beginning of the project until now."
   – "Write major events, successes and disappointments on the timeline."
   – "Draw a line describing your feelings during the project. If you felt great, your line goes far above the timeline. If you felt terrible, then your line must be somewhere very low. I predict this line showing your feelings will look pretty like a snake."
2. Small-group stage
   – "In mixed groups of four share your stories."
   – "Create a common story about this project from the beginning until now on a piece of flipchart paper."
   – "Think about future cooperation and make three wishes."
3. Presenting stories

Check-out (5 minutes):
1. Discussion with the group
   – "How did the workshop go, any surprises?"
2. "Thank you!"

What about the rest of the workshop? Based on wishes of the group we created a common goal, solutions, and an action plan. I will not tell you how to do it, because you should already know (formula and process outline presented and analysed in previous chapters).

What was used and why?

Pair discussion – To focus and connect

Timeline – To process emotions and review their changes and effect over time

Me/We/Us – To create understanding

Case study #3:
Beginning the healing process

The scene

Sometimes relationships sour. Things can start off wonderfully, but over time a good thing turns toxic. This is a fact that most of us can relate to on a personal level, but also professionally too. Have you ever worked with a toxic teammate? You might have been a toxic teammate at one point. Working with a person who is hostile, angry, burnt out, or outright toxic is stressful. Removing the problem person from the organisation is a common step in moving forward, but it does not fix the situation completely. Facilitators are often brought in to help groups move forward. For example, I remember working with a group of hardware developers at Hot Chip, a semiconductor and computer processor manufacturing company. Their Development Team had just lost a longtime member called Jack, a longtime employee who was extremely talented but equally aggravating. I was called in about two weeks after Jack was fired to help the remaining team members move on past the toxic atmosphere that surrounded Jack for years.

The tool for the job

I greeted everyone and explained that today's objective was to share emotions about what had happened and prepare to move forward together without Jack.

"We have 90 minutes today, and I hope by the end of the session, you will have been able to share your feelings about what happened and feel better about moving forward together as a team. The first thing I would like you to do is find a partner. We will have a brief discussion in pairs for about three minutes. The question is a simple one; *Why am I here today?* You have three minutes and can start now!"

Once everyone had the chance to discuss in pairs, I asked three volunteers to share their answers.

"I'm here to try and move past a bad taste that has been in my mouth for the last two years," said Justin.

Anna added, "I want to get rid of the anger I have towards Jack so I can enjoy coming to work again."

Jerri said, "I am here to try and wipe the slate clean and remove the negative feelings and guilt I have."

"Thank you, everyone. I heard something to do with emotions in all your answers, so I think it's important to have a good opportunity to think about how you feel. I heard some of you mention common emotions like shame, anger, and sadness. On the handouts and the whiteboard, I have drawn a wheel and divided it into eight different sections. Each section has an emotion: love, joy, pride, interest, shame, sadness, fear, and anger. Think about how you feel about Jack leaving the company and consider each emotion written in the wheel. If you feel one of the emotions extremely strongly, draw a line on the outer-most edge of the section of the wheel with that emotion written in it. If you don't feel any emotion, then draw a line on the inner-most part of the wheel where that emotion is written. One by one, go through all eight emotions like this until each one is marked off appropriately to reflect how you feel. Once all of the emotions are marked, then connect the lines."

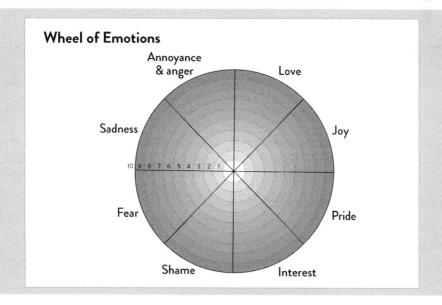

Wheel of Emotions

After a few moments, the Dev Team had finished, so I asked them to get into two groups of four to share their wheels with each other. Up until this stage, the mood had been a bit reserved, with people being quiet. But now, in their groups of four, people were laughing and loudly talking as they compared the similarities and differences in their emotional wheels.

"Joy? How could you have marked joy so highly?"

"I feel sadness more than anything else. It worked out terribly for Jack and us. But at least we managed to perform well as a team results-wise, even if each day with the guy was worse than pulling teeth."

"I scored all eight emotions as moderate or high. I'm excited and joyful that he is no longer around, but I will miss him purely from a performance aspect. He was a damn good programmer, even if he had no clue about how to treat other people."

I listened to a few more comments as the groups continued to share, and then I called for attention to explain what came next. "Now, in these same groups, create a common emotional wheel. This will be a shared story that captures how all of you collectively felt about your time working with Jack."

The instant the instructions left my mouth, several debates erupted around the room.

Justin wondered just what part of Jack's daily degrading and sarcastic remarks should have made him feel Joy. Kari was explaining that her group's collective emotional wheel should score the highest possible amount of happiness because, as she put it, "It was an awesome moment when Jack made a rude comment about Alex's shirt, only to spill coffee all over his new pants. He was so mad and embarrassed, served him right!"

Once the groups had time to create their shared emotional wheels, I called everyone together again, asked each group to present their shared wheel to everyone else. Then I gave the final set of instructions for the session.

"You all have done a great job making the emotional wheels and thinking about how you felt about your time with Jack. We have thought about the present moment enough, so now I would like you all to take a moment and individually think about what you want to feel in the future. For example, when you come to work or are with your colleagues, what emotions do you want to feel? Take a few moments and write down your ideas."

No one had any trouble thinking about the emotions they wanted to feel in the future, and I soon had them share their ideas in groups of four and finally together as one large group.

"OK, everyone, I need an emotion that someone wants to feel in the future. Anything will do!"

"Hope!" someone called out.

"Perfect, hope it is! But why wait to feel hope? I want everyone to join me in a meditation that will fill us with hope, right here, right now! Close your eyes and imagine coming to work, being with this team, and feeling hope. If you are brave and ambitious, try and feel hope as strongly as possible right now!"

People gave it their best try, and while I am not sure how strongly they felt hope, I saw that everyone seemed to be enjoying the meditative exercise. So, I asked for two more emotions that people wanted to feel in the future and repeated the meditation focusing on *happiness* and then *serenity*, before closing the session with a check-out activity where I asked for feedback about how we did reaching the workshop objectives.

Analysis of the Wheel of Emotions and Emotional Goal Setting

I used two tools to help Hot Chip employees move past their experiences with Jack. The tools I used were Wheel of Emotions and Emotional Goal Setting.

The Wheel of Emotions helped people stop and take a moment to analyse what was happening internally. Most of the time, we are looking outward, focused on external events and the actions of others. This is especially true within teams and when we collaborate with others. We are concerned about the group dynamic or how something affects other people more than we are aware of our own emotions. The Wheel of Emotions helps us become aware of what is happening on the inside, and once we have this awareness, we can begin talking about our emotions in a healthy way. I used the Me/We/Us structure along with this tool. The primary objective of the 90-minute session was to help people process their emotions and begin the healing process so that they could be ready to move on past a traumatic event.

The other tool I used was Emotional Goal Setting. Setting emotional goals is much more rewarding than creating action points. I firmly believe that you can decide in the morning what you will feel that day, and by fixing this emotion in your head and focusing on it, you create a self-fulfilling prophecy that helps guide you throughout the day. This commitment to feeling an emotion for the day (Emotional Goal Setting) is just as important as what happens during the day. I can wake up, look myself in the mirror and decide that "today is going to be a great day, and I will feel fantastic for the whole day." This commitment to feeling fantastic will do as much or more for me than the activities I have planned throughout the day, even if the activities are something I tend to enjoy, like fishing or shopping. Sure I love to fish and go shopping, but I have had bad days doing both of those things.

Emotional Goal Setting is a straightforward and powerful tool due to the close relationship between our thoughts and our emotions. It's common knowledge that our feelings stem from our thoughts. In other words, if I think negative things, I will feel bad. This is true, but it is also true that our thoughts stem from our emotions. If I commit early to have a joyful day, my thoughts will fall in line with that positive emotion.

I concluded Emotional Goal Setting by asking the group to think about the emotions they wanted to feel in the future and imagine feeling them now. The session ended on a strong positive note.

Process and participant instructions

Objective: Share emotions related to what happened and prepare for the future

Time: 90 minutes

Check-in (10minutes):
1. Presenting the objective and the workshop process.
2. Pair discussion:
   – Why am I here?
3. Feedback
   – "Would anyone like to share?"

Workshop tool: Wheel of Emotions (75 minutes)
1. Individual stage:
   – "Think about your emotions related to Jack leaving the company. Consider each emotion on its own and on a scale of 0 (low) – to 10 (high), mark down how strongly you feel the emotion. Now join the marks around the circle."
2. Small-group stage
   – "In groups of four share your wheels and explain why or why not you are feeling these emotions."
   – "Create a common story explaining how you feel and why."
3. Presenting stories
4. "Individually think which emotions you want to feel in the future."
5. "Share your future feelings in groups of four."
6. "Let's share with everyone how you want to feel in the future."
7. "Now let's close our eyes. Take a deep breath and imagine yourself working in this team and feeling that specific emotion. If you are brave, you can even try to feel that emotion."

Check-out (5 minutes):
1. Discussion with the group
   – "How did the workshop go?"
2. "Thank you!"

What was used and why?

Pair discussion – To focus and connect
Wheel of Emotions – To raise emotional awareness
Me/We/Us – To create understanding
Emotional Goal Setting – To create a positive mindset

Case study #4:
Dealing with uncertainty, fear, and anger due to workshop results

The scene

Looking around the room, you would have guessed that a fight had broken out or that someone had just hurled a horrible insult at someone else. Papers were on the ground. One person was being lectured by three people simultaneously. A giant sigh accompanied by a curse word came from someone in the back of the room. There was even a plate of cookies that someone had thrown on the floor. So, what happened? Is this a story of a brawl or some horrible misunderstanding? Nope, not at all; this was the aftermath of a successful change deployment workshop. During the workshop, the group agreed to some significant changes, and one person even took it on themselves to resign from their role as they felt it was in the company's best interest. That person was now being lectured to by their shocked co-workers while others sat around the room in a haze. There was fear and uncertainty in the room, along with a marvellous collection of cakes, cookies, and pastries. I was facilitating a session in Benny's Original Bakery.

Caroline, the owner of Benny's (apparently, she chose the name randomly), asked for my help leading a change workshop. The business had gone a bit stale and lost customers to a new restaurant in the area. The results of the change workshop involved one of the lead pastry chefs resigning and the bakery slashing its menu back down to a core selection of offerings. These changes were big news to some of the employees at Benny's, men and women who had been working there for years without anything nearly as eventful happening. For the workshop to end on a positive and productive note, I decided to change my planned check-out activity to a tool that could help everyone process things.

The tool for the job

"I can see that these changes are important to all of you and that you have a lot to say. So, let's talk about it then. I need half of the group to stand up please, this side of the room is fine." Half of the group, about eight people, stood up. "Please stand in a circle and face the outside of the room. You all make the inner circle. Everyone else, stand up and make a larger circle around these guys. Arrange yourself to line up evenly with someone in front of you. You are facing in-wards so that you end up standing face to face. Together, all of you are forming a carousel! Carousels move, so the outer part will rotate clockwise while the inner circle stays still. This way, you are going to rotate when I tell you to."

The bakery employees seemed to understand well, and there were no questions yet. I told them that the topic of their conversations was the emotions that they felt during the workshop. I pointed to the wall and said, "On this wall, I have a list of fundamental emotions; joy, love, surprise, pride, interest, fear, sadness, anger, and shame. You can refer to that list if you need help getting your conversations going. Look at the person in front of you and start the conversation by asking each other, *What are you feeling?* Keep chatting with that person until I say it's time to rotate."

People got to it and began chatting right away. I heard one person focus on the emotion *surprise* and how the resignation of the chef left him feeling a bit stupid; "I thought we were more of a team than that, and I had no idea that he would make such a big decision without consulting the rest of us. What am I supposed to do now that he is gone?"

Another person felt fearful and said that such important changes after years of stability left her scared of the uncertain future. I told the group to rotate every five minutes and eventually asked for everyone's attention after the 3rd round of conversations. "Our carousel has come to a stop. Would anyone like to share a bit about what you talked about? Are there any insights?"

I called on a few people to give them a chance to share their conversations. As I expected, people felt better now that they had the opportunity to talk about how they were feeling. Then I brought the workshop to a close once I confirmed that the room's mood was calmer and more stable.

Analysing the Carousel tool

Carousel

Divide the group into two parts. One part will form the inner circle and the other the outer circle. People in the inner circle will stand facing the outer circle. This arrangement forms pairs (2 people facing each other).

The leader gives questions that will be asked in pairs. The question gets participants tuned in to the meeting, such as: What are your expectations? What is your opinion about the topic? Why did you come to the meeting?

After 5 minutes, the facilitator asks the inner circle to stand still and the outer circle to move one-person clock-wise to create new pairs, and new discussions begin. The facilitator will give new topics between each round of discussion.
Repeat 2 – 3 times.

As the workshop with Benny's Original Bakery progressed, people felt a rainbow of emotions. People talked about significant changes, and one person even decided to resign! These changes caused strong feelings of fear and confusion, so I abandoned the original check-out activity that I had planned and decided to use a tool to help the group talk about their emotions. I chose to use the Carousel tool, but Archipelago of Emotions and Wheel of Emotions also would have worked. The important thing was to give everyone the chance to discuss their feelings.

It is hard to perform at your best if you are preoccupied or lost in your emotions. It is hard enough to organise your thoughts, and it is nearly impossible to listen to someone else, let alone connect with them to understand their logic and create breakthroughs. So be aware of the importance of managing the emotions within a group and come prepared with the right tools to lead effectively.

What was used and why?

Carousel – To deal with emotions. Carousel is a good tool to begin a workshop with. It also is good for reviewing at the end of a workshop. To begin a workshop with Carousel, make the topic expectations instead of emotions. For reviewing, you can have participants talk about key takeaways.

Process and participant instructions

Check-out (20 minutes):

1. "This half of the group, please stand up and form a circle. Now turn around facing outwards. You form the inner circle of a carousel. You stand still and people will come and talk to you with a new question each time. There will be three rounds."

2. "The other half of the group will form the outer circle of the carousel rotating with changing questions. You see the fundamental emotions posted on the wall, your first task is to connect with one of the participants standing in the circle and to discuss which emotions you felt during the workshop."

3. "The outer circle moves clockwise to meet the next person. You still see the fundamental emotions posted on the wall. Discuss which emotions you feel now."

4. "The outer circle moves counterclockwise in order to talk to the 6th person. Take a new look at the fundamental emotions posted on the wall and discuss which emotions you are going to feel after this workshop."

5. "The carousel has stopped now. Anyone wants to share insights?"

6. "Thank you for the workshop!"

The benefits of emotional health for group decision making

If you lead a workshop, your job is to create a plan and execute it to meet the objectives. You are not a therapist, and most workshops that I have led relate more to growth strategies, company goals, or new initiatives than they do to feelings and emotions. However, emotional health plays a major role in effective leadership. Remember earlier when I said that a good leader has calm and approachable energy? Good luck with that if you are not emotionally healthy yourself. It is much easier to be a capable leader if you are in a good place emotionally. In other cases, there will be open disagreements that you need to arbitrate before a group can effectively work together, so be sure to have the tools ready that can help you do this. Using tools that help people understand and share their emotions gives three key benefits; 1) increases trust to create better interpersonal interactions, 2) relieves emotional tensions, and 3) provides a sense of closure to a meeting or a workshop.

Increased trust for better interactions

Self-disclosure creates trust. Think about your own life for a moment. Who can you share your feelings with? I would guess that the list is a short one when you get down to it. You need to trust someone to be able to share on an emotional level. When you share your emotions with someone and vice-versa, it strengthens your relationship and opens the door for other vital interactions in the future. This holds true in workshops, too! Sure, the topics are probably not as intimate as what you share with your best friend but asking someone how they feel increases trust within the group. A light tool for sharing emotions that I like to use is Line. Even people who have difficulties communicating how they feel can place themselves on a line to indicate their mood or feeling and explain their choice.

Emotional Islands, demonstrated in this chapter, can explore emotions on a deeper level. In this chapter, I used the tool to ask how people felt about a company strategy, but you may also use Emotional Islands to explore emotions generally: you simply share what makes you feel that particular emotion of the island where you stand. Compared to Line, Emotional Islands create more discussion about emotions, which results in a higher level of trust within the group.

Relieve emotional tensions

If you are angry or upset, you might feel like you are carrying around that emotion inside you. This creates tension that will remain until either enough time passes for you to forget about what bothered you in the first place or until you have the chance to share the emotion. I use emotional tools to relieve any tension that participants are feeling. I frequently observe people blaming each other at the beginning of the workshop. When you feel tension and want to blame someone else, it is almost impossible to discuss something objectively.

I rely on emotional tools to eliminate this tension and prepare people to talk about the true nature of a problem, challenge, or whatever the workshop topic may be. In Volume 1 of this book, you saw Dynamic Facilitation at work. Dynamic Facilitation is a tool that achieves two important things at once; it helps create an understanding of a situation while letting people talk about their emotions at the same time. The Timeline tool demonstrated in this chapter is similar. It requires people to think about the different phases of a project and how they felt at each point. It is like an emotional audit of a situation and connects emotions with events to give a complete picture. Also, Wheel of Emotions helps someone understand the reasons behind their feelings and emotions.

Discussing emotions gives closure

All workshops need to end with a sense of closure. I usually ask for feedback and a few participant comments or use a simple show of hands to ask people how they feel about the results. But when tensions are high, I use a more in-depth tool that requires people to talk about their feelings. A tool like Carousel is a great choice when emotions run high because it involves several rounds of sharing. The more emotional the workshop, the more time you will need to spend talking about emotions, especially at the end of the workshop. The payoff is a sense of relief for everyone. When people have just gone through a shared process of revealing their emotions, they leave the emotional episode in the past, and they can move forward together with a clean slate.

CHAPTER 4:

Problem Solving with Challenge Mapping

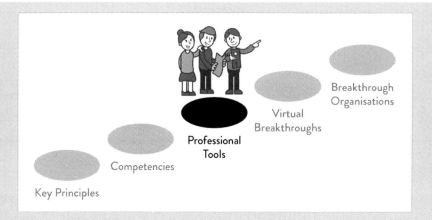

Key Principles

Competencies

**Professional
Tools**

Virtual
Breakthroughs

Breakthrough
Organisations

What's here

- **Case Study:** I used Challenge Mapping with a group of teachers and school officials to tackle rising vandalism in their school.
- **Tools:** Morning Walk, Challenge Mapping, Whip, Me/We/Us

How it helps

Challenge Mapping is a great tool to have at the ready when people get stuck or are searching for solutions to complex problems. It gets to the why that lies behind a problem and leads to discoveries. I find that Challenge Mapping is helpful in both my personal and professional life. The group leadership tools I use professionally also help troubleshoot problems with colleagues and friends.

Problems are simply opportunities for outstanding leadership

Sometimes, there is an obstacle that gets in the way of forward progress. Optimistic people tend to call these things challenges. Others call them problems. And some very frustrated people might call them major headaches. When an unexpected problem comes up, it can cause people to get discouraged and stop pushing forward. Problems can get in the way of effective workshops, just like emotions or disagreements can. What should you do when a group is wrestling with a complex problem without any clear answer? You can't give them the answer. This would break the core leadership principle of remaining content neutral. You need to find another way. Thankfully for you (and all of the people who will be attending your workshops), a tool called Challenge Mapping forces people to ask the right questions. And when you ask the right questions, the answers you need are revealed. This chapter will review a workshop where I used Challenge Mapping as the core tool to help a school deal with its rising vandalism problem. Challenge Mapping is a wonderful way to help people see a problem in a new light. Problems that previously seemed impossible are now understood and can be solved.

An environment to learn

It's been a long time since I have been in one of these, I thought to myself as I entered Marymount Senior High School, located in suburban California, USA. I was not back in school to brush up on my maths or take a test. Instead, I was there to facilitate a problem-solving workshop for a group of nine teachers and school administrators. Usually, I lead groups in office buildings or company headquarters, so it was a nice change of pace to find myself inside a classroom, even if the seats were a bit cramped. A friend of a friend gave the school's assistant principal my contact information. Luckily, I was already in the area to attend a conference, so everything lined up nicely. The school needed help finding solutions to the ongoing vandalism of school property. As I walked through the school grounds towards the meeting room, I saw the issue first-hand. Graffiti covered various walls and signs outside of the school. There was trash littering the parking lot and flower beds, and inside the halls of the school were walls that were scratched and scuffed. The school looked more like the bathroom of a dive bar than a place of education.

The group of teachers and school officials were already waiting for me in the conference room. I must have been wearing a look of surprise because one of the teachers said, "You think this is bad? This is a weekend! You should see how things look Friday afternoon!" The group laughed, and I was happy to see that everyone seemed to have a sense of humour about the situation. After a brief round of introductions, I got down to it and began to give instructions to the attentive group of teachers.

"Today, we're here to identify the key challenges related to the vandalism problem this school has. Then, I will lead you all in an activity that will produce key questions and show what keeps you from solving this vandalism problem. This activity will take place in small groups, and I hope that in 75 minutes, we will see this vandalism issue in a new light."

"Your plan sounds OK, but there is only so much that can be accomplished by talking about this. It is a police issue," said a heavyset bearded man named Karl, who I later learned was the head of custodial staff.

"Thank you for your feedback, and we will wait and see how good my plan is. But first, I would like to start by inviting everyone to stand up. We will all get our brains activated by going for a little walk right now...around this room. Have any of you ever gone for a long walk with a friend and enjoyed a great chat? We are going to capture that same feeling now. So, everyone, please walk around the room, and when I say, 'stop', find a partner and talk with them for two minutes. You are not going to talk about just anything, however. Instead, you are going to discuss this question," I said as I wrote the following on the chalkboard that sat at the front of the room:

1. How are you feeling this morning?

I let the group walk around for about ten seconds before signalling to stop and find a partner. Right away, the pairs launched into discussions about their morning commute, what they had for breakfast, and some more difficult students that they shared. After a couple of minutes, I had everyone walk for another ten seconds or so before having them stop and find a new partner to discuss the same question. After this, I introduced the following question by writing it on the chalkboard below the first:

2. What do you think about the workshop topic?

"Just like the first question, you have two minutes to talk with a partner when I say stop, begin walking!"

Once I stopped the group, I heard bits and pieces of interesting conversations. Based on what I was hearing, it seemed people had very different perspectives about the vandalism issue. For example, in the front of the room, I heard Karl vent about the vandalism problem to a partner; "You teachers only see it. It is my literal job to clean it up! I could be using my time for much better things than babysitting the students or trying to fill the role that a police officer should be taking!"

Behind Karl was another teacher that said the topic of vandalism should really be replaced with the subject of money; "All of this started to increase right when our budget decreased, no surprise there, right?"

After another round of sharing, I introduced the third question:

3. What should happen here today?

I set the group to walking and sharing. I heard a scattering of answers ranging from, "We should be reallocating the budget to allow for spending on more security officers", to "We should be out cleaning this mess up instead of talking about it—at least that way, we would be getting something done and achieve some results, even if they were gone by Monday morning."

"Thank you all! I hope you enjoyed your morning walk. Please take your seats and sit down. I have one final question before we begin: Are the ways of working and the objective clear for today?"

"I understand the objective is finding challenges that relate to our vandalism problem, but what if they are things we cannot accomplish?" asked Jordan, the school's head counsellor. She continued, "We all have been wishing for things and solutions that only come with a larger budget, so these things remain only as dreams. I'm afraid that today will follow this pattern."

"Thanks for sharing your concerns, Jordan. Your objective for today is only to find key challenges and related questions and concerns about vandalism. That is all. You do not need to worry about any budget or other logistical matters. I know that it is not simple to put aside all budgetary concerns, but leave that for another day," I said. There were no other questions about the objectives, and the group confirmed that the working methods were clear, so there was nothing left for me to do but move on to the next set of instructions.

Finding key questions

"The first thing I need is for everyone to split into three small groups. If you look around the room, you will see three flipcharts and tables with pen and paper on them. Choose one workstation to go to now, and no more than three people per group."

The teachers and school workers were quick and obedient in following instructions. Once they had formed three small groups, I continued, "All three groups are going to be working with the same topic, our workshop topic. Can someone remind me what that is?"

"Reducing vandalism in Marymount Senior High School," said the school's principal, a gentleman called Ken.

"That's right. All three groups will be working on the topic of reducing vandalism in this school. We will spend the next forty minutes building maps of key questions and challenges around *reducing vandalism at school*. If you look at the chalkboard behind me, you can see that I have written down some map building instructions for you all."

Map Building instructions

1. Use the topic of the day as a starting point (eat healthier).

2. Turn it into a "How might we..." question: "How might we eat healthier?"

3. Ask a new question about the how might we question: "Why..." or "What's stopping...": "Why do you want to eat healthier?"

4. Answer the questions in a complete simple sentence. "I want to eat healthier to lose weight".

5. Transform the answer into a new sub-topic: "How might we lose weight?"

6. Place the new topic on the map in relation to the original topic and continue.

7. "Why..." questions create new broad questions and answers to why questions build the map upwards.

8. "What's stopping..." questions create specific challenges and answers to these questions build the map downwards.

After going through the instructions, I suggested we practice. "Let's pretend that the topic for the day is to eat healthier. We start with placing this topic on the map and by turning it into a 'How might we...' question," I said while drawing an example on the chalkboard.

Ricky, one of the custodians, had a reply ready; "You can eat healthier by drinking less beer!"

"Great answer, Ricky, but we don't answer the questions at this point. Instead, we ask *Why* in response to the question and then answer. So, the next step is to ask, 'Why is it important to eat healthier?' Can anyone answer this?"

"It's important to eat healthier so that you lose weight," said Jeff, a geometry teacher.

"Thank you, Jeff. Using your answer, we make a new question, 'How might we lose weight?'."

At this point, a few of the teachers caught on and continued to build the map:

"Why is it important to lose weight?"

"It's important to lose weight so I have more confidence."

"How might we have more confidence?"

"Why is it important to have more confidence?"

"It is important to have more confidence so that I can feel happy."

"How might we feel happy?"

The two teachers continued building questions, and the questions became broader and broader until no new questions could be added. I jumped in and said, "Great job! This is a fantastic example of making new questions and building the map upwards. We can also take the original topic and make more specific questions, which build the map downwards, and it is easy to do! Just ask the question, 'What is stopping us from....' This creates specific challenges that we can solve later. Can two other volunteers give this a try and build a map downwards using the original topic?"

Two new teachers took a shot:

"How might we lose weight?"

"What is stopping us from losing weight?"

They paused, considering this new question, before one of them answered, "A lack of knowledge about a good diet is stopping us."

"Good job," I said. "At this point, you can continue to build down from this question by asking what is stopping you from learning about good diets, or you can leave this challenge as-is and build down again from the original topic. Any other ideas?"

"A lack of motivation is stopping us."

Ken, the school's principal, joined in and said, "A lack of self-control regarding doughnuts is stopping us!"

I laughed along with the rest of the room at Karl's joke (that hit a little too close to home for my liking) and thanked the two volunteers.

"Great job. As you can see, the map extends downwards, and specific challenges are produced as we ask and answer what is stopping us. Are there any questions before we try this out for real in our small groups?"

"One question," said Raul, one of the school administrators. "You've explained how to build the map up and down, but can it expand in different directions too? Or should we stick to vertical expansion?"

"Great question. Like real maps that plot the path of a road or river, this map will plot the challenges. If you notice something worthy of discussion apart from our original topic, you can write it down next to the original challenge on the map and then use 'why' and 'what' questions to build up and down from it. Let's get to it. Please spend the next forty minutes in your groups making your maps, and of course, let me know if you have any questions or concerns for me."

Off the three groups went, building their maps. I walked around the room and kept an eye on things to ensure that no questions went unanswered. Each group had a sprawling, multi-level map full of new questions by the end of the forty minutes.

Where does the map lead us?

"All three groups have their own maps. Some of the content may repeat itself, but there are also some great ideas and challenges that other groups have uncovered. Everyone can stand up and take about five minutes to walk around the room and get familiar with the other maps. Think about key questions or challenges that you want to solve as you do this. You can pick as many as you want and post them on this empty wall. Are there any questions?"

There were no questions at the moment, so I gave everyone around five minutes to circulate the room and pick up the key challenges they identified as important. The next step of the activity was to eliminate the challenges that were duplicates and listed multiple times. "I would like a few volunteers to help eliminate the challenges that are exactly the same from the map."

A question came up almost immediately. "You said we are supposed to combine challenges that are the same. Can we put together ones that are almost the same? On this map, one challenge is a lack of funding, and another is a lack of paid security positions. Both deal with money, so I would combine these, right?"

"No," I said. "Combining these two would be a mistake because they are actually different enough; one refers to a lack of general funding and the other to a lack of a paid security position, which makes them different. So don't combine but eliminate challenges if they are identical."

Next, I instructed them to find a partner from a different map-making group and find space in the room to work. "Now that you all are paired up, I am distributing ten dollars to each group."

"That is pretty good pay, especially within the field of education," one of the teachers quipped.

I tempered their excitement by letting them know that the money I was distributing was not for spending but instead for voting. "You will notice that the ten dollars I am giving you are not real money. In fact, it does not even exist. You and your partner have the money to invest. To spend it, you just use your pencil to write down a dollar amount next to a challenge you wish to solve. This is a voting activity, and you and your partner are to invest the money into the key challenges. If you think there are several good ones, you can put a few dollars here and a few there. If you only find one challenge worth discussing, you would invest all your money into that single idea. The point is to put your money now where your mouth is and back the key challenges with your ten dollars. Are there any questions?"

One hand went in the air, and a math teacher asked, "These challenges are so different that it makes it hard to treat them all as one group. When we asked 'why' and built the map up, they became broader and at the top of my map is something like a motto or vision. And as we went down the map, concrete actions sprung up, specifically quantifiable things. How can we vote between the two? I see the broad and the specific both being important."

The math teacher raised a valid concern. The challenges outlined on the maps pertained to different levels and scope, but that does not matter now. "Great question," I said and then continued, "But that does not matter now. You can invest in any challenge you find important, be it very broad or something specific. Just make sure to have a good discussion about the logic behind the challenges you consider to be most important and choose with your partner where your ten dollars should go."

The teachers and school employees began enthusiastically investing. They had no problem enjoying an activity that required a bit of imagination, and they seemed to be having a bit of fun, too. *This group of teachers is excellent to work with*, I thought to myself. *After all, they spend most of their professional lives leading kids in activities that require imagination and creativity, so it is no surprise that they embrace the activities I am showing them.*

I noticed that everyone had just about finished investing in their groups, so I left my thoughts, returned to reality, and asked everyone to organise the challenges based on the amount of money invested into them.

"Everyone can take their original seats," I said as I positioned all three Challenge Maps at the front and centre of the room. "On the wall are the challenges with the amount of money you invested into them. These results are great, but they are a bit cluttered. Let's make a new list of the top challenges with the total investment amount next to them on this blank flipchart. I assume that as teachers, you would be good at these types of things. I will leave this task completely to you."

After the results were tallied and the challenges with the most investment were summarised into a list on the flipchart, I instructed everyone to take a look. There were ten challenges with investments, but three of them came out as having far more money invested into them than the others. After a moment, I asked, "How did it go? Did we reach the objective?"

A geography teacher called Kevin replied, "I think that we did. Before the workshop, I thought that solution was simply to hire more janitorial staff. It looks like I was wrong. The results clearly frame the issue as a larger one about educating students about respect and also for us to create an environment more focused on learning and less on consequences."

Prioritised challenges: How might we...

Increase student pride in school – $29
Fund cleaning – $17
Make school better learning environment – $14
Illustrate consequences to behaviour – $3
Find safe and appropriate environment for graffiti – $3
Shape good habits – $2
Educate students further about good habits – $2
Create positive atmosphere – $2
Reward good behaviour – $1
Get more security officers – $1

Short and sweet feedback

"Before we go, I want to hear your thoughts about the workshop, but before you begin preparing long monologues for me, I don't want to hear that much. All I want is just one word from each person. So please stand up and arrange yourselves in a circle. Then, think of one word that best describes your feelings about the workshop. You have ten seconds to get ready!"

Everyone jumped up and arranged themselves into a circle. Once it was formed, I said, "Now we're going to begin with Mike here. When I say go, Mike will say his one word, and as soon as he does, the person next to him will say their word until the whole circle has shared. Let's see how quickly we can go around the circle. Ready, Mike? Go!"

The group was good (teachers are lovely to work with!), and feedback slashed around the circle like an informative boomerang.

"Great!"

"Interesting."

"Different."

"Useful."

"Fun!"

"Engaging."

"Revealing."

"Good."

"Illuminating."

"Optimistic."

I completed the circle with two words that I wanted to share with the group: "Thank you!"

Analysis

Questions before answers

Problems are easy to find, unfortunately. They can appear suddenly and quickly, almost anywhere! We have all been in a situation where a problem is staring us in the face, and we do not have an answer. Often, answers are hard to find because we are not asking the right questions. Challenge Mapping is just what you need to help ask the questions to get you on the path to solving complex problems. It creates understanding and attitude change by reframing a problem through repeated rounds of questioning. I trust this tool, which has helped me resolve crises with friends and family members. It can be demanding to use, but it delivers consistent and impactful results.

Benefits of Challenge Mapping

- Creates many questions that open new opportunities

- Creates a thorough understanding of the issues surrounding a problem; from minor obstacles to broad beliefs and ideologies

- New problems and challenges emerge as the original problem is explored

- Creates deep understanding of an issue

Other tools such as Dynamic Facilitation help us identify the root of a problem, so what is different about the results Challenge Mapping provides? Dynamic Facilitation identifies the different levels of a problem throughout a free-flowing conversation that the group leader records and categorises. Challenge Mapping is excellent at identifying the different levels of a problem, too, but it goes further and does even more. Challenge Mapping examines the broader motives behind a problem by asking, "Why?". Also, it forces participants to outline specific challenges and obstacles to solving a problem by asking, "What is stopping us?". This way, the tool explores multiple levels of a problem. It generates new issues and challenges that cover various levels. When I first began the session with the school employees about the issue of graffiti in their school, many of them thought the police should have handled the matter. By the end of the workshop, their new emergent problems to work on included raising student pride within their school and providing a safe place for students to graffiti and make art.

Just how and why does Challenge Mapping provide these results? In his article, *Reducing Complexity in Conceptual Thinking Using Challenge Mapping*, Min Basadur states that a hierarchy emerges when using Challenge Mapping and that the different levels can be labelled:

- Vision
- Mission
- Objective
- Strategy
- Programs

Specific tasks fall into the *programs* level, and the content becomes broader and more open-ended as the hierarchy extends to the *vision* level. Unlike other tools that do not create cohesion and understanding across levels, Basadur noted that creating a Challenge Map helps someone understand how everything connects to the core problem, creating more investment and ownership of tasks and actionable steps.

How to make the map

Challenge Mapping begins with a core issue or problem. In my workshop with the Marymount High School employees, the problem started as *reducing vandalism in Marymount High School*, and I changed that question into the positive form of, "How might we reduce vandalism in Marymount High School?" The positive question opens new opportunities and automatically evokes answers in our heads. Then the questions continue. First, we asked "Why is it important?" questions to build the map upwards and to broader levels and then explored specific challenges by asking "What is stopping us?" questions. These questions expand the map downwards, and if a new challenge appears on the map, you can place it next to the original challenge and build the map downwards again.

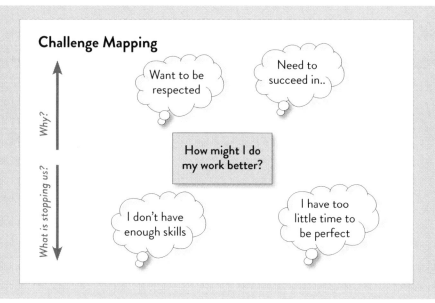

A common concern for those new to using Challenge Mapping is knowing when to stop building the map upwards. Is there a suggested amount of *why* questions? Should the map stop after a certain point? The answer here is quite simple. The Challenge Map will reach a top limit and regulate itself. You will notice that the answers to the why questions will get broader and broader until the participant building the map will begin answering in circles and reach a point where they cannot go to a broader level. You will know you reached this point when people start to give answers about their childhood, parental issues, or other vague Freudian replies. Once the top is reached, you can begin building the map downwards.

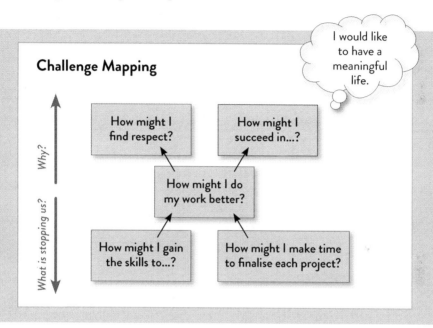

The map should also be expanded. Any issues appearing on the Challenge Map can become the centre of the mapping process, and you may construct new branches using the *why* and *what's stopping us* questions. I usually explain how people can do this by building a map using the original challenge and then making new maps out of the challenges they find interesting. People end up making maps that look like spider webs expanding outwards, upwards and downwards. There is no limit to how large a map can be.

In this workshop, three small groups created their own Challenge Maps using the original issue of reducing vandalism and then expanded their maps as they saw fit. But when it came time for everyone to review all three maps and prioritise the challenges, a lot of the content overlapped, and it was an easy process for everyone to understand the maps of the other groups.

Earlier, I said that Challenge Mapping produces more in-depth results than most problem identification tools, so why don't I use this all the time? Well, there are a few reasons. First off, it does not work well in large groups. Imagine a group of thirty people asking for the reason *why* behind a topic. People tend to have their own logic systems, and they would be debating the answer for a few minutes at least. Challenge Mapping means asking why repeatedly, and in large groups, it causes too much disagreement and debate. Yes, it would create passionate discussions, but progress moves too slow for Challenge Mapping to work efficiently. I mostly use Challenge Mapping in personal sessions with people facing complex challenges and up to groups of twenty (which needs to be split up into small groups of a maximum of three people per group).

Challenge Mapping is a tool that examines a topic profoundly, and it will make a seemingly impersonal topic quickly become a talk about someone's family, core beliefs, or self-worth. This is what happens if you keep asking, "Why is this important to you?" Take our case study here; the topic was originally about picking up litter and removing graffiti, but the upper levels of the Challenge Maps contained challenges about being a good person and leading by example. If you ask for the *why* behind these ideas or beliefs, you enter very personal territory.

By asking questions about a new challenge, Challenge Mapping halts our default thinking patterns and creates confusion. Once the mind is confused, it will search for new answers, which leads to a deeper understanding and breakthroughs. This is not easy for the participant and requires a great deal of introspection and constant participation.

The Process of Challenge Mapping

1) Write a "How might we / I..." question
Place the questions on the wall.

2) **Create a map upward-one question at a time:**
A) Ask: **Why?**
B) Answer with a complete sentence.
C) Transform the answer into a new, "How might we / I.." question
   without changing the content

3) **Create a map downward-one question at a time:**
A) Ask: **What's stopping us?**
B) Answer with a complete sentence.
C) Transform the answer into a new "How might we / I.." question
   without changing the content

4) **Continue...**
Building the map to all different directions. Link questions and figure out
the interconnections. Repeat stages 2 and 3.

5) **Select the questions that open the biggest knots.**
With a group you can use, e.g., Dot Voting. Usually that's not enough as
the outcome could be deeper understanding that cannot be presented
on a single Post-it. Discuss the outcomes in small groups and write new
Post-its if necessary. This can be put on the wall in a reason-outcome
order.

6) **Discuss the outcomes and how to move into creating solutions.**

Simplify the map

When you use Challenge Mapping, there are a few ways to simplify
the process and make it easy to follow. First off, be sure to visualise
as much as possible. Write down clear instructions that are visible to
everyone at all times; participants will be referring to them throughout
the process. Also, demonstrate the tool and explain how to build the
map, how the questions can build the map up or down, and how new
challenges can be added and expanded on.

Constructing the rest of the workshop

Challenge Mapping was the star of the workshop, but other tools also played an important part. Like any good workshop, this one had a distinct check-in stage where I explained the objective and ways of working to the group. I also used a warm-up tool called Morning Walk to energise the participants, get them moving around the room and talking about a mix of questions, some just for fun and some related to the workshop.

Morning Walk

How it works

Participants start to walk around the meeting room. The leader gives a sign when participants need to find a partner to talk to. The leader assigns the discussion topic, and the pairs discuss for 2 minutes. To be repeated 2 – 3 times. Examples of questions:
- How was your morning?
- What energises you?
- What are your expectations for this meeting?

Purpose
- Walking is energising; participants tune in to the event better by moving than being static in their chairs.
- It is recommended to let the participants talk about an easy topic first. Afterwards, it is easier for them to start discussing the actual meeting topics.
- It's easier to speak in pairs than it is in front of a large group. This makes Morning Walk a good warm-up activity.

I incorporated a Me/We/Us structure to use along with Challenge Mapping. For the convergence stage, I had people look at the other maps individually (Me). Then, I asked them to eliminate the duplicate entries and vote in small groups about which challenges were the most important with the Investing Activity (We). Finally, they made a list of the top ten most important challenges using the results of the Investment Activity (Us).

I wanted to end the workshop by getting some final feedback from the group. I used Whip to do this, which requires only one word of feedback from each person. Whip is a tool that American teachers created as a way to get even the quietest students to share. If you attended primary school in the United States, you might remember a teacher using the Whip tool.

Whip

This is a fast and energising way to ask for feedback.

Steps

- Participants stand in a circle
- Everyone thinks of one word that best describes their feelings, how the meeting went, etc.
- Everyone shares their word by taking turns

Application

- To ask for feelings or expectations in the beginning of a workshop
- To check how things are going for participants during a workshop
- To ask for feedback at the end of a workshop

The group was small, so I wanted to hear from everyone, and Whip was a good fit. If you ever have the chance, give Whip a try with large groups, too. It is an impressive sight to watch 100 people sit in a circle spitting out words as quickly as possible to complete the round of feedback!

Workshop process

Objective: To find the key challenges
Time: 75 minutes

Check-in (15minutes):
1. Presenting the objective of the stage and the workshop process.
2. Morning Walk with three questions:
   – "How are you feeling this morning?"
   – "What do you think about our workshop topic?"
   – "What should happen here today?"
3. "Is the objective of the workshop and way of working clear?"
   – short discussion

Emergence tool: Challenge Mapping (40 minutes)
1. "I have prepared spots for working in groups of three. Please choose your spot!"
2. "Write a, *How might we...* question related to the topic and place the question on the wall."
3. "One question at a time-create a map upwards."
   A) Ask *Why?*.
   B) "Answer with a complete sentence."
   C) "Transform the answer into a new, *How might we...* question without changing the content."
4. "One question at a time-create a map downward."
   A) Ask, *What's stopping us?*.
   B) "Answer with a complete sentence."
   C) "Transform the answer into a new *How might we...* question without changing the content."
5. "Continue building the map to all different directions. Follow your intuition and begin with any question you like and repeat stages 2 and 3."

Convergence tool; Me/We/Us (20 minutes)
1. "On your own take a look at the challenges of all the groups and choose the ones we should solve."
2. "Lets eliminate the duplicates."
3. "With a pair from the other group, invest $10 into the challenges we should solve."
4. "Lets organize the challenges based on how much money was invested into them."
5. "Did we reach the objective?"

Check-out (5 minutes):
1. "Think of one word that best describes your feelings about this workshop."
2. "Now we shall share our one word fast like a whip slashing through the room. Mike, you start!"
3. "Thank you!"

What was used and why?

Morning Walk – To focusing and connect participants

Challenge Mapping – To create a deeper understanding of a challenge

Me/We/Us – To create understanding

Investment Activity – A polling tool to prioritise challenges

Whip – To collect feedback and end the session

CHAPTER 5:

Navigating Difficult Group Situations using the 3-Step Intervention Model

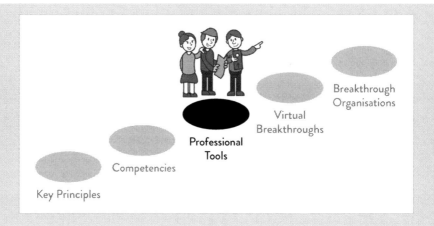

What's here
- **Case Study**: Three examples where intervention from the group leader is needed to deal with disrespect, disobedience, or a lack of confidence.
- **Tools:** 3-Step Intervention Model

How it helps
The 3-Step Intervention Model can be applied to diffuse emotional situations and find logical steps to move past potential conflicts.

Control: do not reach for it once you have lost it

Leading groups is not always easy, especially when things do not go according to plan. I can guarantee that you will encounter difficult situations along the way. I am not using the term *difficult situations* to talk about ordinary things like time management, transitioning between workshop stages, or what to do if your pen runs out of ink. I am referring to challenges that are more confrontational in nature. What do you do if someone blatantly disrespects you? Ignores your instructions and walks out? Gets visibly upset and angry at the outcome of the workshop? What would you do if someone called you an "incompetent fool" to your face? Are these examples a bit too dramatic? You might think so, but all of them have happened to me during my facilitation career.

When these things happen to you, it may feel natural to try and regain control. I know I instantly tried to get back control the first few times I faced adversity when leading a group. I would create more ground rules for people to follow, or I became more enthusiastic and talked louder to try and dominate with my energy. Using controlling tactics worked OK for me, and I later learned that they were common ways used by group leaders.

Controlling tactics might be effective in the short term by redirecting the energy and focus of the group, but they also can feel hollow. More importantly, they are ineffective because they typically do not address the problematic behaviour or explore the motivations behind the behaviour. For example, if someone calls me an idiot during a workshop and I simply redirect them by using a controlling method, I do not explore why they feel this way, and I ignore the elephant in the room. As a facilitator, I constantly ask for feedback, and then I use that feedback to shape the workshop to the group's needs. Controlling methods are a stark contrast to this—they ignore serious situations that come up during the session.

Controlling tactics and their shortcomings

- **Talking about company goals:** People pick up on the topic change and real reason behind it (attempt to regain control of the meeting).
- **Creating ground rules:** Implementing additional rules to curb a behaviour can make people agitated.
- **Increasing your energy level:** This does not address the reason behind the behaviour and can be seen as a distraction.
- **Trying to connect individual motivations with group motivation:** Nice in theory, but it feels fake when used to control people.
- **Giving praise to try and win over people:** Can seem insincere.

It is human nature to try and combat conflict by exerting your control over the group, and yes, it often works. However, there is another way to handle difficult and combustible situations: the 3-Step Intervention Model. Here is how it works.

A difficult situation arises

Step 1 – Behaviour: Summarise what happened, and let people comment on or correct your summary of events.

Step 2 – Interpretation: Give your interpretation of why the situation happened, and let people comment and share their thoughts.

Step 3 – Proposal: Suggest a way of moving forward that works toward the workshop goals and takes into account the information shared in steps one and two.

Let's take a look at how this works in practice.

Case #1: What did you call me?

About ten years ago, I facilitated a strategy workshop for the print division of a large media company based in Italy. The situation was bleak; digitalisation and changing consumer habits left this company with reduced profitability; layoffs were imminent. It was a high-stress situation, but the session was going OK. I was summarizing the results of their small group discussions when one of the employees, Franco, interrupted me and said, "Just stop it already you incompetent fool!"

I was shocked, first by the level of disrespect and second by the gentleman's vocabulary. English was his second or 3rd language, yet he was pretty creative in his insult. I recovered a bit and pressed forward with the Intervention Model by first summarizing the behaviour as objectively as possible.

Behaviour: "Franco, you just called me an incompetent fool, right?"

Franco nodded and said, "Yes, I did. I don't see you demonstrating anything worthwhile here. Your 'talents' are a waste of our time."

Ouch, I thought to myself. I stopped myself from allowing my emotions to take over, and I gave my interpretation of the event.

Interpretation: "You don't respect me, do you, Franco?"

Franco thought for a moment before replying, "I do respect you. Or, at least, I did not mean to disrespect you. I'm sorry. It is the meeting that frustrates me. I think that you are trying to manipulate us into accepting new policies that are poor and that this workshop is designed to manipulate our feelings about these new changes."

We were beginning to touch on the heart of the matter, so I decided to dig deeper. "The group came up with solutions to deal with the current situation, but you think I am trying to manipulate things somehow?"

Franco considered this and said, "I might just be a bit horrified by the prospect of the upcoming layoffs. I love my team, and many of us have been working together for well over a decade."

Happy that Franco expressed himself more productively than name-calling, I finished the Intervention Model by making a proposal.

Proposal: "Can you give me five minutes to finish summarizing the group's work first, and then we will talk about how to deal with the lay-offs? I promise you will have the chance to share any concerns and objections that you may have."

This sounded good to Franco, and he agreed to give it a try. So, after a brief and uncomfortable detour, the workshop was back on track.

Case #2: Where did everyone go?

A few years back, I led the solutions stage of a change workshop in China. We were a few hours into day one, and I thought things were going great; I was my usual happy self, and the group seemed engaged. I was basing the workshop around the Café method, which called for everyone to spend an hour rotating between different small groups. After setting up the activity, I was confident and leaned back against the desk in the front of the room to observe. Imagine my surprise when the group of twenty-five dwindled to about half its original size within a few moments. Almost half the group had left without saying a word!

I was in shock, but I did not chase them down. Instead, I helped the remaining participants finish the activity while trying my best to calm my internal voice that was shouting angrily. The activity ended, and we took a break for lunch.

When the afternoon session began after lunch, most of the group had returned. Since a good portion of the group had outright ignored my instructions and left the session, I felt I needed to apply the Intervention Model.

Behaviour: "We are a group of about twenty-five, and around ten of you stayed and participated in the workshop. The rest left the workshop completely without saying a word, right?"

The participants could not help but to sheepishly agree to this fact.

Interpretation: "The meeting topic is not interesting or relevant to you?"

Right away, a few of the deserters quickly rushed to explain themselves.

"The topic is interesting. Of course, we should be involved with finding our own solutions. But you said yourself that we could go where we were most needed."[*]

I replied, "That is true, but I meant within the workshop, not running off to chase down a latte and a bagel!"

"But Pepe, we can't influence these changes. This workshop is useless!"

I was surprised by this new bit of news, and needless to say, I had no clue what was going on. We had a good talk about the changes, what the participants really can influence in the company, and whether the workshop was needed or not. There had been many workshops before, but none of them had been impactful due to a lack of follow-up and management support. After a while, I had an idea about how to move forward.

Proposal: "How about if we make a plan about how to follow through the changes and how to get the key stakeholders to provide more support?"

Everyone agreed, and we got back to work.

---

[*] They are referring to the "law of two feet" which states that you trust your own intuition to take yourself to wherever you are most needed. Their interpretation of this rule, while a bit surprising in how it was applied, was accurate.

Case #3: Upsetting results

I was wrapping up a one-day strategy implementation workshop. I was standing in a semi-circle with the participants reviewing the road map where they prioritised their actions. All of a sudden, a voice behind me said loudly and firmly, "Stop! Enough!" The voice belonged to Mark, a quiet guy who was one of the team leads.

Mark went on talking, his voice getting louder and his face getting redder; "This is garbage! Trash! These new plans undo about half a year of hard work. Half a year of late nights and not seeing my family... for what? A new plan that that was created in only a few hours? No!"

Mark was getting more and more upset, and I obviously needed to intervene.

Behaviour: "Mark, are you saying that the result of this workshop undoes your hard work?"

Mark responded, "The answer is in that damn roadmap of yours; do you see any of my projects there? I sure don't."

Interpretation: "You feel that I led a session that devalued the hard work you have already done. Something like this?"

"Yes, that's exactly how I see it," said Mark.

Proposal: "How about this; you add your key actions on the road map, and we ask the group if everyone is ok with it. Would this work?"

Mark agreed, and the intervention tool took him from yelling at a piece of paper to calmly consider the session's results, their potential benefits, and how to move forward.

Case #3 shows the power of the Intervention Model in diffusing tense situations. Mark was quite upset initially, and it was a volatile moment when he was shouting about the workshop's outcome. He was upset, and his display of anger could have made others in the workshop uncomfortable and upset, too.

I tried to remove all emotion from the situation when describing the behaviour in step one of the Intervention Model. This analytical approach caused Mark to think about the situation and check if my description of events was correct, and this got him outside of his emotions and thinking more calmly.

From that point, we were able to discuss our interpretations peacefully in step 2, and finally, in step 3, Mark was relaxed enough to accept a proposal on how to proceed. This was a quick turnaround that occurred quickly, within a few minutes.

Analysis

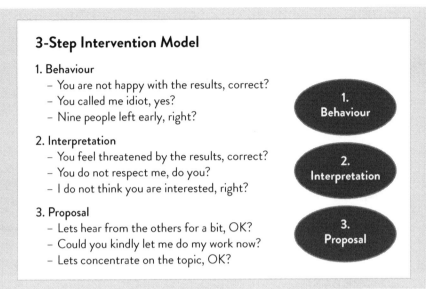

3-Step Intervention Model

1. Behaviour
- You are not happy with the results, correct?
- You called me idiot, yes?
- Nine people left early, right?

2. Interpretation
- You feel threatened by the results, correct?
- You do not respect me, do you?
- I do not think you are interested, right?

3. Proposal
- Lets hear from the others for a bit, OK?
- Could you kindly let me do my work now?
- Lets concentrate on the topic, OK?

The 3-Step Intervention Model is simple and reliable, and I have used it to smooth out many difficult situations over the years. I would love to take all of the credit for developing this tool, but I cannot. It is a simplified version of a tool called the six-step cycle for diagnosis and intervention introduced by veteran consultant and facilitator Robert Schwarz in his book, *The Skilled Facilitator*. The six-step cycle for diagnosis and intervention can be divided into two parts. The first part of the model is called *internal content*, consisting of the thoughts, logic, and opinions held on an individual level. According to the intervention process, anything inside a person's head is classified as internal content.

Schwarz's cycle of diagnosis and intervention

Internal Content (Diagnosis)	External Behaviour (Intervention)
1. Observe behaviour	1. Describe observation
2. Infer meaning	2. Test inferences
3. Decide if intervention is needed or not	3. Help the group decide how to change behaviour and move forward

The second part is *external behaviour*, which consists of any actions or behaviours visible to the entire group. The cycle begins with an observation of the environment which then leads to conclusions. Based on these conclusions, the group leader decides whether to act or not. If they choose to act, they share their observation with participants and check if they agree. Then the group leader explains their conclusion and checks whether the group is on the same page. If a decision is made to act, an action is suggested. Then the leader checks how the group feels about the proposed action.

Schwarz's six-step cycle is well-designed, but I prefer to cut out the first three stages. These diagnostic steps all take place internally and almost reflexively. It has been my experience that I never need to consciously consider if it is worth intervening or not. The answer is usually obvious. The first three stages over-complicate things; I almost always go towards simplicity whenever possible, and it is easier to remember three stages than six.

Intervention for everyone

It is easy to think of the Intervention Model as a tool to curb unwanted behaviour, and it is. But it also kept me from losing my cool and entering a counterproductive mindset. For instance, in the second case in China, I was shocked when I observed a large part of the group seemingly disregard my instructions and leave the session. Even though I understood the group was not interested, I also took this as a direct sign of disrespect. The Intervention Model forced me to begin by simply describing the behaviour and then my interpretation of the situation. These two steps required me to slow down, and each step allowed the participants to explain their side of things, too. Instead of becoming angry and resorting to giving more ground rules or attempting to assert control over the group, the Intervention Model enabled a logical intervention that removed emotion from the equation and helped me understand the underlying motives of the participants that left the session. Finally, we were able to create a win-win solution.

I sincerely hope you do not encounter too many difficult situations as you begin to guide groups in decision-making, but you will find yourself in at least a few. All leaders do. By applying the 3-Step Intervention Model, I am confident that you will handle them without a hitch.

CHAPTER 6:

Discovering True Customer Needs with STP Analysis

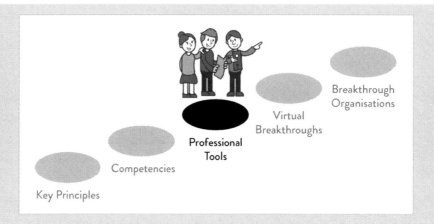

What's here
- **Case Study:** A planning session with two clients whose wants do not match their needs.
- **Tools:** STP Analysis

How it helps

I use STP Analysis before I outline my service proposal to clients. What the client thinks they want and what they need are two completely different things. STP Analysis helps them understand the current situation and allows the group leader to implement the correct workshop.

Every workshop starts the same

How does a workshop begin? You might think that a warm-up activity always starts things off. Close, but think beyond the workshop schedule. What happens before that? Planning the materials by gathering pens, flipcharts, and nametags? Getting closer, but something else needs to happen first. The first stage of a workshop occurs days or even weeks before the actual event: the client meeting. This is your chance to find out what they want while identifying what they really need. I have never met with a person who did not have some ideas about what they want. Hearing this, you might be thinking to yourself, *Pepe, this sounds too easy! You're describing a meeting where the client knows what they want and what outcome they wish to see! This is as simple as can be, right?*

It may sound simple, except for one key and crucial detail:

What people want and what they need
can be two completely different things.

People usually know what they want, and they often have a fixed idea of what they want you to do. Unfortunately, following their fixed idea would not get the results they hope for, so it is on your shoulders to help identify the client's true needs. Identifying a client's true needs and planning an appropriate workshop to meet these needs is a key competency of a successful group leader. Fortunately for us, there is a tool that helps identify true needs: STP Analysis. STP Analysis reveals the difference between a business or organisation's current reality and the version they wish to be in the future. STP Analysis gets its name from the three categories it explores: Situation, Target, and Proposal. Unlike the other tools mentioned in this book that can be the core of a workshop, I never use STP Analysis in a workshop. Instead, I use this tool to plan the workshop with the client. These planning sessions usually occur in one-on-one meetings or, at most, in groups of three or four. Let's take a trip to China together to look at STP Analysis in action in the following case study.

Rapidly expanding spaces

"Our business is based on providing things that you and I take for granted every day: reliable internet, comfortable desks and chairs, and hot coffee. Look around you. Replicating this simple room in cities worldwide has created a global phenomenon. We can barely keep up with our newfound success."

I politely looked around the room and through the large glass window that served as a wall looking out into a larger office. I saw rows of desks, each equipped with a display monitor and a charging station. I was in the headquarters of Work It Coworking Spaces, a Chinese start-up company that catered to the rapidly expanding number of remote workers around the world. Work It Coworking rented out space and equipment using contracts that ranged from just a few hours to multiple years.

They were one of the first companies to offer space as a service within China, and they were currently expanding rapidly, both domestically and internationally.

I met with two senior employees; founder Yu, a serious-looking woman in her early forties, and CFO Bei, a gentleman who was slightly younger but equally serious.

I could tell by the dynamics between the two that they both were the decision-makers within the company. The two of them had been there from the beginning when Work It Coworking opened their first location in Sanya, a popular coastal tourist destination. Yu and Bei suggested that I lead a three-hour team building activity for the company's management team of around fifteen employees.

"We have a very talented and energetic management team. They are the stars of the company and a huge asset to us," said Yu.

Bei added, "It makes sense to develop this group of managers. They are the force behind our fast expansion and success. We need a fun team building session with games and energising activities for them."

Before Bei could continue, I stopped him and said, "I would love to hear what both of you think would be most beneficial to your managers, but first, let me back things up a bit."

What is the situation?

"I want the three of us to thoroughly understand the situation of Work It Coworking so that we can go forward with the most beneficial workshop for your managers. To do this, I am going to post three pieces of flipchart paper on the wall and take notes on them while we talk," I said as I wrote *Situation*, *Target*, and *Proposal* on the top of each piece of paper before taping them to the wall.

Yu and Bei looked on politely as I explained the way of working. "Your role is to share your knowledge, and my role is to ask questions and to keep a written record of our conversation. In the end, I will ask you to summarise each topic. Then, once the three of us have a common understanding of what is needed, I will share my proposal about what type of workshop I think would be most constructive for your group of managers. Does this sound OK?"

"Let's give it a try," said Yu.

I stood by the flipchart paper labelled *Situation* and took the cap off my marker, getting ready to take notes. I asked Yu and Bei what the current situation was for Work It Coworking.

Bei explained that they have a high-energy management team responsible for carrying out most of the day-to-day operations. Yu added that Work It Coworking was in rapid expansion, both inside China and internationally. She continued, "We went from just four branches of coworking spaces 18 months ago to around 200 locations now. The structure is that each manager oversees a cluster of around 20 offices. They are responsible for keeping the equipment up to date, organising any local promotions or business partnerships within their area, and hiring and managing the employees that work in their coworking offices. The managers then report to the upper-level employees directly, consisting of Bei, our CEO, VP, me, and a few others."

I wrote all of this down as Bei began explaining the problem; "As we grow, we put more and more responsibility on our management team. Now they are even in charge of headhunting and hiring new employees in some cases. As each manager has their areas to look after, they are isolated and not collaborating with their peers. This is the main issue, a lack of collaboration. They are getting the job done as is, but things could be so much better if they pooled their knowledge and worked together more."

Yu interjected, "Bei is on the right track but wrong in his assessment of the problem. The problem is a simple lack of trust! We started in one city with one office. Everyone knew each other, and we all had confidence in our fellow man or woman. Now, within our team of managers, there are eight different nationalities represented, which oversee our 189 different coworking locations that are spread out over eighteen different countries! No wonder people don't trust each other—they hardly even know each other! There was one case where a manager filled in and oversaw the operations of a coworking office while their colleague was sick. The thing was, she did not give control back! She thought that her processes were so much better that she contacted me and said that the other manager was incompetent and that the office was in better hands now. I know both employees involved, and they each do a fine job. They just need to trust each other more."

I thanked Yu and Bei for the detailed description of the situation and asked, "What is your target? What do you wish to change here?"

"More trust among managers," said Yu. Bei added, "More collaboration among the team. I want people to know each of their co-workers better, so there is more synergy in their work."

Yu agreed with Bei and added that if the managers knew each other better, they would be more likely to trust one another.

Moving on, I turned to the flipchart marked *Proposal* and asked Yu and Bei what they proposed.

Yu said that the answer was team building activities. "We have three hours booked for next month, and I want to try out activities that will force our managers to build bonds with each other and become friends. This is how the company culture was when we were much smaller, and there was much more collaboration then."

Bei added, "I like the idea of team building. They can play games that require teamwork and working in unison, which may carry over into their regular daily work. I agree with Yu that there should be some get-to-know-you games and some real group challenges."

Yu and Bei had given their proposal, and all three flipcharts were filled with notes. We were not finished with our analysis yet, though. We were just getting started.

Digging deeper

I began jumping around from topic to topic and asked Yu and Bei questions about their descriptions of the Situation, Target, and Proposal. "Why do you think that there is no trust between your managers?"

Bei answered that people choosing to silo themselves off and work individually proved that there was a lack of trust, and Yu added that some managers were constantly questioning the work of others. She said, "Many managers do not share any common goals, either. This makes it hard for them to understand the motives of their fellow managers, and they become frustrated."

"Wait a moment," I said. "I don't understand. What is stopping you from creating a common goal for the management team?"

Yu and Bei considered my question for a moment, and Bei replied, "We are just too busy and never have time to meet to discuss it. Also, I am not sure if I believe that common goals are possible. The business is emerging and growing extremely fast. Our management team is spread out across different cities and, in some cases, different countries! Each region has variables which make their priorities different; in some places, the focus is logistical; hire the right people and get the right equipment in the coworking space so that it can run."

Yu jumped in and added, "And in other places, the managers are in charge of an established office, so they focus more on marketing and other initiatives like reducing the carbon footprint of the business and establishing local business partnerships."

I continued with my line of questioning and asked them what else was causing the lack of trust. Bei replied that the decision-making was not transparent, which negatively affected the company culture. The managers are stepping on each other's feet and fighting for the same clients. During this period of rapid growth, the practices adopted were now damaging to morale. Yu added, "Our managers are doing enough to survive and keep their offices up and running, but I know that they can do more than just survive; if they trusted each other and worked together more, then they would be thriving, which is what I want for my employees. It is not enough for only the business to grow and succeed; we need the same for our team."

I continued with my line of questioning until we explored all of the topics. Then I asked Yu and Bei to summarise each flipchart while I wrote down their summaries on the bottom of each.

Bei summarised *Situation* by saying that day-to-day operations were too hectic to allow employees to collaborate with each other and that working practices had become siloed during Work Its period of rapid growth.

Yu summarised *target* by explaining the aim to have the managers trust each other more, create a common goal, and recapture the spirit of collaboration and closeness between co-workers. *Proposal* was first summarised with Bei and Yu's idea to have a half-day workshop filled with icebreakers and team building activities to help create trust and collaboration between employees. Then Bei and Yu looked at each other, and Yu suggested, "That is definitely not enough. There is no trust because there are no common goals and no decision-making model. The poor managers are fighting for power without clear direction, and yet, they still somehow manage to do a great job!"

Bei continued: "Yes, we have to clarify the goals first, and then go for the decision making, roles and responsibilities."

I thanked them for their great analysis and put forth my proposal.

"Thanks for your help and insightful comments. Now I have enough information to make my own proposal about what we should do. I propose to start with a two-day workshop focused on outlining goals and clarifying roles and responsibilities. Once your managers identify and create these together, trust and collaboration will come. After the goals are clear, we will develop a collaborative way of following up the success in your hectic business environment."

Bei and Yu agreed. After all, my proposal came directly from their own analysis and beliefs.

Situation	Proposal	Target
• Rapid expansion to different markets	• Short 3 hour workshop	• More trust within management team
• Management team growing	• Management team will attend	• More collaboration within management team
• Isolated working practices	• Focus on team-building activities	• Co-workers know eachother and feel like they are a team
• Variation in procedure from office to office	• Building trust and teamwork through games	• Everyone on the same page
• Infighting among team	• Building teamwork through light group activites	• A culture of support for the management team
• Lack of shared goals		
• Increased responsibilities	• No follow up session needed	• Create manageble workload so employees can thrive, not only survive
• Company values and culture have changed (weakened) during growth period		
• Managers barely know their co-workers		

Analysis

Planning with a client is sometimes a funny thing. They frequently know what they want, but it is not what they need. They know that something needs changing, and they have taken the first step in enlisting help from a colleague, facilitator or a consultant. But their idea of what needs to happen usually is a surface-level solution that does not address the core issues. You know better and try to share your knowledge with them and help by suggesting something more effective, but they do not even consider what you have to say. People cannot take your answer before they have understood the big picture and internalised the solution themselves. We saw this exact scenario play out in the case study above; Yu and Bei correctly identified an issue (lack of trust due to a rapid expansion of business), but their proposal to have a few hours of team-building activities was superficial. It would not have led to impactful results. It wasn't until STP Analysis was applied that they saw the whole picture.

This is why STP Analysis is such an important tool to use with the client; it allows them to see the nuances and details of the situation to get on board with a proposal that addresses their true needs.

When I was early on in my facilitation career and just beginning to plan sessions with clients, I could not get my head around why it was so difficult for them to trust my assessment of their needs. I felt that they were often-times resisting my proposal, and even a bit surprised that I had the nerve to question the details of their situation and the contributing factors.

Eventually, I realised two key things to remember when working directly with the client to plan a session. First, the client already knows what they want you to do before they even meet with you, and second, they probably see things differently than you do. My clients are usually upper-management, board members, executive officers, and other high-ranking people. They already know what they want. It can be difficult to suggest an idea to someone accustomed to making decisions and telling others to follow their lead.

Business consultants approach working with clients differently than I do. They try to understand the situation themselves to provide insight and give value to the client by asking questions and writing down thoughts and ideas. This method may help the consultant understand the problem, but it does not help the client understand the situation or avoid mistakes or inefficient working methods.

My style is a bit different. I want to take notes too, but I record them to be always visible to everyone in the room. As the client talks and sees their ideas being written down, they let go of their original ideas and want to go deeper into the situation. Suddenly the original proposal looks a bit small, and they realise that it is not suitable. They know that they require a different solution, but they do not know what.

STP Analysis

1. Write the following headings on three pieces of flipchart paper (one word per paper): Situation, Proposal, Target.

2. Introduce the way of working: "Let's analyse the case. I will ask some questions and take notes on these flipcharts."

3. Begin the conversation by covering each topic in order; first situation, then target, and lastly proposal. Write down as much as you can.

4. Now jump between all three topics and try to dig deeper by asking:
   • Why?
   • What's stopping you?
   • Can you elaborate a bit?
   • What happens if you do not reach this target?

5. When the conversation seems finished, ask the client to summarise each topic. Write down their summary and underline it.

6. Thank the client for their contribution and begin building and presenting your own proposal: "I like your idea to have a 2-day strategy development workshop. Now let me give a concrete proposal that shows what this workshop could look like."

STP Analysis is a form of gap analysis that shows the difference between the current state of a business or organisation (the situation) and the desired state (target). Gap analysis is an old tool used in strategic planning, process development, marketing, and project management. STP Analysis requires people to discuss the current situation and future targets. Once everyone agrees on the key points, they summarise the situation and targets. After this, a proposal on how to proceed can then be accurately created.

This combination of STP Analysis with visualising ideas using group memory is extremely powerful. The key with STP Analysis is to record the key points of the conversation in the client's own words. Then, as the clients continue talking about the Situation, Target, and Proposal — your notes for the three categories you are writing on the flipcharts serve as the group memory, a map that paints a cohesive picture of everything. This picture also enables more profound conversations as people refer to it mid-conversation and lets them draw on the captured information.

STP Analysis shares some things in common with Dynamic Facilitation. Both tools involve the leader recording a group discussion on flipcharts that people can refer to as the conversation continues. Both tools also involve dividing conversation into different categories (STP Analysis = Situation, Target, Proposal; Dynamic Facilitation = facts, concerns, key questions, solutions). However, unlike Dynamic Facilitation, STP Analysis requires that the topics are discussed in a specific order. When the discussion begins, the leader starts with situation, moves to target, and finally finishes with the proposal. Then, the leader asks a series of questions designed to clarify and get participants to elaborate on key points. There is no needed order during this questioning phase, and the discussion jumps from topic to topic. Finally, the leader asks participants to summarise each category before giving their own proposal of what should be done. Whereas in Dynamic Facilitation, the leader becomes a recorder, in STP Analysis, the leader guides the discussion with questions and controls the conversation.

I mainly use STP Analysis for planning with the client because I have limited time to get results. When I lead a workshop, I usually use my favourite tool, Dynamic Facilitation, which leaves more room for emotions and creativity.

STP Analysis is a fantastic way to begin a relationship with the client because it creates a strong understanding of the best course of action, and it leads to good decision-making and planning. Most workshop attendees don't realise that a successful workshop started days or weeks earlier in these preliminary meetings. Yet these meetings lay the groundwork for a successful workshop, and they provide an opportunity for even the most stubborn of clients to learn what they actually want.

What was used and why?

STP Analyses: To help the client understand their true needs during the workshop planning meeting

STP Analysis process and participant instructions

Objective: To create a deeper understanding of the situation and outline genuine client needs.

Time: 80 minutes

Check-in (15 minutes):

1. Discuss the objective of the meeting and the way of working.
   - "I want us both to thoroughly understand the situation. To achieve this, I will post three flipchart papers on the wall, and we will discuss the situation, the target and a proposal of how to work towards this. Is this OK?"
   - "Your role is to share your knowledge. I will ask questions and keep a written record. At the end of the discussion, I will ask you to summarise. When we will have a common understanding of what is needed, I will start preparing my proposal. Is this OK?"

Divergence tool: STP Analysis (60 minutes)

1. "I have written down Situation, Target, and Proposal on flipchart papers. Could you first tell me about the situation?"
2. "And what is your target?"
3. "And what is your proposal?"
4. Ask questions related to the Situation, Target, or Proposal. You do not have to do this in any specific order. You are a private investigator looking for the truth. Some good questions are:
   - *Why, why, why, why, and why.*
   - *What is stopping you?*
   - *What else?*
   - *Questions related to team or organisational effectiveness*: Are the roles clear? Is there a common goal? Is there an agreed way of working? How do the team members communicate with each other? Has it been agreed how decisions are made? How do people feel? How is this affecting different levels of the organisation? How often do people meet or collaborate?
5. "How would you summarise the discussion?"
6. "Did we reach the objective?"

Check-out (5 minutes):

1. "How do you feel about our discussion?"
2. "Now I have enough information to prepare my proposal. Let me explain how I would deal with the situation next week (or you can continue with your own proposal building on the findings you just made)."
3. "Thank you!"

CHAPTER 7:

Storytelling

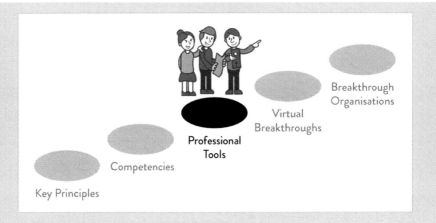

What's here
- The role storytelling plays in group leadership
- Anchors, spines, and common storytelling terminology
- Change Equation
- Success Stories

How it helps

Great group leaders use storytelling to get people to open up. Storytelling helps people reveal information that they usually keep to themselves. Use storytelling to break down defences and get to the heart of an issue.

Let me tell you a story

Great leaders all know a thing or two about storytelling. I'm not saying that all great leaders can spin tales about past events and capture everyone's attention by launching into a monologue. Doing that would make someone a good storyteller, something altogether different. I am referring to storytelling, a technique that skilled leaders use to get people to open up about themselves. This is not as straightforward as it sounds. If I put you on the spot and ask you to tell a story, you will probably find it challenging. Great leaders know how to facilitate storytelling by using the right tools and the right approach to make it feel effortless and natural for participants to tell their own stories and open up about themselves. Perhaps an example would be best.

Take a moment and look around the room. Yes, you, dear reader. Look around the room and pick up an object that is special to you. Go ahead. I'm waiting! Once you have chosen an object, think about why it is important to you. Is it a gift from someone special? Do you use it every day? If someone asked me to do this, I would look at the top of my cluttered desk and pick up a pen. But not just any pen. I would pick up a gold pen that I always keep on the top right corner of my desk. This pen was a gift to me from an important client I worked with for over fifteen years. He even engraved it with my name and the date our first project together commenced. This pen reminds me of a job well done and of the client who provided me with many professional successes over the years. What are you holding in your hands? I asked you to pick up an object that is dear to you. I bet you can easily talk about it for a while, right? You will not have any trouble explaining why it is important. You know the object and its history well. This is storytelling.

Great leaders ask the right questions to get people to open up and share stories about themselves. Through stories, we create understanding and connect with other people. We empathise and feel emotions and gain knowledge of someone else. Stories are memorable, so great leaders rely on storytelling as an important part of what they do. Once people connect by sharing stories, hidden motivations and emotions come to the surface, and collaboration becomes more straightforward. One of the basic principles of effective group leadership is not dominating the session. In other words, let participants do most of the talking. You might have entertaining and insightful stories to tell but save them for the bar after the workshop ends. Workshops and meetings are the place for participants to tell their own stories, not the group leader.

Anchors, spines and stories

Storytelling can be simplified by looking at the terms and concepts that support it. After all, you can't just step in front of a group and suddenly say, "Alright, everyone, today we are going to be each telling some personal stories that reveal our emotions and feelings. Who's first?" That blunt approach would probably result in folks racing for the door! Instead, it's better to ease everyone into sharing stories by using activities and objects that prompt people to share their stories. These are called anchors and spines.

An anchor is an object that prompts people to start talking. It can be anything. In the example above, I asked you to find an object and explain its meaning. The anchor was the object you chose and the story you shared revealed personal information. In my case, the anchor was the pen. I shared a story about the client who gave it to me and how the pen symbolised the beginning of a rewarding relationship. The specific anchor that the leader uses or asks people to choose does not matter. It is the stories that people share. The anchor just serves to break the ice. You can have everyone start with the same anchor, or you can have people choose their own. Either way will get the job done. An example of using the same anchor for everyone can look like this. Hold up a frisbee and ask everyone to think about how the frisbee symbolises their organisational challenges, strategy, or future goals. No matter how strange the object is, people will relate it to themselves and their own stories. People are very creative, don't forget that! Or, if you want everyone to start with their personal anchors, you can ask them to pull out their phones and open an app they use the most. Then ask how their organisation can learn from what this app does well. The anchors are interchangeable, and there are no limitations on what works as an anchor. Be creative too, when selecting anchors for your groups to use! I once saw an excellent facilitator point to a small scar on her elbow and use that as an anchor to get a group to talk about mission statements!

Great leaders often create activities around their anchors to make storytelling even easier. For example, a fun prompt for groups is to give a bunch of Legos and ask them to build the anchor and then talk about it. I did this once at the beginning of a workshop focused on corporate values. I instructed the group of serious-looking businesspeople to think about what they value most at work (this was the anchor I used). Once everyone had something in mind, I pointed to a large box of Legos and told them to now build it! I love to use Legos because it requires folks who are almost always in front of a computer screen or perched behind some fancy desk to get on the floor and dig through a box of coloured building blocks. As a result, people are forced to let their guard down, which gives them the perfect mindset to tell their own stories.

Another twist you can use with anchors is to ask everyone to first think of an object and then write a story about it or draw a picture of it. These activities also help people loosen up and let them have some fun with their anchors before they launch into storytelling.

A spine is a series of anchors. Spines are used when the discussion topic is complex enough to require longer stories and a high degree of self-disclosure. A well-known example of a spine comes from the classic line that starts off most fairy tales: *Once upon a time...* This is the prompt that starts a story. Then, the next part of the spine can be, *Suddenly...* This asks people to explain a problem or event that happened in the middle of a story. The last part of the spine could be, *Then...* This is asking for a resolution. You may finish the story simply with, *Finally, they all lived happily ever after.* To summarise, the spine above asks for three distinct parts of a story: the beginning, the conflict, and the resolution. It requires that the stories address all three aspects, whereas an anchor elicits simpler stories. Sometimes, a group leader will run a session to deal with a problem, long-term challenge, or conflict. In this case, a spine would be better than an anchor because it is crucial to cover the entire history of the issue.

Spines are like anchors in that you can use different prompts tied together to form spines as long as they elicit a multi-part response. For example, you can ask participants to draw three pictures representing their company's past, present, and future. Then you can ask them to tell the story depicted in the pictures or act it out.

Spines and anchors are important prompts that a leader uses to help people open up and tell their stories. There are also dedicated storytelling tools. I will share two of my favourites, Change Equation and Success Stories, with you. Before I explain how each tool works, I will share a story where I used it. Then I will analyse how it was applied and explain why it is an excellent tool for you to use.

Cleaning up messy content

They say that there is no such thing as a boring business. As long as a company is financially successful and has a positive working culture, then any industry or business venture can be exciting. As a professional facilitator, I agree. I believe that people make a company exciting or not, not the actual products it produces or if it has a fancy office. I am excited by most organisations I have the privilege to work with. However, I remember one key example when my optimism was put to the test. I was working with a large European company that produced industrial cleaning supplies and fertilizers. The company was called CleanTech. It was not the industry that made working with this company boring. I don't have anything against cleaning or fertilizer. The challenge resulted from the inconceivable thoroughness of all business documents distributed by the CEO, Raul Paulo. In other words, CleanTech's CEO had a problem editing himself and shortening his message to a manageable size. I was called in when a problem occurred after he attempted to hold a meeting to share the updated company strategy. Raul explained that for some reason, his usually dedicated group of employees had real trouble staying focused.

"I could not believe it. I was just getting into the heart of the new strategy, and I noticed people beginning to slouch in their chairs and struggle to keep awake. I was only on slide twenty of the presentation and just getting started!"

Fearing that I had misunderstood Raul, I asked for some clarification. "Did you say slide twenty, Raul? How long was the entire presentation?"

"It was seventy slides long, but a brisk seventy slides."

Seventy slides? No wonder Raul saw some of his managers lose interest. The thought of trying to stay engaged during a dense seventy-slide presentation almost made me begin to yawn on the spot. I suggested to Raul that he shorten the presentation and focus only on its key aspects, but he insisted that it could not be any shorter than it already was.

"I can't shorten it any further, Pepe. This new strategy has many moving parts, and I have already cut the presentation down to seventy slides from the 100 or so slides I had originally."

"Don't worry, Raul. You don't have to cut down your presentation any further. Tell me, were you able to get through the entire presentation with your managerial team?"

"Yes, I did. But people looked bored. I doubt it made much of an impact. My managerial team is supposed to relay this new strategy to the rest of CleanTech. I am talking about thousands of employees! How can they motivate the rest of the company if they were bored themselves by the new strategy?"

I eased Raul's doubts and told him not to worry. "Think about the new company strategy. Don't try and visualise all seventy slides, but answer these three questions…"

1. Dissatisfaction. Why do we need to change now?
2. Vision. How will our job be better once the new change is made?
3. Process. How will the new strategy be implemented within our team?

Raul paused and began looking through the PowerPoint slides while jotting down notes to himself. Finally, after a few moments, he nodded and said he was done.

"Good job, Raul. Your answers to these questions are what you should be relaying to your managerial team! This is your change story, and it clearly explains the reason why the new company strategy is needed. This will be much easier for your employees to understand and build around than the seventy slides would be. You can always give out the detailed version of the new strategy after your managerial team understands the reasons why the change is important."

I asked Raul to book a half-day session with the managerial team, and a week later, I was in an immaculate conference room at CleanTech HQ. Raul began the session by explaining his change story first, and then the group was tasked with customizing it to fit each of their departments. I gave them some Legos to help get their creativity flowing, and CleanTech managers got to building all sorts of things. I watched them build towers, shapes, and animals with Legos. They talked with each other and excitedly examined parts of the new company strategy. By the end of the session, the strategy was clear to everyone, and the floor was littered with Danish building blocks.

Most importantly, everyone on the managerial team now had a change story prepared to tell their own teams. Raul was a very happy man, but as we walked out of the conference room, he made sure to ask someone to clean up the Legos that remained on the conference room floor. After all, the CEO of CleanTech hated to leave a mess behind.

Change Equation analysis

The tool I used as a spine with CleanTech is called Change Equation. The three questions I asked Raul and CleanTech's managers to focus on related to the three components of the Change Equation. The Change Equation is a formula originally used for measuring the possibility of change. Richard Beckhard and Reuben Harris developed this tool in the 1980s to assess the probability of success or failure of a proposed change in the workplace. It states that change will occur if dissatisfaction, vision, and the accessibility of the change process are all greater than resistance to change.

Change Equation

Change will occur if;

$$C = D \times V \times P > R$$

Dissatisfaction and **Vision** and **Process** of change are greater than **Resistance**.

In other words, if the positives outweigh the negatives, then change will take place. You can't quantify each part of the Change Equation like a simple numerical math equation, so there is no concrete way to measure each component to see which is more significant.

Each component of the Change Equation can be defined as follows:

D – Dissatisfaction (Motivation or urgent need to make a change)

V – Vision (What will the change do for you? How will things be better if you make this change?)

P – Process (How will you make this change happen? What are the short-term steps to take? How about the long-term steps?)

A good rule of thumb is that change will not occur if one area of the Change Equation is weak or missing. If dissatisfaction is weak or absent, there is no push to change, even if the benefits and steps to achieve the change are evident. If process is weak or missing, people will feel frustrated and helpless. You will want to change but will not know how to change. If vision is weak or non-existent, you might be running around like a headless chicken. You will be very busy trying several different things to change and ease the dissatisfaction, but you do not know where you are going, and very little will get done. As you listen to people share their stories, you will tell which components of the Change Equation are strong and which components need more development.

Elements of a Change Story

D = Dissatisfaction: External and internal reasons for change

V = Vision: What is the outcome of change

P = Process: How do we move towards the vision

Most importantly, people going through organisational change typically do not see the forest from the trees. They explain details but do not communicate the most important elements of change. Change Equation gives you these key elements and works fantastic as a spine for storytelling.

Now I want to share another storytelling tool that all leaders should know, Success Stories.

Sharing success

Sometimes it is hard to see the positive side of things. As I stood in front of a room full of eighteen frowning strangers, I could tell that no one saw anything positive at the moment. I was leading a workshop for a management team of a wholesale fruit company called, Apples to Apples. The company was going through a rough adjustment to new market conditions brought on by a larger competitor recently entering their market. Now they had to deal with a huge company undercutting their prices. Apples to Apples reacted by streamlining their company profile by cutting costs and letting some workers go. The Sales Team even suggested a strike after hearing that their sales targets had gone up again. Everyone was stressed and focusing only on problems and negative news. Instead of thinking about new and better ways to do their jobs, people became stuck in their routines and tried harder to hit the new, more challenging sales targets.

A workshop was called to address organizational changes that needed to be implemented. The management team lacked confidence, and I would help them focus on their strengths instead of any obstacles in their way.

I started by talking about a recent workshop I led in my own company where my leadership trainers and I brainstormed company mission statements. After the session, everyone felt very positive and focused. I told this story to share an example of the success I experienced recently. Then I asked each person to write down an example of success that they experienced at Apples to Apples. Matt, a long-time Apples to Apples employee, seemed to want to derail my plan almost immediately. "And what should we write down if there are no positives? I could think and think, but I doubt I'll come up with anything."

I stopped Matt in his tracks and did not let him continue any further. I wanted to focus on positivity, not problems. "Then write down an example that you heard from someone else. Or something you observed somebody do. Any example of success, big or small, will do. If you can't think of a story, don't worry about it. Just listen to others sharing their stories, and you might be inspired to think of something."

The room was quiet. People seemed to be thinking, but they weren't writing anything down. I started to worry but soon breathed a sigh of relief. These things just take time, and sometimes the group leader just needs to have a bit of patience. Gradually everyone began to write down their thoughts, and after a few minutes, I let everyone know their time was up and gave out the next set of instructions; "Split up into groups of four. Share the positive experiences you wrote down with each other."

Everyone quickly divided into groups of four people and shared their success stories. I kept a close eye on things and walked around the room to offer support and eavesdrop a bit. I passed one of the groups and heard Barry, a long-time Apples to Apples employee, reminisce about making his first sale in a new district. "Time flies, but I remember it like it was yesterday! When the client signed the sales receipt, I almost forgot to give them their carbon copy of the receipt!" Barry recounted to his group. I chuckled to myself and thought that perhaps only a few people in the room were old enough to remember carbon copies. After all, that outdated system of receipts was replaced in the mid-1990s!

I kept walking and stopped by another group to hear what Sales Manager Laura had to say. "My biggest success was working with another salesperson to hit my sales goals. The person who helped me was a veteran salesman named Dale, who is retired now. I thought that there was no way I could manage to hit my goals, but he took the time to help me and give me the tips that he learned over the years. I try to continue what he did for me by paying it forward and helping others, too!".

I continued to make my way around the room, becoming more and more inspired as I went. It seemed like Matt's worries about not being able to find any positive examples of success were irrelevant. The whole room seemed to be buzzing with positive energy stemming from everyone remembering their moments of success. Once everyone finished sharing, the group was full of energy and excitement. I wanted to harness this positive energy, so I asked for a volunteer from each small group to share with the entire room a success story. Nicholas, an eager and ambitious guy who had the distinction of being the youngest ever employee to become a sales manager for Apples to Apples, raised his hand and shared his success story. "I remember thinking that it would be impossible to succeed in my assigned sales district. Our top competitor dominated us at the time and did something like 85 % of all produce sales in the district. We were barely there. But after some time and a lot of hard work getting to truly know the customers, I began to close more and more deals and strike new contracts, and now we own 32 % of the market share there. And it's rising!"

Nicholas smiled, and some of the other managers even clapped a bit. Andrea, a friendly woman and long-time Apples to Apples worker, congratulated Nicholas and said they were all proud of him. "Keep up the good work, Nicky! You are just getting started!"

A hand went up in the front row, and I called on Carlie to share her story. Carlie pointed at Andrea and said, "I have been working with Andrea and this wonderful group of men and women for almost 15 years. The group's support, help, and warmth has created a great workplace for me and transformed some supportive co-workers into lifelong friends. Carlie was even one of my bridesmaids at my wedding a few years ago!"

I thanked everyone for sharing their examples and let them know I was impressed. Then I told them what to do next.

"Now that we have had time to hear about successes that you all have enjoyed while working at Apples to Apples, it's time to think about them on a deeper level. Why did they happen? Do your success stories share something in common?"

"That's obvious, Pepe. I'm at the centre of all the successes. But, it's our team that makes the magic happen," said Carlie. I smiled at her confidence but elaborated as to what I meant.

"You're right, Carlie. This group of amazing people is at the centre of all the success and achievements. But be more specific. What did you do? Who helped you? The idea now is to think about the ingredients for your successful moments. What common factors do your success stories share? Take a few minutes to think about these things and write down what comes to mind. This is an individual activity, so no talking, please. You can begin!"

Everyone got to it and began to write their ideas down. After about five minutes, I asked everyone to form groups of four. "In these small groups, share the success factors you identified! You have about ten minutes to do this, and if you have any questions, ask me!"

I moved around the room as people shared success factors in small groups, and I managed to catch bits and pieces of the different conversations. I was happy to hear that Matt had a lot of positive things to say. Earlier in the session, he doubted if he could even think of a single positive thing to say. Now, he was excitedly telling his group how using existing tools like the Apples to Apples training materials and employee knowledge base helped him push through obstacles at work.

In a different corner of the room, Laura shared one of her secrets to success with her group. "For me, I look for help outside of our Sales Team if I am stuck or need a new viewpoint. I remember once I had trouble managing a difficult client. This person would email me at all hours of the day, and once, they even called me at 11 p.m. just to ask a question that I had already answered! I was at a bit of a loss about what to do. The business deal was fine, but managing this person was turning into a nightmare. It occurred to me that we have people in our company who specialize in this sort of thing, our HR Team! So, I booked a meeting to chat with Tim, a Human Resource Officer. He gave me some good tips about how to communicate in a way that can make a difficult client feel empowered and become less bothersome."

I gave everyone a few more minutes to share their success factors in small groups, and then I called for everyone's attention. "Great work! Now let's join back together as one large group. I need each group to write down the success factors you discussed. I have passed out a piece of flip chart paper and a pen to each group, so you should be ready to go. Once you have made your list, take it to the front of the room and tape it to the wall."

Once the flip charts were taped to the front of the room, I asked everyone to stand up and come to the front of the room to read the results. "Does anyone have anything to add to these success factors? Anything that you want to elaborate on?"

"Accountability," Barry said. "We all agreed that it is much easier to perform your best if you have someone else to answer to."

Joel, another Apples to Apples Sales Manager, added, "Yes, Barry is right. If I feel that other people think what I do is important, then it makes me take everything more seriously."

Matt raised his hand to share his group's success factors. "We all agreed that working with others to close a sales deal or even having a few different people help a single client is best. The old way of doing things used to be one sales manager assigned to a client. We used to work a lot on our own, focusing on our own clients and our own personal sales goals. It felt a bit like you were on an island by yourself. We realized that the best moments of our careers and the best things we have achieved are shared successes with others. When we collaborate, we usually succeed," concluded Matt.

I thanked Matt for his comments and gave the final piece of instructions to the group. "As you can see, you all have a lot of success factors! Now it is time to choose the best ones. When you're ready, come up and write your initials next to the top two or three success factors. Choose the ones that you think are the absolute best of the best. Go ahead and get started!"

One by one, everyone got to it. Some people like Carlie knew exactly which factors were the best. She came to the board immediately and wrote her initially next to *cross-team collaboration*. Other folks were more hesitant, but everyone had signed their initials next to at least one success factor after a few minutes, and our job was done. There was a positive feeling in the room, and the Apples to Apples Sales Team had a new perspective on things now that they had the ingredients to their success written down and understood by all. I usually am not the type to brag, but I thought this workshop was nothing short of a huge success.

How to use Success Stories

1. Sharing success
   - write down personal experiences
   - share stories in small groups
   - choose the best stories to be shared
   - share the most inspiring stories with everyone

2. Success factors
   - analysis of success factors individually
   - exploring and finding key factors in small groups
   - posting, presenting and prioritising

Success Stories analysis

I used Success Stories in my session at Apples to Apples. I chose this tool because I could see that the entire group was preoccupied with challenges and problems. I wanted to energize them and redirect their focus onto something more positive.

First, I explained how the activity worked and shared one of my own success stories. Next, I continued the success stories session using the familiar tool Me/We/Us (individual thinking, small-groups, and finally sharing with everyone in the room) and asked everyone to think of a moment where they experienced some professional success. Time to think individually is essential. If you asked people to share success stories without giving them time to think, it would not be successful.

After individual thinking, small groups were formed for sharing. Sharing in small groups is an easier transition from the individual stage than a group-wide discussion. Once everyone had a story in mind, they shared it in groups, which completely changed the atmosphere from negative to positive. Finally, volunteers were asked to present a few examples to the whole group, but not too many. Too many presentations can quickly kill the positive energy.

Next, people began to look for factors present in the success stories. What caused these things to happen? What factors are behind the events?

They started analysing their own examples of success and continued building on each other's ideas in groups of four. Finally, they posted their key success factors on the wall.

We first shared success stories, and next, we discovered the key success factors. Just sharing success stories can be energising. We have used them in large groups to celebrate the year and the beginning of a new season. It is inspiring to have hundreds of people share their stories in small groups. Groups always choose the best story before joining another group and sharing the best stories again until only a few are left. Finally, you have these very best stories shared in front of everyone.

We have created company values based on success stories. First, we shared the stories. Next, instead of asking for success factors, we asked for values that help us succeed.

After finding success factors, you may continue by creating solutions for strengthening each factor and finalising the workshop with a concrete action plan; what, who, when. I did this when I was working with a street food franchising company. After initial fast expansion, their success began to fade. The concept had gone through many changes, and it had been forgotten what had made the restaurant a hit in the first place. With the help of storytelling, we found the key success factors and made a plan for ensuring future success.

In our case with Apples, I continued the following week with the Clarifying-Solutions-Action structure. We first created a common goal, followed by solutions and an action plan.

You can use success stories for energising teams, strategies, projects or even your relationships if you desire. In my experience, people remember workshops and meetings that celebrate success much better than sessions that revolve around challenges or problems.

> ## The benefits and challenges of using Success Stories
>
> Benefits
> - Encourages positive thinking
> - Energises participants
> - People remember positive examples better than problems
> - Develops relationships and strengthens the bonds within a team
> - It is inspiring to talk about your successes
>
> Challenges
> - Storytelling does not work if there are no inspiring examples of success to share

A time and a place for stories

You may use storytelling in everyday situations. I was working with a software company, and I was brought in to help a group of programmers review a post-mortem incident report following an extended service outage. It is a bit of a tired stereotype to say that programmers can be a bit shy when talking about themselves, but in this case, the shoe fit. No one wanted to say anything. I thought that this was an excellent time to dust off a storytelling tool, so I dropped an anchor and asked each of them to think of their favourite video game and then explain why they liked it and what could be learned. With this anchor (storytelling prompt), they were off and chattering a mile a minute and talking about their childhood, favourite games, and what made the games brilliant pieces of art. Storytelling got everyone engaged and communicating. And as anyone with any group leadership experience knows, getting participants engaged and sharing is the starting point for all great meetings and workshops.

Highly regarded professional group leaders, facilitators, consultants, coaches, and managers all use storytelling tools to get participants to open up and create self-disclosure. Using storytelling makes content personal and more memorable. It also has the power to frame challenges or ideas in a new light.

CHAPTER 8:

Virtual Breakthrough Decision Making

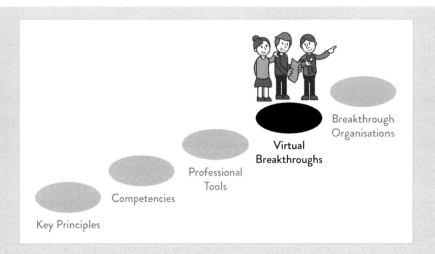

What's here

- **Case Study**: I guide Bonaventure Banking's Marketing Team through a creativity workshop where the goal is to develop a new slogan to be used in the brand relaunch of the bank. The unique thing about this session? I conducted it remotely using virtual meeting software to bring together a group that was scattered around the globe.
- **Tools**: Self-portraits, Idealogue, virtual meeting software

How it helps

Remote work is becoming more and more common. Leading groups remotely is different from face-to-face leadership, and this chapter shows what a virtual session looks like and demonstrates key practices for successful virtual leadership.

Creative differences

I had just hung up the phone after wrapping up a friendly conversation with a Bonaventure Banking Corp representative. She was reaching out to request my services to help their marketing team develop a new slogan for the bank to serve as the centrepiece of their rebranding efforts. "I will send over the details," she said as her parting words.

A few moments later, I received an email from her laying out the specifics; I would lead a two-hour workshop for a group of ten, which would take place as soon as possible. The attendees would be directly involved with the brand relaunch; the brand manager, marketing director, digital marketing specialist, and other key members of the Bonaventure Team, such as the Chief Business Officer and the Public Relations Director.

As I finished reading the email, I was impressed. Their proposal made sense, and so far, and based on my phone call with the secretary, this seemed to be an intelligent and capable group. I scanned the rest of the email. Below the farewell and signature were the official details of the bank; contact information, office locations, and the slogan we would replace; *Bonaventure Bank: Let your banking be an adventure!*

Let your banking be an adventure?! An adventure is the last thing you want when it comes to money, I thought to myself incredulously. The current slogan clearly showed why Bonaventure Bank wanted to have the workshop as soon as possible. Filled with a sense of purpose and a bit of embarrassment due to their shoddy slogan, I got right to work.

An important invitation

Three days before the workshop took place, I emailed an invitation to all the participants. I wanted to make sure that they knew how to download and set up the virtual meeting software. I also informed them when the session began and how long it would last.

It might have been the first time some people were using virtual meeting software, so I made myself available the night before the session. In the orientation email, I wrote, "I will be available from 5 p.m. to 6 p.m., Eastern Standard Time the night before if any of you wish to sign in to the virtual meeting software and check that it is set up properly."

I also needed to make sure that everything was working well on my end and also that I was familiar with the software features that I planned on using, like the shared writing space and breakout rooms.

How do you feel today?

The day had arrived, and the session was underway. I glanced at the clock on my computer screen and saw that we were already a few minutes into the meeting. The virtual meeting software was open, and the following screen was displayed:

I saw that eight people managed to follow my instructions of *Draw a self-portrait of yourself in a creative mood and write your name.* Unfortunately, that meant that two people were running late.

As I waited for the final two people to complete the activity and confirm their presence, I glanced at the self-portraits. I saw a few smiles which were easy to interpret. A few of the drawings were a bit more abstract and harder to read. But I didn't see any self-portraits with tears, frowns, or eyes shooting fire out of them, so I was off to a good start. Two more names appeared on the screen, both placed under self-portraits that were a bit rough but happy looking, so I knew that everyone was there and that we could begin.

Pushing the microphone icon on my screen, I thanked everyone for attending and complimented their drawings. "We have some happy-looking people here today. Well, I assume that we are all people—that was not entirely clear from the drawings. Anyway, our objective today is to have a two-hour creativity session where you all will come up with a new slogan for Bonaventure Banking Corp."

I toggled up the relevant slide that summarised the plan.

Meeting objective and format

Objective: To create a new slogan for Bonaventure Bank

Time: 2 hours

Process:

1. Individual brainstorming
2. Stealing ideas from each other
3. Choosing the best slogans

"If you have any questions about the meeting or our objective, please type it into chat now." I let around twenty seconds pass to give time for any questions to be submitted. So far, there were none. I continued, "We are all meeting virtually today, and to ensure that it will be the best meeting possible, I have outlined some ways of working that will help us have the best virtual session possible. You can see them all on your screen now. Please take a moment to read them over while I explain."

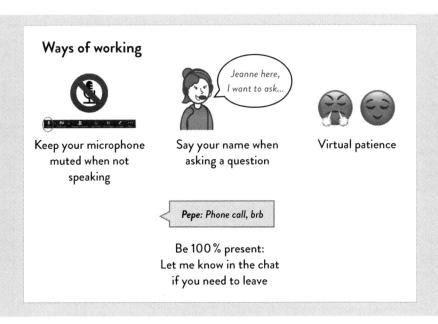

Ways of working

Keep your microphone muted when not speaking

Say your name when asking a question

Jeanne here, I want to ask...

Virtual patience

Pepe: Phone call, brb

Be 100 % present: Let me know in the chat if you need to leave

"It's important that you state your name before speaking and let the group know via chat if you need to step away for a moment. These simple actions keep the conversation running smoothly."

Suddenly, I heard the crackling of a microphone, followed by a voice: "What do you mean by..., oops, sorry. Let me try again. Linda here; I have a question for Pepe. What do you mean by 'be 100 % present'?"

"Great question, Linda, and nice job stating your name before speaking. Being 100 % present means announcing to the group via chat if you need to leave for a moment. It also means focusing on the meeting content and minimising distractions for yourself during the meeting. For example, if we were sitting here together in one conference room, I am confident that you would never pull out a newspaper and begin reading it while I am talking. And I am sure that you would not start your own conversations with friends during our time together. And I know that you would never pull out your phone and bury your head in the screen when someone is talking to you, so please kindly refrain from doing these things during our virtual meetings, too."

A few good words

With the way of working clear and the ground rules explained, I proceeded to the heart of the session, which was using Idealogue to create and decide on new slogans for Bonaventure Bank. Idealogue works the same virtually as in face-to-face workshops, so I did not need to change the instructions.

"You have ten minutes to think of slogans individually and write down as many as you can. You can record the ideas on a notepad on your computer or by using pen and paper, whichever you prefer. You can start when you are ready!"

I sat back and gazed at the screen. The only noise was the smacking sounds of someone chewing gum while working, and this soon disappeared when they remembered to mute themselves a moment later. After fifteen minutes were up, the next stage of Idealogue called for repeated rounds of idea theft in rotating small groups. This was the same format that Idealogue follows in face-to-face meetings.

"We are going to have three rounds of idea theft in groups of three. Your task is to collect the best ideas for yourself by sharing, listening, eliminating, and changing slogans. I have opened breakout rooms for each group, and I will automatically divide you into new groups and rotate you every fifteen minutes until we have completed three rounds of sharing."

I pulled up a list of the ten participant names within the meeting software client and clicked to divide them into three groups: one group of four and two groups of three. Each group was linked to their own conference call while still having access to a shared whiteboard.

"I am here to help out with any technical issues or questions that come up, so please feel free to get a hold of me via chat if I can help with anything!" I reminded the group as they began sharing and stealing from one another.

After the first round, I explained that two more rounds of small group discussions would occur in breakout rooms. By now, everyone was used to the meeting software, and the small group discussion was going well.

Virtual convergence

"Now that you have searched the room for slogans to steal, we are going to come together once again in small groups to find out what the best ones are. You will see a shared virtual whiteboard on your screen where you can add your favourite slogans by typing them. Please take a moment with your new group of three-four participants and choose the best slogans you have."

Add ideas for new slogans by typing them into the chat.

- Bonaventure bank: Your new favorite trip
- Banking made easy
- Banking without the adventure
- Bonaventure for a bon voyage
- Bonaventure; where you want to be
- The bank of the future
- Your needs of tomorrow given today
- Your future problems solved today
- Tomorrow's needs provided today
- Providing for the future in the present
- Bonaventure: giving the gift of a secure future
- Bonaventure: the present of a secure tomorrow

- Bonaventure: the gift of time by managing your money
- The people's bank
- Honest banking made easy
- Wherever you need us, we're there.
- Bonaventure Bank: For the long journey
- Don't let your bank meander
- Stability through the quest
- Banking for the journey of life
- Stability in unstable times
- Timeless, trustworthy, avant-garde
- Bonaventure bank: timeless innovation
- Bonaventure Bank: It really is this easy

Type new slogan here to add to virtual whiteboard...

After fifteen minutes, we got back together, and it was time to conduct the Investment Activity virtually. I usually hand out stickers for groups to invest in face-to-face meetings, but virtually it is a bit different, depending on the meeting software you use. This time the meeting software had a polling feature where points could be assigned to a specific idea by writing the number of dollars next to the best ideas. I gave the instructions as I usually would. The only difference was that the investment was completed and displayed on the virtual whiteboard instead of on a piece of paper with stickers and markers, as is the case in face-to-face meetings. The group of marketing experts, P.R. reps and content strategists had done well. After investing ten dollars in pairs, the top slogans were displayed on the virtual whiteboard as shared property.

Investment Activity results

Solutions for tomorrow's world today – $21

Bonaventure Bank: peerless and timeless, today and tomorrow – $11

Bonaventure Bank: stability in the face of change – $9

Bonaventure for a bon voyage – $3

Bonaventure Bank: it's that easy – $3

Bonaventure Bank: Journey with us – $3

Checking out and following up

"Fantastic work, everyone! I'm no marketing expert, but I think these new slogans are a vast improvement over Bonaventure Bank's current slogan. We're almost finished, but I want to revisit your moods before we go. Remember the beginning of the session where you drew a self-portrait in a creative mood? I have a similar activity for you now. Look at our shared meeting screen. On it, you will see different pictures. Please write your name next to the picture that best represents your mood."

The names clumped together next to the smiling or laughing emoticons, and I was ready to wrap up the virtual meeting and label it a success.

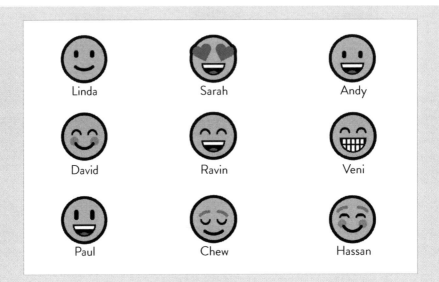

"Let's close today by getting three comments," I said.

"Hassan speaking. I am so relieved we finally came up with a viable slogan. I was not able to do it alone."

Next, the director of PR added her thoughts. "Sarah here. I am excited to take this new slogan forward and share it with the world!"

Lastly, Paul, the digital marketing director, added, "We came together today better than we do in person!"

I smiled behind my screen and typed out a big "Thank you, everyone!" which appeared in the virtual meeting space. Then, I explained to the group that I would send out an email that summarised the session and included all the content written on the virtual whiteboard.

Analysis

Successful virtual meetings are not a mystery. The key is learning how to use one of the many virtual meeting software programs available, becoming comfortable with it, and mastering the use of features like breakout rooms and a shared virtual whiteboard. New programs are constantly entering the market and becoming available, and I will not endorse a specific one. Instead, just make sure that it is easy to use and has two key features: a virtual whiteboard that anyone can edit within the meeting, and breakout rooms for collaboration in small groups.

For this session, I also made sure to select tools that work well virtually. Idealogue can be used just about the same virtually as in a face-to-face session. The repeated rounds of sharing in pairs and small groups can be handled using the breakout rooms built into the virtual meeting software. By selecting the correct tool for the job, I created a scenario where group members could enter the emergent zone where shared understanding is developed, and new ideas are born.

Essential features you need in virtual meeting software

- The ability to divide one large group into pairs or smaller groups.
- Polling software
- A shared chat room
- Virtual whiteboard that can be edited by anyone within the meeting
- Teleconferencing that can easily create new groups and quickly change from group to group.

We know what features the virtual meeting software needs to have, but what about the group leader? What about you? As I see it, there are six keys to succeeding as a virtual meeting master:

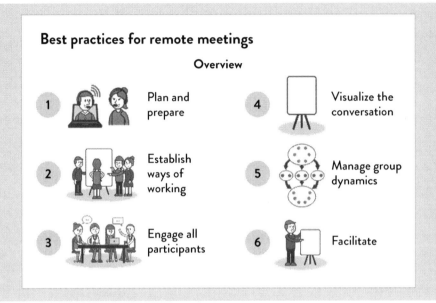

Let's review each one and see how I executed it in the case study.

1. Plan and prepare

The work starts before the session does. After meeting with the client, the first thing I did was send an invitation to the meeting participants with a link to the virtual software. By doing this, I gave the workshop participants a chance to become familiar with the technology. I also informed them about the workshop details, such as the starting time and duration.

During the planning stage, I map out the workshop and decide what tools to use and how much time to spend on each part of the meeting. I also prepare the meeting slides and any other content I plan on using during the workshop.

2. Establish ways of working

I prepared everyone to participate effectively by presenting clear ground rules. The ground rules I typically use are;

1. Keep your microphone muted when you are not speaking
2. 100 % participation (excuse yourself before leaving the session)
3. Virtual patience
4. State your name before talking or asking a question

By outlining clear rules, you ensure that you will not be surprised by unexpected behaviour during the meeting. Agreeing on and sticking to a set of ground rules is even more critical when participants aren't physically in the same location and can't see each other.

It is important that people say their names before speaking. This way, there is no confusion and stating one's name before speaking also avoids situations where people begin to talk over each other. It also calms and prepares the other participants to listen to what the speaker says.

My favourite rule for virtual meetings is *100 % participation*. This means that people attending the meeting must give 100 % of their attention to the meeting. They need to actively listen to whoever is speaking. No one can check their emails, look through customer contacts, or text their friends. In physical face-to-face meetings, this rule does not need explaining. It would be insulting and potentially career-ending if someone pulled out their phone to read the news in front of the rest of the company. But it is different in virtual meetings. Many people use the internet with multiple tabs open, and technology makes it easy to multitask. I like to remind groups of the 100% participation rule a few times throughout a session. It is that important!

Focused participation also helps eliminate background noise. In order to be 100 % focused and tuned into a meeting, participants should find a quiet place to use to attend the virtual meeting. There is always background noise in public areas. For example, if you're waiting for a train, not only is there lots of background noise, but it is a task itself and will prevent you from actively participating. Ground rules and clear instructions are also needed before any issue is opened up for group discussion. As the meeting leader, how do you want the group to discuss something? How much time do you wish to spend on this discussion? Imagine asking a group of twenty to decide on something in a virtual meeting without giving the group any guidance. You need a clear set of ground rules to prevent chaos and keep the group on track.

If the group is using a new virtual platform for the first time, it's also good to have a *technical support person* who can help participants with technical problems while the leader guides the group through the tools and the meeting's process. By tasking a person with the job of helping clear up any technical issues, you can focus on more important things and don't need to worry about getting interrupted every few minutes if there are repeat technical issues.

3. Get everyone engaged

Without passion and enthusiasm, nothing worthwhile gets done. This holds true for meeting leaders and attendees, too. If the person running the meeting is not interested and engaged, how can the attendees be expected to care? It is crucial to lead sessions in an engaging, purposeful way. Have a plan you believe in and be decisive in guiding the group through your plan. Think about when there should be a break for coffee or to stretch. If there is a long presentation, the group will need a break afterwards. Even half an hour of focused listening is tiring. To get a group to refocus, use activation tools to get people focused and alert. The shared virtual whiteboard is an excellent piece of technology, and you can do all sorts of things with it, including using smileys and voting icons, polling, drawing, and writing. Use these techniques to ensure the group is paying attention and to refocus participants.

When leading a virtual meeting, it is best to start with a dynamic activity. This can be a game to get people thinking or conversation in small groups to get people to talk to each other. After the group is activated, the meeting leader can proceed with the agenda and monitor the groups' attention level. If people seem impatient or distracted, give the group a short break or start a new activity to draw them back into the workshop.

4. Visualise the conversation

Using group memory is an integral part of great group leadership. Group memory functions as a mechanism for storing the ideas produced during a meeting. Simply put, group memory means that issues important to the group are written down and made visible to participants. In doing so, no ideas are neglected or forgotten, and conversation is enhanced. People can only remember a few things at a time, and the visual aid of writing everything down becomes an extension of the mind. This extension of the mind is the group's memory. By writing down all the ideas produced together, the original owner of the idea, the person who thought it, is made irrelevant, and the ideas are allowed to stand on their own. The idea has become the property of the group.

5. Manage group dynamics

Incorrect group size can cause a leader all sorts of headaches. If a group is too big, it is common for a few talkative people to participate while everyone becomes distracted or uninterested. It becomes a challenge for many people to be engaged in large group sessions. The energy level dramatically decreases when there are over fifteen people in a group. While it is true that more people in a group means more resources to draw from, the group's focus, energy level, and collective intelligence decrease when it becomes too large. When thoughts and ideas are first refined together in a small group, they are often better formed than individual opinions. You should use activities that divide a large group into several smaller groups. It increases engagement, and it is easier for participants to express themselves without the pressure of speaking in front of a large group.

6. Facilitate

Virtual collaboration can be a real challenge. Some people think that virtual meetings are nothing more than a short vacation. They believe they can attend the virtual meeting successfully while keeping an eye glued to their T.V. set, watching the latest soap opera or football match. Other people want to participate, but it is a new format for them. They might be unsure of the technology and not know how to participate. As a group leader, you must remember one of the most important rules of facilitative group leadership; focus on the process. Focusing on the process will allow you to guide people through any distractions and uncertainties that may arise, freeing up the group's energy and brainpower to focus on the task at hand.

Make the trend

Virtual meetings are nothing new. Some organisations have been running virtual meetings for decades, and the current trends indicate that virtual meetings will only become more and more common in the future. The COVID-19 outbreak of 2020 made face-to-face meetings impossible for people worldwide. It forced many companies to close their offices and adopt policies that only allow remote work and virtual meetings. The good news for you is the virtual meeting practices presented in this chapter are an excellent foundation for successful virtual meetings. New and improved virtual meeting software is released all the time, which means that it will only get easier to meet virtually going forward.

What was used and why?

Self-portraits – To activate people within the first minutes of the online meeting. This is very important in a virtual meeting where people tend to disappear somewhere
Idealogue – Key tool for emergence
Choosing a picture – To get feedback about the workshop

Key requirements for virtual meeting software
1. A shared whiteboard where everyone can write
2. Breakout rooms for discussions in small groups

Process and participant instructions

Check-in (15 minutes)
Draw yourself in a creative mood (choose any mood you like!) + add your name
- Group leader pointing at pictures -> How do you really feel?

Presenting the schedule and way of working
- Expectations in chat + checking the participant expectations
- Introducing the way of working

Emergence (55 minutes)
Individual thinking, group leader opens a whiteboard with text (10 minutes):
- Write down ideas for a new slogan individually
- Develop your ideas in silence

Stealing with Pride (3 × 15 minutes)
- "I will be opening breakout rooms soon and you will be developing ideas in groups of three. Your task is to steal with pride."
- "Share, listen, and develop the ideas you hear from others."
- "Collect the best ideas on your own piece of paper. You may use the whiteboard to visualise ideas but keep the best ones on your own paper. We will change groups three times and I do not want you to lose your treasures!"

Convergence (40 minutes)
- "In your groups of three choose the best ideas."
- (Everyone together) "Write your very best ideas on the whiteboard."
- "Look at the ideas and on your own, choose your favourites."
- "With a pair, explain, influence and get ready to invest $10 into best ideas!"
- "Ok friends, enough talking. Invest $10 with your pair in the best slogans."
- "What do you think about the results? Do we have a winner?"

Check-out (10 minutes)
Write your name on the picture that best reflects your feeling now
Short round of comments
"Thank you!"

CHAPTER 9:

Breakthrough Organisations

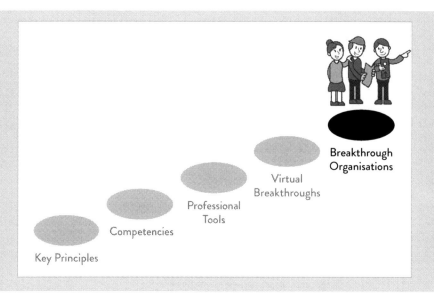

What's here

- The six key features of breakthrough organisations: clear focus, rapid transformation, efficient processes, happy clients, connected employees, systematic leadership
- Case studies demonstrating how these features are unlocked using dialogue and breakthrough decision-making tools
- Thinking beyond business to create a breakthrough society

How it helps

A breakthrough organisation is a system connected by dialogue. This dialectic connection creates better decision making and alignment. This chapter shows how to apply breakthrough decision-making tools, workshops, and meetings to develop a unified, aligned, agile, and efficient organisation.

A unified system
connected by dialogue

When two people take the time to understand each other and align their priorities, great things happen, and the results often exceed even the most optimistic of expectations. The power of collaboration grows when a group of people puts their heads together to create a unified front and work towards a singular goal. Still, we can dream even bigger and take things to the next level, the organisational level. The idea of improving organisations comes from the field of organisational development. Organisational development involves studying successful organisations and their structures, seeing what works, and applying it in other contexts. The field has been around since the 1930s, when researchers observed that some organisational structures resulted in higher productivity and better results than average. Organisational development requires more stages and much more time than group leadership and workshops. Instead of a session that takes place over a few hours, organisational development can take months or even years to implement. The person who is tasked with leading this development across an entire organisation is called an organisational development practitioner (or OD practitioner). A large organisation may have dedicated OD practitioners on staff who work with managers and team leads to teach collaboration tools. An OD practitioner may also be brought on temporarily to work with management to train them in leadership skills and demonstrate the cycle of meetings and events needed to strengthen collaboration within an organisation. The OD practitioner's role is to oversee the significant changes that should occur, and they often work with influential stakeholders (management and decision-makers). Organisational development is similar to how communication and alignment are built within groups. The same breakthrough decision-making tools from previous chapters are the tools you use to create a breakthrough organisation.

A breakthrough organisation is:

An agile and aligned system that is connected by dialogue on all levels

Once a breakthrough organisation takes shape, the following features emerge and become stronger: clear focus, rapid transformation, efficient processes, happy clients, connected employees, and systematic leadership.

Breakthrough Organisation

1. Clear Focus
2. Rapid Transformation
3. Efficient Processes
4. Happy Clients
5. Connected Employees
6. Systematic Leadership

These features need to be developed and strengthened by regularly holding workshops and meetings that use breakthrough decision-making tools. People are required to communicate and collaborate as they participate in these sessions. As these tools are used more and more, the entire organisation becomes connected by dialogue and a positive feedback loop is developed; as the elements of a breakthrough organisation are strengthened, they positively benefit the organisation, which further supports the features of a breakthrough organisation.

You need to be aware of the six features of breakthrough organisations as you practice organisational development. You should notice them as they emerge in your organisation, but if for some reason you do not, then it is time to revisit your methods and review your meetings, workshops, and use of group tools. Keeping track of six different features of a breakthrough organisation probably sounds like a lot of work, right? Well, it is. One piece of advice is to focus on just one at a time. For example, as you use breakthrough decision-making tools throughout your organisation, concentrate on *clear focus*. Do you notice a clear focus throughout your company? Does your organisation benefit from having a clear focus? When you can confidently answer yes, then move on to the next feature and see if you can observe it as you continue to help build your very own breakthrough organisation. Let's look at each of these features to see what they entail and how they look in practice.

1. Clear focus

Want to test out something? Next time you are at work, ask your team what their top short-term priorities are. You can also ask them what the long-term goals of the entire organisation are. If you try this out and receive the same answer repeatedly, then congratulations; your breakthrough organisation benefits from having a clear focus. But if each person answers differently, you should spend some time reflecting on your organisation and how it could benefit from having a clear focus. Look for areas where you can host a meeting or run a workshop to align people around the same goals. If anyone could possibly think that they already had things developed to a point where focusing on focusing wasn't needed, it was me, a professional facilitator who has founded his very own company that trains people in leadership principles around the world. I am sorry to say it, but I was foolish enough to make this mistake within my own company.

We are a small team at Grape People. Ten of us manage to handle all the operations of the entire company. Since we are all so educated and experienced in communication and facilitative leadership, I thought we must always be aligned and on the same page. I was wrong. The realisation first hit me during a moment of frustration. It was an anonymous day in March, and I was standing in the office kitchen, contemplating a recent disappointment. A week earlier, Jaakko, our Head of Marketing, told me that he had been declining all digital ad campaign proposals from our ad partners. "I mean, they would be nice to have, but obviously, with our current business climate, it just isn't going to happen," Jaakko told me over a cup of tea.

Trying not to do a double-take, I said, "And what climate is this, Jaakko?"

He proceeded to explain to me that his decision was based directly on the annual winter strategy meeting that took place in January.

"You remember Pepe, the meeting where we agreed to act in the best interest of the company by focusing on what we do best, our core competencies and all that?"

Jaakko finished explaining himself and left the room, and I was at a loss. Had we really agreed that? I remembered the meeting Jaakko referred to, but I saw it entirely differently; we talked about our product offerings, not advertising or marketing efforts! How could I be so misunderstood? Here we are months later, and I was waiting for a boost of new customers coming in from new ad campaigns while Jaakko was doubling his efforts in the same channels we had been using for years!

Discouraged, I looked aimlessly around the kitchen until my eyes fell on a bookshelf that stood against a wall. My eyes moved from title to title as I wondered just how we got ourselves into this mess. I was beginning to reach severe levels of self-pity when I picked up a book from the shelf, *The GE Workout*. I remembered that this book covered how General Electric implemented massive changes in the 1980s, which streamlined the organisation and set it up for success in the decades following. I was not interested in the whole story, but I remembered a detail from the book that could help my current situation. I quickly leafed through the pages until I found what I was looking for; a section detailing General Electric's use of follow up meetings to help people remember and stay true to implemented changes or procedures. I spent a few moments reading the section and familiarizing myself with the importance of having regular review sessions that follow planning meetings. I kept reading and began devising my plan of action.

The next day I called Jaakko and everyone else around the coffee table and called for their attention. "Do you see this book? It is our key to success!" I proudly announced.

"You want to sell fridges and washing machines?" deadpanned Kara.

"No, but that was not a bad joke, Kara. Forget about G.E. and the title of the book for a moment. The secret behind General Electric's success was to review its progress. We created our strategy together to stay focused and aligned, but it is simply not enough. We are human, after all. We tend to forget and lose focus over time. From this point forward, that all changes. We will have review sessions regularly to help us keep focused and stay true to our strategy. There is a lot of time between our winter and summer strategy sessions, making it easy to forget our core goals or go off on our own paths and pursue something else altogether. Our first strategy review meeting is next week, and we will have another one about a month later. We are all experts in communication, but we also need to formally review our goals for us to be our best."

The whole Grape People Team was on board, and that was the day review workshops became a regular and important part of our workflow.

Clear focus analysis

Focusing is the practice of stringing workshops together over an extended period of time to agree on common goals, remind people about goals and decisions, check in on the progress made towards reaching these goals, and examine any obstacles that may have come up. The general formula is to run a goal-setting workshop and follow it with one or more review workshops. Keeping people in contact with each other and requiring them to use breakthrough decision-making tools repeatedly will make them examine points of view other than their own. Doing this enables someone to adopt new ideas more efficiently and understand what is best for the entire organisation.

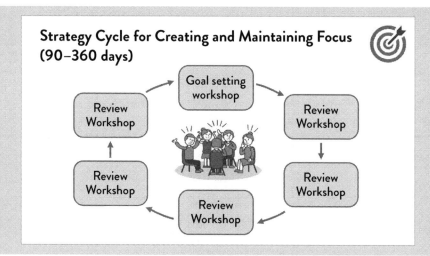

Strategy Cycle for Creating and Maintaining Focus (90–360 days)

Goal setting workshop

Review Workshop

Review Workshop

Review Workshop

Review Workshop

Review Workshop

By having frequent review workshops, you also make sure that momentum is not lost. The reoccurring workshops require people to revisit previous goals and decisions. The book I found on the office bookshelf, *The GE Work-Out*, by Kerr, Ulrich and Ashkenas, explains how General Electric pioneered this strategy. The company made itself famous in the 1980s by devoting significant time and resources to transforming its organisational structure. They always began with a planning workshop and then followed it with four review workshops. The review workshops were held 30 days, 60 days, 90 days, and 180 days after the initial planning workshop*. They imposed a 180-day deadline for all projects, having identified this amount of time as ideal. They found that anything shorter tended to feel rushed, and anything longer was challenging to commit to because the end date was so far away. These changes helped modernise the company and set it up to succeed in the decades to come.

At my company, Grape People, we use this as a template to keep everyone focused. We are a small team of fewer than ten people, yet each person is an expert in their own area. Some people are focused on digital marketing, others on sales, others running training sessions, etc. We need to come together and outline a company-wide strategy so all know how we can act in the best interest of Grape People and its long-term goals. Our timeline for focusing is to have a strategy workshop followed by a review workshop every one or two months until it is time for the next strategy workshop.

2. Rapid transformation

Roger was not having a good day. In fact, he was having one of the worst days of his professional career. Roger sat in the fancy office of one of the suite-level employees, the Vice President of Product, Ms. Broom, to be exact. Ms. Broom was nice enough, but Roger usually did not have to cross paths with her in any significant way. She was typically just a name on the bottom of a strategy update email or a signature on some official company letterhead detailing stock options

---

* I hold a workshop 120 days after the initial workshop, too. Three months without reviewing performance is just too long.

or some other official formality. For Roger to be face to face with Ms Broom, something must have gone wrong. This is why Roger found himself in Ms Broom's well-decorated office, listening to her politely but firmly question Roger just why he had messed up so badly.

"Help me to understand just how it went wrong, Roger. Two months ago, we had the strategy update where we decided to push our new product offering by upselling it to existing clients when it came time for them to renew their contracts with us."

Roger nodded. This was not new information to him; he was at the very same meeting and clearly remembered Ms Broom making the same point then. "I remember that well, Ms Broom. I can assure you that I relayed the message to my team, too." Roger was sure he had told his sales team about the initiative and then turned them loose. However, he was unsure what the specific problem Ms Broom was referring to, so what better way to find out than to ask. "I understood the point and told my team, so is there a specific issue that I do not know about, Ms Broom?"

"The issue is that within your team, we do see a slight increase in new sign-ups for the new product offering, but there is a significant decrease in renewals for our legacy offerings. It's almost like your team isn't trying to upsell but simply sell the new product at the expense of our other offerings. These are supposed to be complementary, not an either-or situation."

Roger knew this and had to bite his tongue from letting out a loud, "Duh!" Instead, he chose a more diplomatic reply. "I'm aware of this, Ms Broom, and I reported to my team the direct results of the strategy session upper-management had together. But, apart from that, I am at a loss about what else could have been done."

Ms Broom thought for a moment and had a realisation. "How did you inform your team about the results of the strategy session?" she asked Roger.

"I emailed the notes to everyone and had a brief question and answer session," he replied.

"I thought so. Do you remember the strategy session yourself? You were there."

Roger nodded and said yes. He remembered the strategy session well. It was nearly two days long and led by some leadership expert who called himself a facilitator. The facilitator had a bunch of exercises to get everyone talking and sharing ideas, and while Roger began the session a bit sceptical, he had to admit that the methods worked. By the end, the upper managers agreed about what needed to be done, and everyone was eager to share the news with their teams. As Roger thought about how great the strategy session was, he began to have the same realisation as Ms Broom.

"Our strategy session was effective because we spent so much time talking about it and making sure that everyone understood it inside and out. But then we just carried the message to the rest of the company by dumping an email into their inbox and offering a few minutes for questions. You don't think that this could be the problem, do you?"

Ms Broom was not sure, but she had the sinking suspicion that they had found the weak point. It was not Roger's fault, but it was everyone's fault for following a poorly-developed workflow. Significant time and resources had been spent to hold the strategy workshop, but the fruits and benefits of the workshop were carelessly delivered to the rest of the company in such a way that greatly limited the effectiveness of the new strategy. Ms Broom began outlining a plan for the following strategy update, including a dedicated workshop for each company level where the strategy is presented and explained. While she couldn't be 100 % positive that this would be the solution to their problem, she had a hunch that things would be much better for her and Roger next time.

Rapid Transformation Analysis

Organisations do not follow the same structure. Depending on their size, industry, or company culture, the number of levels in an organisation varies. On one side are flat organisations that use a modern approach where everyone has agency and is involved in decision-making. On the other side are more traditional organisations that have a distinct hierarchy. These are your classic organisations that have a pyramid-shaped leadership structure.

The size and structure of an organisation affect communication and how new ideas and policies are understood and adopted throughout the entire organisation. Breakthrough organisations are unified and nimble. You need to know how to communicate change clearly across multiple organisational levels to create a system that can genuinely be called a breakthrough organisation.

The main challenge is making sure everyone is on the same page. You may be thinking of your own working life now and saying that adopting change is simple enough. Perhaps you have received an email from your boss in the past that details a new initiative or updates company procedure. You can simply read what to do and put it into practice, right? And if the same email gets sent to a team of 50, then it is a safe assumption that all 50 of you would read the email and instantly be ready to provide a unified front that executes the new initiative without a hitch, right? Unfortunately, it is not so simple. For example, think back to when you were six or seven years old, back in primary school. Did your teacher have you play the game telephone? Everyone stands in a line and the teacher whispers a message to one of the kids at the end of the line. The message is passed down the line one whisper at a time until it reaches the other end, where it is repeated aloud again. This game is fun and worth playing because, without fail, the message gets distorted every time. What starts as *I love pancakes* could end up as *I eat poodles*. Distorting a message is fun for kids playing telephone, but it can be disastrous for business. Unfortunately, messages get misinterpreted as they pass through different levels of an organisation.

Luckily, there is a solution; run a dedicated workshop for each level of the organisation to help them understand the new change. Continue as needed with workshops as you work your way down the levels of the organisational structure until you have traversed from the top to the bottom of the organisation. Doing so will interject dialogue throughout the organisation and allow it to rapidly transform as it pivots to a new strategy or adjusts to large-scale changes.

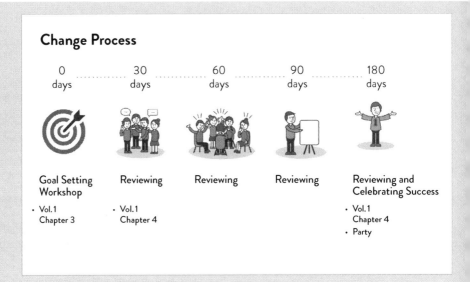

Change Process

0 days	30 days	60 days	90 days	180 days
Goal Setting Workshop	Reviewing	Reviewing	Reviewing	Reviewing and Celebrating Success
• Vol. 1 Chapter 3	• Vol. 1 Chapter 4			• Vol. 1 Chapter 4 • Party

You can start with a goal-setting workshop for upper management. Once they are aligned, you can move down a level and give an implementation workshop to communicate the goal and make an action plan to outline how things will get done. Finally, applying the practical transformation model of General Electric, you can follow up with review workshops at regular intervals held 30 days, 60 days, 90 days, and 180 days after the initial goal implementation workshop. I like to modify General Electric's workshop schedule just a bit and add in an additional review workshop that takes place after 120 days. This extra workshop eliminates the long gap between the 90-day and 180-day workshops. Three months without a review workshop is simply too long, in my opinion.

3. Efficient processes

At the GlobeCom head offices in Stockholm, Michael pushed the ENTER key on his calculator with a flourish and said, "If we skip this proposed problem-solving workshop and elect for teleconferencing instead, the total savings would be over $42,450. That is enough money to pay the annual salary for a junior accountant, which I could use in my team, by the way."

GlobeCom CEO Jules Hoff smiled at Michael, who was going well into his second decade as GlobeCom's head of accounting. "Michael, you know how things are done here. When a business need arises, we spare no cost! It has been this way since you started here, and I believe that I would be doing this company a disservice if I were to change that."

Michael frowned. Jules was right; for as long as he remembered, GlobeCom had always pulled out the stops and arranged meetings or workshops to react to issues ranging from lacklustre performance to internal bickering. These meetings always involved all relevant employees, even if that number swelled into the hundreds, which it could, considering that GlobeCom was the world's 3rd largest telecommunications company. Michael even remembered when 500 employees received an email that they were required to attend a leadership summit that would begin the following week in the Italian Alps. Michael shuddered to think how much that week must have cost.

"Jules, I know that the track record of calling everyone together for a workshop is important, but all I am saying is that perhaps we need to begin picking our spots a bit more carefully. Do we stand to gain more than $42,450 worth of value by flying 21 employees to...where did you say that the workshop is taking place?"

"Vienna," said Jules. "And yes, I think we stand to gain that much in value, and then some. The whole point of this workshop is to align our sales and marketing processes. It seems that there are lots of frustrations, especially in the new markets. The group of employees I want to invite are all from markets that we have recently entered, so it is a new experience for all of them. The problem-solving workshop makes sense, but I will do things your way. Instead of the summit, I will arrange for someone to plan a remote session with teleconferencing and emails. That should cost us about five per cent of what it would if we did it together in Vienna. This time we try it your way and see how it works."

Michael had been working with Jules for years, and he thought he knew the man very well at this point. But he was in shock now! This was the first time he had ever seen Jules deviate from his policy of prioritising these types of meetings over a budget. He thanked Jules for the chance to try things a different way, and he optimistically left the office and began to eagerly think how well that $42,350 in savings was going to look in the *cash assets* section of the company's balance sheet.

Meanwhile, Jules smiled as he watched Michael scurry out of the office. He was not confident that cancelling the workshop was a good idea, but he was willing to try it. After all, he could always reschedule it again a month or two in the future, if needed.

~Two months later ~

Michael dejectedly pushed the ENTER key on the calculator and said, "The total cost for the emergency workshop is going to be $141,800. The flights and accommodations for everyone are more expensive this time around as it is now tourist season in Vienna. Unfortunately, the list of required attendees has grown from 21 to 51, making the event substantially more expensive."

Jules nodded. He thought that this might happen. GlobeCom tried to host the event remotely, but the workshop's effectiveness paled in comparison to their tried and true format of face-to-face workshops. He was not angry for trying; at least it confirmed to both he and Michael that their standard way of prioritising the needed meeting or workshop over financial considerations was the way to go. He gave Michael the OK on the new proposed expense report and began looking forward to the upcoming meeting in Vienna. The extra $100,000 in costs made this a costly lesson that they only needed to learn once.

Efficient processes analysis

If you could view an entire organisation as a whole and see how different parts work together, you might see something that resembles an engine. Or better yet, your view of the organisation looks like the inner workings of a fine watch; different parts spinning and rotating, pushing and pulling, all working together to create an output.

It might feel like your organisation is completely unified on good days, but there are likely problem areas. Unlike an engine or a watch where the entire system is connected, an organisation consists of different teams or departments with their own goals and ways of working. For example, your Accounting Department will be focusing on expense reports, while your Digital Marketing Team will be concentrating on advertising campaigns. Each team has an expected output that they are focusing on. As the teams work to produce their expected outputs, they work in isolation and independently of other teams. Processes do not work because they are not synchronised.

The problem is that grey areas exist between these silos, with no clear delegation between teams. These grey areas are where tasks get lost, forgotten, or mishandled. In the previous example with Globe-Com, the silo existed due to the distance between managers and their offices. Sure, they could compare notes via email and try to learn from each other over the phone, but the best and most effective intervention was to get everyone together for a problem-solving workshop.

Why is a workshop so effective in solving organisational problems? You get key stakeholders together; you create a shared understanding of the fundamental issues, solve them and create a concrete action plan. When people get back to the office, they understand what needs to be done and are committed to action. Problems get solved.

What was wrong with dealing with the problem online? Nothing, online workshops can be very effective. However, very few organisations can do participatory workshops online. Instead, people tend to hold long monologues online and send emails that no one reads.

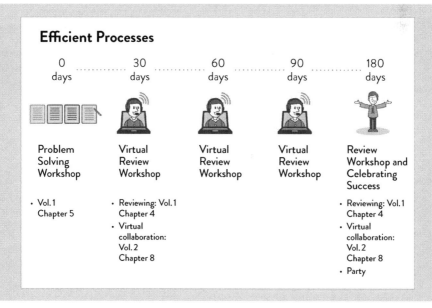

CHAPTER 9: BREAKTHROUGH ORGANISATIONS **441**

A key trait of Breakthrough Organisations is a willingness to quickly evaluate what is needed and get people together to make it happen. I have observed that organisations with this trait own a distinct strategic advantage over their competitors that do not. For example, if you are not scheduled to have a review meeting until next month, but you notice that people seem lost or uninspired, then immediately take action to fix the issue. Take the time and spend the money needed to get all key participants together to solve the problem so that the organisation can perform at the level it should be. This ensures that challenges disappear as quickly as they arise, and this is a very effective practice.

4. Happy clients

An online workshop was bringing together two worlds that often remained separated. One end of the call was broadcasting to a large and bustling warehouse, Pro Package Packers, commonly known as PPP for short. They were a mid-sized logistic and freight company that specialised in delivering throughout Australia. On the other end of the call was the office of Brandhouse, an ambitious e-commerce platform that was selling designer items and home goods. Brandhouse and PPP were entering a new partnership together. PPP was going to run a large warehouse located just outside Melbourne to serve the entire Oceania region. The conference call was not aiming to broker a deal but rather serve as a workshop to agree on common goals between the respective managerial teams of PPP and Brandhouse. Whitney, the marketing director for Brandhouse, whispered to a colleague of hers, "They are shipping our items, about as straightforward a job as you can ask for. So why are we talking to them again?"

Her colleague shrugged; he did not know either. In fact, for most of the Brandhouse employees, this meeting with the logistics company was something new and out of the ordinary. They worked with four other logistics companies, and no one ever insisted on having an online workshop. Still, there they were, listening to Stuart, an enthusiastic team lead for PPP, and setting common goals together. Agreeing on common goals was fast and easy; logistical operations should be fast, reliable, and flexible to accommodate customer needs. While the participants created solutions, Stuart explained how they liked to work with their clients.

"At PPP, we like to take a hands-on approach and collaborate as much as possible with our clients. This means that we will get to know your business a bit and understand your priorities and wants beyond the simple need for a delivery agent. For example, if orders are delayed across the board, would you prefer an itemised recovery approach or..."

Stuart continued to describe different shipping methods to deal with an order backlog. Unfortunately, Whitney didn't know a ton about different logistics strategies, and as she heard Stuart asking about a preference between SKU-based or FIFO, she found herself asking a question.

"Whitney from Brandhouse here. Can you please tell me what FIFO is?"

"Sure thing," said Stuart. "FIFO is a term used in managing inventory that means first-in, first-out. That is, orders will be processed in the order that they are placed. The advantage is that no specific order will be too delayed, but it takes longer to clear a backlog this way. An alternate strategy popular during heavy times like Christmas is to focus on SKUs instead. In other words, we would process all pending orders for a specific item, clearing out one area of the warehouse at a time. Since we are staying in one place to deal with all orders for a specific item, we can clear a backlog of orders more quickly this way, but the one disadvantage is that you may see newer orders being sent out sooner than older ones that have been waiting a while. Great question, Whitney."

Interesting, Whitney thought to herself. She continued to listen as she began contemplating what strategy would be best for Brandhouse, and she also was beginning to see the point of this virtual workshop, after all.

Happy Clients analysis

A consumer might buy something from an online store, like Brand-house, and then decide if they like the experience or not. They might like the shirt they bought, consider it is well-made and sold at a fair price. But the shipping was slow, and the customer service agent they spoke to was a bit rude. The consumer weighs all these factors and decides if they will buy from Brandhouse again.

The reality is that the experience Brandhouse provides its customers is reliant on a few different companies. PPP handles their logistics, they outsource manufacturing and customer service to India, and a third-party marketing consultant develops their web and advertising content. Brandhouse is the client for each of these companies, and they all collaborate with Brandhouse to varying degrees. PPP did a great job by meeting with them to outline goals and preferential workflows. This is not the norm, but it should be, and I encourage you and your organisation to do the same.

When talking about process efficiency, we learned that departments and teams operated in silos. Interestingly, the organisations are enormous, isolated silos themselves. The Sales Director and the Purchasing Director talk about money and make a deal. Typically, there is little or no discussion about cooperation and optimal workflows. Instead, contractual details are discussed, and prices are negotiated. Once an agreement is reached, the companies retreat to their respective offices to fulfil the contractual duties before re-joining a year or so later to enter a new round of negotiations. It is no surprise if the client is not happy.

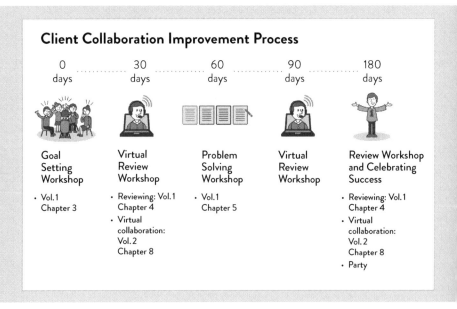

Client Collaboration Improvement Process

0 days	30 days	60 days	90 days	180 days
Goal Setting Workshop	Virtual Review Workshop	Problem Solving Workshop	Virtual Review Workshop	Review Workshop and Celebrating Success
• Vol.1 Chapter 3	• Reviewing: Vol.1 Chapter 4 • Virtual collaboration: Vol.2 Chapter 8	• Vol.1 Chapter 5		• Reviewing: Vol.1 Chapter 4 • Virtual collaboration: Vol.2 Chapter 8 • Party

Establishing common project goals, holding occasional problem-solving workshops, and reviewing progress can make miracles happen. Best of all, the benefits only increase as projects become more complex.

5. Connected Teams

A gentle *ping* alerted me that my virtual meeting with HR Head Ann from the logistics company Flow Logistics was scheduled to begin in five minutes. I took a moment to pull up the email Ann sent me weeks earlier, where she explained the challenges that her company was facing. As I read it, the details came flooding back to me.

Ann's company Flow Logistics had a central office of about 30 employees that looked after its network of 25 warehouses scattered across North and South America. The office ran smoothly, and its employees reliably rated Flow Logistics as a great place to work. The company was thriving, and there seemed little need for outside help from a facilitator like myself. Unfortunately, all of that changed in the early months of 2020 when the COVID-19 global pandemic caused the entire office to shut its doors. As a result, all Flow Logistics employees were forced to work from home.

The Flow Logistics staff felt lucky because business was still good, despite the pandemic. Everyone was grateful to still have their jobs. But as she detailed in her email, people struggled to work as effectively as a team remotely as they did when they all shared an office. Ann finished her email with a plea for help:

> Less than two months have passed since we transitioned to remote work, and things are already going off the rails. I anticipate that our shift to a remote office may be permanent. We need to figure out how to regain the sense of community and share knowledge with each other if we hope to have any bit of the success that we had before.

Ann called me to discuss further the problems outlined in her email. As she told it, the office workers used to communicate very effectively in unofficial channels; breaks, casual conversations in the office kitchen, dropping by a colleague's desk to chat about weekend plans. Now that everyone was virtual, they could not replicate this communication using the tools they had at their disposal. Ann began to get pretty worked up just thinking about how her beloved team struggled to transition to a virtual working world. "We used to have an atmosphere that made outsiders jealous! An office visitor has asked me on more than one occasion what our secret was, and I always said that the only thing we ever worried about was finding the right person for the job. I still believe that we have the best people, but now everything is different, and not in a good way," said a dejected Ann.

"Don't worry, Ann. I think I can help. I propose that we have a few workshops for your team that we will hold virtually. I aim to create a common team goal to define what kind of team the members want and make a pathway for getting there. Later we will solve some of the challenges they face virtually and review the new goals. I think that by the end of it, your team will be well on the way to getting back on track."

Ann liked the sound of my plan, and a week later, I was hosting a virtual workshop for all 26 central office employees of Flow Logistics.

Keeping Flow Logistics Connected

The problems: Replacing the benefit of personal face-to-face conversations, maintaining valuable company culture after forced shift to remote work, learning how to interact with co-workers virtually

The plan: 3 virtual workshops: goal setting workshop, review workshop #1 30 days later, review workshop #2 60 days later

The desired outcome: Goals created and actions put in to place to reach the goals (goal setting workshop, tracking progress and making needed adjustments (review workshops)

Connected Teams analysis

Dysfunction can strike an organisation at any level. Team health needs to be maintained, reviewed, and analysed. Once problems are identified, a workshop needs to be called to address these issues. Breakthrough organisations work to maintain a healthy ecosystem throughout all levels of the organisation.

If a team has an emotional problem or a conflict between members, then a problem-solving workshop can fix the issue. Once the conflict is removed, the team's emotional health will dramatically improve, and performance will improve, too.

This example showed how a goal-setting workshop helped create a team vision. Review workshops were also required to help them rediscover their team culture and the habits and ways of working that were temporarily lost during the switch from an in-office team to a virtual one.

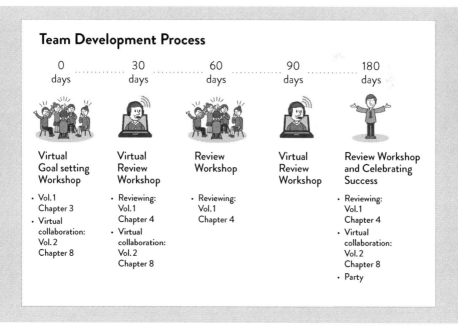

Team Development Process

0 days	30 days	60 days	90 days	180 days
Virtual Goal setting Workshop	Virtual Review Workshop	Review Workshop	Virtual Review Workshop	Review Workshop and Celebrating Success
• Vol. 1 Chapter 3 • Virtual collaboration: Vol. 2 Chapter 8	• Reviewing: Vol. 1 Chapter 4 • Virtual collaboration: Vol. 2 Chapter 8	• Reviewing: Vol. 1 Chapter 4		• Reviewing: Vol. 1 Chapter 4 • Virtual collaboration: Vol. 2 Chapter 8 • Party

6. Systematic Leadership

Systematic leadership is the final feature of breakthrough organisations. This is achieved by combining the previously mentioned five features to deal with problems through routine interventions and communication systematically. When an organisation uses breakthrough methods, people begin to believe that they can solve any problem. Leaders may use different types of workshops depending on what current need arises. If the organisation lacks focus and needs a new strategy, then a goal-setting workshop might be the key. When teams are not productive, you develop the teams. When the processes are not working, you get the right people together and fix the problems.

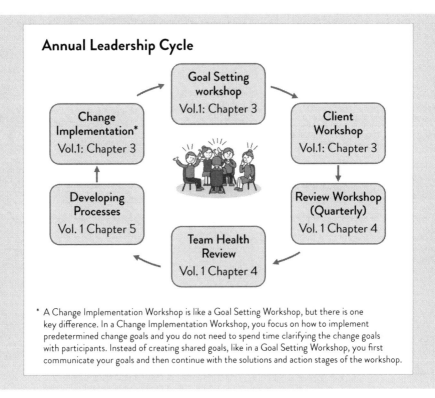

Annual Leadership Cycle

* A Change Implementation Workshop is like a Goal Setting Workshop, but there is one key difference. In a Change Implementation Workshop, you focus on how to implement predetermined change goals and you do not need to spend time clarifying the change goals with participants. Instead of creating shared goals, like in a Goal Setting Workshop, you first communicate your goals and then continue with the solutions and action stages of the workshop.

However, I like a systematic, planned approach to organisational development and to have most annual activities planned in advance to make sure they all happen.

In a breakthrough organisation, the individual members are connected to their peers and feel that they have a voice and can affect change instead of simply feeling like an anonymous cog of a large machine. This feeling of connectivity is even more important when there has been a significant shift to remote work.

Wishing for a breakthrough society

I am a dreamer, and I am blessed (or sometimes cursed) with the desire to take something that is already impressive and make it even bigger. I want to push the envelope further. I appreciate breakthrough organisations, but I still want more. I dream of breakthrough societies: *connected civilisations utilizing dialogue that results in better decisions and alignment*.

Before you call me crazy and disregard these words as idealistic fluff tossed into the end of a long book, there is a reason why I choose to end on this note. The tools demonstrated in this book and the principles of effective group leadership can help your meetings and workshops. Then you can think bigger and apply to a long-term leadership cycle to help execute ambitious projects. Then you can take things even further and use them to create breakthrough organisations. So, why would we stop there? Imagine the principles of the breakthrough organisation on a societal level; true democracy instead of the standard polarizing voting habits, collaboration that spills over borders and ethnic or religious divides, and more profound understanding and more empathetic and better solutions. I have seen examples of these tools and principles applied in areas outside of the business world. I remember helping my son a few years ago (or trying to at least!) with his homework. When he mentioned that he needed help with his social studies homework to design a platform for a fictional presidential candidate, I thought it would be as simple as writing down some ideas on a piece of paper or helping him type out some thoughts in a word document. Instead, he handed me a tablet, told me to click an icon to open the specific app for this class, and then browse the message boards where he and his classmates shared ideas. I don't know about you, but this level of collaboration did not exist when I was at school, and it was thrilling to see it in action and imagine the countless ways it could be applied within education. This software is similar to existing virtual meeting software, and I hope that virtual meetings and virtual classes continue to become more common.

Flashes of a breakthrough society have emerged from the field of politics, too. No, I am not talking so much about the sensationalised headlines that leaders of state shout into microphones or tweet out to their millions of followers. Instead, I refer to the recent trend of crowdsourcing public opinion about proposed projects or the best use of government funds. This allows the average person to have more active participation in their government, and it helps identify true needs much more so than old-fashioned bureaucracy does. This involvement also helps people understand the reasoning behind governmental decisions. Just like an initiative needs to be clearly explained to each organisational level of employees for it to be understood and supported, the same can be said for the actions of a government. Unfortunately, this is not usually the case, but if we are going to dream, we may as well go for it and dream big, right?

Building a Breakthrough Society Together

I sincerely hope that my wish for a breakthrough society will soon be obsolete. Not because we don't need it, but because it has already arrived. Perhaps, dear reader, these words bring a wry smile to your face because you find yourself in a breakthrough society already. That said, I know that effective leadership, clear communication, and strong emotional health are timeless goals. I believe that slowing down to listen to others, dealing with emotions, and being a supportive and engaging leader contributes toward achieving these goals. Now you have the professional facilitation skills to contribute towards these goals and lead some great meetings and workshops along the way.

Let's connect!

I am passionate about social psychology and organisational development, and I regularly share methods and insights that inspire me. I am always happy to connect with people who share these interests. It would be an honour to connect with you!

LinkedIn Pepe Nummi https://www.linkedin.com/in/pepenummi/

Grape People World https://www.linkedin.com/company/grape-people-world

Our training solutions: **www.grapepeople.com**

Bibliography

1. Guilford, J.P. *The Nature of Human Intelligence*. McGraw-Hill, 1967.

2. Guilford, J.P. "Creativity". *American Psychologist*, 5, 444–454.

3. Patnoe, Shelly. *A Narrative History of Experimental Social Psychology: The Lewin Tradition*. Springer-Verlag, 1988.

4. Osborn, Alex. *How to Think Up!*. McGraw-Hill, 1942.

5. Doyle, Michael, and Straus, David. *How to Make Meetings Work*. Playboy Press, 1976.

6. Schein, Edgar H. *Process Consultation: Its Role in Organizational Development*, Addison-Wesley Publishing Company, 1969.

7. Owen, Harrison. *Open Space Technology: A User's Guide*. Abbott Publishing, 1993.

8. Kaner, Sam, and Lenny Lind. *Facilitator's guide to participatory decision-making*. San Francisco: John Wiley & Sons/Jossey-Bass, 2007. Print.

9. Larsen, Diana, Derbey, Esther, and Schwaber, Ken. *Agile Retrospectives: Making Good Teams Great*. Pragmatic Bookshelf, 2006.

10. Brown, Juanita, and Isaacs, David. *The World Café: Shaping Our Futures Through Conversations that Matter*. Berrett-Koehler Publishers, Inc., 2005.

11. Mantere, Veikko. *GroupExpo*. Innotiimi, 2004.

12. Kimmel, Allan J. *Ethical Issues in Behavioral Research: Basic and Applied Perspectives*. Blackwell Pub, 2007.

13. Lewin, K. (1947) "Group Decision and Social Change." In: Newcomb, T. and Hartley, E., Eds., Readings in Social Psychology, Holt, Rinehart & Winston, New York, 197–211.

14. Brehm, Sharon, and Kassin, Saul. *Social Psychology*. Houghton Mifflin, 1993.

15. Rill, Bryan, and Hämäläinen, Matti. *The Art of Co-Creation: A Guidebook for Practitioners*. Palgrave MacMillan, 2018.

16. Bockelbrink, Bernhard, et al. *Sociocracy 3.0- A Practical Guide. 2019, Sociocracy 3.0*, https://sociocracy30.org/. Accessed 12 April, 2019.

17. Nummi, Pepe. *Beyond Brainstorming-Idealogue*. Grape People Oy, 2016.

18. "IAF Core Competencies," 2018. https://www.iaf-world.org/site/professional/core-competencies. Accessed 29 April, 2019.

19. Gray, David, Sunni Brown, and James Macanufo. *Gamestorming: a playbook for innovators, rulebreakers, and changemakers*. Sebastopol, Calif: O'Reilly, 2010. Print.

20. Bono, Edward De. *Lateral Thinking: Creativity Step by Step*. Harper Perennial, 2015.

21. "About us: Our history," http://dynamicfacilitation.com/about_us/About/history.html . Accessed 8 January, 2020.

22. Haggbloom, Steven. "The 100 Most Eminent Psychologists of the 20th Century." Review of General Psychology, Vol.6, No. 2., 2002, 139–152.

23. Basadur, Min. "Reducing Complexity in Conceptual Thinking Using Challenge Mapping." Management of Innovation and New Technology Research Centre, 2002.

24. Schwarz, Roger. *The Skilled Facilitator: A Comprehensive Resource for Consultants, Facilitators, Managers, Trainers, and Coaches*. Jossey-Bass, 2002.

25. Schwarz, Roger M. *The Skilled Facilitator Fieldbook: Tips, Tools, and Tested Methods for Consultants, Facilitators, Managers, Trainers, and Coaches*. Jossey-Bass, 2005.

26. Izard, Carroll E. *The Psychology of Emotions*. Plenum Press-New York and London, 1991.

27. Ulrich, David, Steve Kerr, and Ronald N. Ashkenas. *The GE work-Out: How to implement GE's revolutionary method for busting bureaucracy and attacking organizational problems--fast*. New York: McGraw-Hill, 2002.

28. Huhman, Heather R. "How to Remove Emotions from the Business Equation." Forbes Online. June 27th, 2011 (Accessed June 29th, 2019. https://www.forbes.com/sites/yec/2011/06/27/how-to-remove-emotions-from-the-business-equation/#32fb55632dfa

Tool Index

Me/We/Us (Vol. 1, Ch. 3.1, 3.3, 4.3, 5.1): A basic tool you can use to get everyone involved. Me/We/Us is typically used when you have one question to facilitate.

Wishing (Vol. 1, Ch. 3.1): Use this tool to help people set goals and become emotionally invested.

Dartboard (Vol. 1, Ch. 3.1): Use this tool to visualise priorities.

Dot Voting (Vol. 1, Ch. 3.1, 4.1): Use this tool to visualise priorities.

Silent Moving (Vol. 1, Ch. 3.1): A tool to help create understanding and get people to agree on priorities.

Café (Vol. 1, Ch. 3.2): A method to help groups efficiently talk about multiple questions (or topics) simultaneously. It is especially good at creating meaningful dialogue between people.

Investment Activity (Vol. 1, Ch. 3.2): Use this to help visualise priorities.

Group Ranking (Vol. 1, Ch. 3.2): Use to prioritise many questions simultaneously. Group Ranking is particularly good at creating a shared understanding of the logic behind each idea.

Blossom (Vol. 1, Ch. 3.3): Use this tool to visualise priorities.

One Breath (Vol. 1, Ch. 3.3): Use this to end the session and collect feedback in a fun way.

Force Field Analysis (Vol. 1, Ch. 4.1): Use this for in-depth review. It identifies the key underlying factors behind any strategy, process, service, or project, and it also can be used to assess team health.

Field of Two Criteria (Vol. 1, Ch. 4.1): Use this tool to visualise priorities.

Bus Stop (Vol. 1, Ch. 4.2): A tool for dealing with multiple questions at once and creating meaningful discussions.

Dragons (Vol. 1, Ch. 4.2): Use this tool to visualise priorities.

Earth Energy (Vol. 1, Ch. 4.2): A tool to energise the group.

Kanban (Vol. 1, Ch. 4.3): A tool to visualise action points.

One Step (Vol. 1, Ch. 4.3): Use this to end the session and collect feedback in a fun way.

Hello (Vol. 1, Ch. 5.1): A tool for collecting information at the start of a session.

Dynamic Facilitation (Vol. 1, Ch. 5.1): A comprehensive tool for dealing with conflict and heavy topics.

Signature (Vol. 1, Ch. 5.1): Use this tool to visualise priorities.

Six-Zero (Vol. 1, Ch. 5.2): A tool to energise the group.

Open Space Technology (Vol. 1, Ch. 5.2): A method to help groups discuss multiple topics thoroughly.

Consent Decision Making (Vol. 1, Ch. 5.2): A tool to develop solutions and make decisions collectively as a group.

Five Fingers (Vol. 1, Ch. 5.2): Use this to evaluate results and collect feedback.

Idealogue (Vol. 1, Ch. 5.3): A method to explore one topic thoroughly and create meaningful discussions and understanding.

Roadmap (Vol. 1, Ch. 5.3): A tool to visualise action points.

Floorball (Vol. 1, Ch. 5.3): A tool to energise the group.

Talking Stick (Vol. 1, Ch. 5.3): Use this to end a session and collect feedback in a fun way.

Emotional Goal Setting (Vol. 2, Ch. 3): A tool to help people recognize the emotions they are feeling and take control of their emotions.

Group memory (Vol. 2, Ch. 2): A visual record of the shared knowledge and information. A key tool for focusing people and helping decision making.

Archipelago of Emotions (Vol. 2, Ch. 3): A warm-up tool for creating trust through self-disclosure.

Timeline (Vol. 2, Ch. 3): A tool for reviewing past experiences and dealing with emotions.

Wheel of Emotions (Vol. 2, Ch. 3): A tool to help people recognize and process their emotions.

Carousel (Vol. 2, Ch. 3): A warm-up or ending activity. Carousel can be combined with emotional disclosure to increase trust.

Morning Walk (Vol. 2, Ch. 4): A warm-up activity.

Challenge Mapping (Vol. 2, Ch. 4): The perfect method for clarifying a problem when you need to dig deeper.

Whip (Vol. 2, Ch. 4): An ending tool to share experiences and collect feedback.

3-Step Intervention Model (Vol. 2, Ch. 5): A tool that provides concrete steps for dealing with difficult situations.

STP Analysis (Vol. 2, Ch. 6): A tool to identify actual needs instead of simple preferences or desires.

Change Equation (Vol. 2, Ch. 7): A formula that assesses the probability of change occurring.

Self-portraits (Vol. 2, Ch. 8): A warm-up tool that is very effective in virtual meetings.

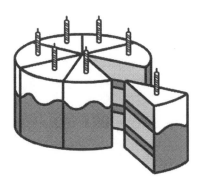

Made in the USA
Monee, IL
18 November 2021

eaa937ea-6b20-4ffc-9bfb-3b681cce41a2R01